W9-AEL-556

International and Development Education

The *International and Development Education Series* focuses on the complementary areas of comparative, international, and development education. Books emphasize a number of topics ranging from key international education issues, trends, and reforms to examinations of national education systems, social theories, and development education initiatives. Local, national, regional, and global volumes (single-authored and edited collections) constitute the breadth of the series and offer potential contributors a great deal of latitude based on interests and cutting-edge research. The series is supported by a strong network of international scholars and development professionals who serve on the International and Development Education Advisory Board and participate in the selection and review process for manuscript development.

Titles:

EDUCATION AND GLOBAL CULTURAL DIALOGUE

A TRIBUTE TO RUTH HAYHOE

EDITED BY
KAREN MUNDY AND QIANG ZHA

palgrave
macmillan

EDUCATION AND GLOBAL CULTURAL DIALOGUE

First published in 2012 by
PALGRAVE MACMILLAN®
in the United States—a division of St. Martin's Press LLC,
175 Fifth Avenue, New York, NY 10010.

Where this book is distributed in the UK, Europe and the rest of the world,
this is by Palgrave Macmillan, a division of Macmillan Publishers Limited,
registered in England, company number 785998, of Houndmills,
Basingstoke, Hampshire RG21 6XS.

Palgrave Macmillan is the global academic imprint of the above companies
and has companies and representatives throughout the world.

Palgrave® and Macmillan® are registered trademarks in the United States,
the United Kingdom, Europe and other countries.

ISBN: 978–0–230–34010–7

Library of Congress Cataloging-in-Publication Data

Education and global cultural dialogue : a tribute to Ruth Hayhoe /
Karen Mundy and Qiang Zha, editors.
        p. cm.—(International and development education)
     ISBN 978–0–230–34010–7 (hardback)
        1. Education—Social aspects. 2. Multicultural education. 3. Education
and globalization. 4. Comparative education. 5. Hayhoe, Ruth. I. Mundy,
Karen E. (Karen Elizabeth), 1962– II. Zha, Qiang.

LC191.E42335 2012
306.43—dc23   2012022500

A catalogue record of the book is available from the British Library.

Design by Newgen Imaging Systems (P) Ltd., Chennai, India.

First edition: December 2012

10 9 8 7 6 5 4 3 2 1

Contents

Figures and Tables

Figures

Tables

Contributors

Robert F. Arnove, Chancellor's Professor Emeritus of Educational Leadership and Policy Studies at Indiana University/Bloomington, is an Honorary Fellow and past President of the Comparative Education Society (CIES). He led an exchange program and taught courses at Hangzhou University in 1983, and has returned over the years to China to participate in comparative education conferences at Beijing Normal University and Zhejiang University. On a number of occasions, he has been an Advisory Professor at the Hong Kong Institute of Education, especially when Ruth Hayhoe was the first Director of the Institute. He has written extensively on educational and social change.

Yeow Tong Chia is a Lecturer in the Faculty of Education and Social Work at the University of Sydney. He received his PhD from the Ontario Institute for Studies in Education/University of Toronto (OISE/UT). His research emphasizes the use of comparative and historical approaches to study history education, citizenship education, as well as education and state formation. His publications include "The Elusive Goal of Nation Building: Asian/Confucian Value and Citizenship Education in Singapore During the 1980s" in *British Journal of Educational Studies* (December 2011). Along with Karen Mundy and Qiang Zha, he was one of the co-organizers of the "Education and Global Culture Dialogue Conference: A Tribute to the Work of Dr. Ruth Hayhoe" that was held on May 6, 2011, at OISE. This book is an outcome of that conference.

Irving Epstein is Professor of Educational Studies at Illinois Wesleyan University. His publications include the edited volumes, *Chinese Education: Problems, Policies and Prospects* (Garland, 1991); *Recapturing the Personal: Essays on Education and Embodied Knowledge in Comparative Perspective* (Information Age, 2007); and the six-volume *Greenwood Encyclopedia of Children's Issues Worldwide* (Greenwood, 2008), where he served as General Editor. From 1988 to 1998, he was an Associate Editor of the *Comparative Education Review*, and from 2006 to 2011, he was Coeditor of the *Asia Network Exchange*. He is most proud of his continued service on the Advisory Board of the *Scholars at Risk Network*, an international consortium of over 200 universities dedicated to scholar protection as well as the preservation of and advocacy for academic freedom.

Joseph P. Farrell is Professor Emeritus of Comparative and International Education at the OISE/UT, where he has served on OISE's graduate faculty since 1968. He served as Founding Director of the Comparative, International and Development Education Centre and Graduate Program. He has undertaken field research related to educational planning and policy change in more than 40 nations, and has published eight books and more than 200 articles, book chapters, technical reports, and given an equal number of conference presentations. In recognition of his work, he has received awards from the Comparative, International and Development Education Society for Outstanding Scholarship, Outstanding Leadership, and was in 2007 designated as an Honorary Fellow of that Society (a lifetime-achievement award). He has also been, for more than 60 years as boy and man, a Scout.

Ruth Hayhoe is Professor at OISE/UT. Her professional engagements in Asia have spanned 30 years, including Foreign Expert at Fudan University in Shanghai, 1980–1982; Head of the Cultural Section of the Canadian Embassy in Beijing, 1989–1991; Visiting Professor at Nagoya University in 1996; and Director of the Hong Kong Institute of Education, 1997–2002. Her recent books include *Portraits of 21st Century Chinese Universities: In the Move to Mass Higher Education,* coauthored with Jun Li, Jing Lin, and Qiang Zha (Hong Kong: Comparative Education Research Centre, University of Hong Kong and Dordecht: Springer, 2011); *Comparative and International Education: Issues for Teachers*, coedited with K. Mundy, K. Bickmore, M. Madden, and K. Madjidi (New York: Teachers College Press and Toronto: Canadian Scholars Press, 2008) and *Portraits of Influential Chinese Educators* (Hong Kong: CERC and Springer, 2006).

Wing On Lee is Dean of Education Research at the National Institute of Education, Singapore, and is currently President of the World Council of Comparative Education Societies. He has previously served at the Hong Kong Institute of Education as Vice President (Academic) and Deputy to the President, Chair Professor of Comparative Education, Founding Dean of the School of Foundations in Education, and Head of two Departments. He has also served at the University of Sydney as Professor of Education at the Faculty of Education and Social Work and Director (International) at the College of Humanities and Social Sciences. Earlier in his career, he was Founding Director of the Comparative Education Research Centre at the University of Hong Kong. In 2003, Lee received the Medal of Honour awarded by the Hong Kong Government. He was also awarded the Bronze

Education Award and Education Innovation Award from the Educational Art Research Association and the Educational Development Forum in Beijing. In 2010, he received the Hong Kong Soka Gakkai International Award for his contribution to values education. He is known for his research in comparative education and civic and moral education.

Karen Mundy is Professor and Canada Research Chair at OISE/UT. Her award-winning research has focused on the politics of international education assistance in the developing world, educational reform in Africa, the role of civil society advocacy in educational systems, and global citizenship education in North American schools. Her recent research, published in more than two dozen journal articles and chapters and in her five coedited volumes, is concentrated on the evolution of global efforts to ensure "education for all"; the role of the World Bank in education; and civil society activism in Africa. Mundy has carried out sponsored research for such organizations as UNICEF, UNESCO, Hewlett Foundation, the World Bank, MasterCard Foundation, the Canadian International Development Agency, the Open Society Institute, UNESCO, and USAID. She is also the founder and cochair of the Canadian Global Campaign for Education, a coalition of NGOs, teachers unions, and universities committed to advancing education for all.

David Post teaches comparative education and sociology of education at The Pennsylvania State University. Currently, he also edits the journal *Comparative Education Review*. He has lived off-and-on in Hong Kong since 1986, and so he has tried to conduct, in Hong Kong, some of the same research agenda on social stratification that he developed while working previously in Peru and Mexico. Other areas of interest include legal and economic policies on child labor.

Haiyan Qiang is Professor of Comparative Education in the Faculty of Education, South China Normal University, in Guangzhou, China, and holds the post of Associate Director of the Centre for Women's Studies in the same institution. She has pursued graduate studies at the University of Massachusetts in the United States, the Institute of Education at the University of London, and OISE/UT. She is the Editor of a series of books and textbooks and has published numerous articles in education journals in that country.

Heidi Ross is Director of the East Asian Studies Center and Professor of Educational Policy Studies at Indiana University. She also codirects the Australian National University–Indiana University Pan Asia Institute. Ross earned her PhD in Educational Foundations, Policy, and Administration at the University of Michigan. Ross has taught and consulted at numerous institutions in East Asia and has served as President of the Comparative and International Education Society, Coeditor of *Comparative Education Review*, and Chair of Educational Studies and Director of Asian Studies at Colgate University. Ross has published widely on Chinese education, gender and schooling, and qualitative research methodology, and her books include *China Learns English* (Yale), *The Ethnographic Eye* (Garland), and *Taking Teaching Seriously* (Paradigm). She is currently leading two field-based projects on student engagement in Chinese higher education and girls' educational access and attainment in rural Shaanxi. In 2011, Ross received Indiana University's prestigious Presidential Award for excellence in teaching, and in 2012, Indiana University's Ryan Award for her leadership in international studies.

Hongcai Wang holds the position of Professor of Education at Xiamen University, where he is the Director of Educational Theory Studies. He received his PhD from Beijing Normal University. Hongcai Wang holds the honor of "Top Youth Social Scientist of Fujian," "New Century Excellent Talent" of the Education Ministry, and was elected as Vice President of Chinese Society of Higher Education Theory Studies in 2010. He has published over 100 articles and 10 books.

Vilma Seeberg is Associate Professor for International/Intercultural Education at Kent State University. She has previously been a teacher, a school principal, consultant with the World Bank, and a Visiting Professor in China. She has a long history of studying Chinese education and published, among others, two books on literacy and basic mass education under Mao. More recently, she has been reporting on field work in girls' education in remote Western China, for example, "Schooling, jobbing, marrying, what's a girl to do to make life better? Empowerment capabilities of girls at the margins of globalization" (2011). She founded and runs the Guanlan Scholarship Foundation for village girls in a remote region of China.

Yimin Wang is a Doctoral Candidate in the Educational Leadership and Policy Studies Department with a concentration in International and Comparative Education at Indiana University. Prior to coming to Indiana University, Wang worked as a Research Associate at the National Institute of Education in Singapore, where she was actively involved in several large-scale projects aiming at nationwide curriculum reform funded by the Ministry of Education. At Indiana University, she was awarded a Proffitt Fellowship, an International Enhancement Grant Fellowship, and a Robert Arnove Travel Fund Award among other scholarships and awards. With Professor Heidi Ross, Wang has served as a Co-guest Editor of two special issues of the journal *Chinese Education and Society* on college entrance examination reforms in China. Her current research interests include environmental education, education for sustainable development, reforms of Chinese higher education, and comparative education methodology.

Rui Yang is Associate Professor and Assistant Dean (Research Projects and Centres), Faculty of Education, The University of Hong Kong. He has worked in different higher education systems, with particular interest in cross-culturalism in education policy, higher education, and sociology of education. After nearly a decade of teaching and research at Shantou University in Guangdong, he received a PhD from the University of Sydney in 2001. He has then taught and researched at Universities of Western Australia, Monash, and Hong Kong. He has written extensively in the field of comparative and international education. His current interest is focused on comparative and global studies in education policy and higher education internationalization.

Qiang Zha is Associate Professor at the Faculty of Education, York University. His research interests include international academic relations, global brain circulation, globalization and education, internationalization of higher education, East Asian and Chinese higher education, differentiation and diversity in higher education, theories of organizational change, and issues with new immigrants' settlement. He has written and published widely on these topics in journals such as *Compare, Higher Education, Higher Education in Europe, Harvard China Review*, and as book chapters. In 2004, he was a corecipient of the inaugural IAU/Palgrave Prize on Higher Education Policy Research. His most recent books include a coauthored book (with Ruth Hayhoe, Jun Li, and Jing Lin) *Portraits of 21st Century Chinese Universities: In the Move to Mass Higher Education* (Hong Kong: Comparative Education Research Centre, University of Hong Kong and Dordecht, the Netherlands: Springer, 2011), and an edited volume *Education in China: Educational History, Models, and Initiatives* (Great Barrington, MA: Berkshire Publishing, 2012).

Ningsha Zhong received her PhD degree at OISE/UT, and is currently affiliated with the University of Toronto. Her research experience has included the study of university autonomy in China and the cultural impact on Chinese higher education in modernity.

Acronyms and Abbreviations

CCULP	Canada–China University Linkage Program
CIDA	Canadian International Development Agency
CIE	Comparative and International Education
CIES	Comparative International Education Society
CPC	Communist Party of China
CRC	Convention on the Rights of the Child
EEIP	Early English Immersion Program
ERASMUS	European Community Action Scheme for the Mobility of University Students
GATE	Global Alliance for Transnational Education
GDP	Gross Domestic Product
HK	Hong Kong
HKIEd	Hong Kong Institute of Education
IR	International Relations
KMT	Kuomintang of China (Nationalist Party of China)
MBA	Master of Business Administration
MOE	Ministry of Education
NICS	Newly Industrialized Countries
NGO	Nongovernmental Organization
OECD	Organisation for Economic Co-operation and Development
OISE/UT	Ontario Institute for Studies in Education of the University of Toronto
PISA	Programme for International Student Assessment
PRC	People's Republic of China
SAR	Special Administrative Region
SCHK	Save the Children Hong Kong
SU	Shaanxi Normal University
TNHE	Transnational Higher Education
UGC	University Grants Committee
UN	United Nations

UNESCO	United Nations Educational, Scientific and Cultural Organization
UNICEF	United Nations Children's Fund
WCCES	World Council of Comparative Education Societies
WOSM	World Organization of the Scouting Movement
WTO	World Trade Organization
WUN	Worldwide Universities

Series Editors' Introduction

As the *International and Development Education Book Series* editors, we are especially pleased to introduce this volume—*Education and Global Cultural Dialogue*—which expands on the life work of Professor Ruth Hayhoe, University of Toronto. Recognized as a pioneer and leader on many fronts, Hayhoe has established a lasting legacy in the area of comparative and international education among policy makers, scholars, and practitioners all over the globe. Especially significant has been her pioneering work on educational change and development in China. Her work has influenced an entire generation of scholars, both within and outside China, who have benefitted enormously from her critical insight on and understanding of this complex subject. She continues to work with and mentor junior scholars, including several aspiring scholars from China. To give one example of her recent capacity-building initiatives, Hayhoe has helped in strengthening the journal *Frontiers of Education in China*, one of the leading English-language, scholarly publication in China.

Among the many former students and scholars Hayhoe has mentored over her distinguished career are the editors of this volume—Karen Mundy of the University of Toronto and Qiang Zha of York University. Mundy and Zha have assembled a group of 16 international scholars and practitioners who have contributed 14 chapters to this volume. While most of the chapters discuss Hayhoe's exemplary leadership and scholarship in higher education, academia, and service, some go beyond Hayhoe by building on her legacy. Joseph P. Farrell's chapter 3 gives a historical account of the World Scouting program as an exemplary model of a century-old nongovernmental organization involved in building cultural and spiritual dialogue across and within many nations. Robert F. Arnove (chapter 9) includes a historical accounting of how Chinese higher education has evolved since the establishment of the People's Republic, and highlights the important role Hayhoe has played over time as the "foremost scholar of Chinese higher education."

This volume is cosponsored by the Higher Education Special Interest Group of the Comparative and International Education Society, which awarded Hayhoe with its inaugural Lifetime Contribution Award in 2009. This volume is an important addition to the literature for those interested in China as well as those who are interested in learning more about one of the standard bearers in comparative and international education—Ruth Hayhoe.

JOHN N. HAWKINS
University of California
W. JAMES JACOB
University of Pittsburgh

Introduction

Education and Cross-cultural Dialogue: A Celebration of Ruth Hayhoe's Scholarship

Qiang Zha and Karen Mundy

The Origin of This Volume

We feel privileged to introduce this volume to our readers. It originates from a conference held on May 6, 2011, at the Ontario Institute for Studies in Education of the University of Toronto (OISE/UT), convened as a tribute to Ruth Hayhoe. As a comparativist and sinologist, Ruth has devoted her life and career to the study of Chinese education and culture. Arguably, her work over the years serves to bridge education philosophies and ideas across cultures in the East and the West. In the past three decades or so, numerous Chinese students and scholars have used Ruth's work as milestones for their academic journeys in the field of comparative education, while many of their Western peers benefitted from the East–West bridge that Ruth has helped build in broadening their career horizons. Among them certainly are the two editors of this volume.

When the year 2011 was approaching, a group of Ruth's former and current students suggested organizing a conference to celebrate her scholarship. An immediate reason behind this suggestion was that the year 2011 marked the centennial anniversary of the Revolution of 1911 (or Hsinhai Revolution) in China, a remarkable event that signaled China's interaction with modern democracies globally and its integration into the modern world. There were also other reasons that prompted this event. Specifically, the US Comparative and International Education Society (CIES) decided to convene its 2011 annual conference in Montreal, Quebec, from May 1 to 5. This would bring many of Ruth's international colleagues and friends to Canada. More significantly, Ruth was named an Honorary Fellow of the CIES, and was officially awarded the honor at the CIES 2011 conference in Montreal. This was a recognition of her contribution over many years to research, teaching, and scholarship in the field of comparative education, as well as of service to the CIES. When these different elements were put together, there seemed to be no better occasion for a gathering to celebrate Ruth's scholarship and accomplishments in the field of comparative education.

It would be a pity if we proceeded without dedicating a paragraph to describing the one-day conference, which was no less than a splendid event, attracting close to 200 scholars and students from Canada, the United States, Hong Kong, Singapore, Japan, and of course, mainland China. Among the participants (some even made a special trip to attend) were five former presidents of CIES, including Ruth herself. In addition, the participants included the current President of the World Council of Comparative Education Societies (WCCES), the Editor of the *Comparative Education Review*, a flagship journal in the field, and three former and current presidents of the Comparative Education Society of Hong Kong. In total, 40 presentations were made at this one-day conference, and 14 of them now make up the chapters in this volume. Lastly, we were privileged to have such sponsors for the event as OISE/UT, the Munk School of Global Affairs of the University of Toronto, the Asian Institute of the University of Toronto, the York University Center for Asian Research, *Frontiers of Education in China*, and the Education Office of the Chinese Consulate General in Toronto.

A Celebration of Ruth Hayhoe's Scholarship

As colleagues, students, and friends of Ruth, we gathered for the purpose of celebrating her scholarship. Ruth is by any definition an influential and prolific scholar. Her publication record is nothing short of breathtaking, including five full-length books (including a recent coauthored one), and more than 80 journal articles, in addition to several edited volumes. Her work has been well known in the field, as evidenced by a 2004 survey of the most influential scholars in comparative education. In this survey, Ruth was ranked among the top ten most-cited comparativists (Cook et al. 2004). As a figure of outstanding influence in our field, Ruth has over the years nurtured a unique scholarship.

First and foremost, Ruth adopts a distinctive historical culturalist approach to comparative education, which stresses "the integration of specific historical-cultural contextual details into the analysis" (Hayhoe 1989, 174). This approach is described as having "sharpened her sense for cultural specificities and her ability for cross-cultural dialogue" (Bray 2009; see also Wing On Lee, this volume). As a culturalist, Ruth strongly advocates the recognition that there exist different knowledges and different ways of knowing this world. "Of greatest importance is the readiness to listen to the narrative of the other, and to learn the lessons which can be discovered in distinctive threads of human cultural thought and experience," she once asserted (Hayhoe and Pan 2001a, 20). For her own research, Ruth pays enormous attention to "the ways in which Chinese syncretism manifested itself in historical and contemporary contexts within the realm of higher education," as Irving Epstein notes in this volume. This historical culturalist approach, together with the multidisciplinary perspectives that it entails, has enabled her research to "illuminate the paths to more equitable education systems, more just societies, and, hopefully, to international understanding and peace" (Robert F. Arnove's chapter in this volume), and distinguishes Ruth's study of Chinese education as being "shaped like no other scholar of her generation" (Ross 2009). Second, Ruth's work features a strong sense of self-reflexivity. She has been at the forefront of scholars advocating a deep philosophical reflection about the epistemological nature of knowledge, and how people know and learn in different cultural traditions. Throughout the years, she has been searched assiduously for "a way of looking at knowledge itself and its possibilities in the international arena," as she firmly believes that "a consideration of the nature of knowledge itself, apart from its political or economic implications, is fundamental to an analysis of international educational and knowledge relations" (Hayhoe 1989, 170). Such a sense of self-reflexivity might be best embodied in her courageous and penetrating autobiography, *Full Circle: A Life with Hong Kong and China* (Hayhoe 2004).

Furthermore, throughout her career, Ruth has committed herself to building cultural and academic dialogue across civilizations. Essentially, this is a natural extension from her culturalist methodological position. What Ruth envisions for our field are "interactions....as a true dialogue among ready listeners rather than a struggle among contending interests such as Huntington portrayed in his 'clash of civilizations' " (Hayhoe and Pan 2001a, 21). Over the years, Ruth has written so passionately about Chinese culture and China's educational system, and "contributed tremendously to bringing the world into China and China into the world" (Yang 2009). Ruth's compassion and commitment to intercivilizational dialogue encompasses more than China, and has "led her to look for and build intellectual and institutional bridges across cultures which extended beyond China to other cultures and civilizations, including Africa, India and the Arab countries" (Gu 2009). This commitment is most eloquently manifested in her edited volume *Knowledge Across Cultures: A Contribution to Dialogue among Civilizations* (Hayhoe and Pan 2001b). By modeling intercivilizational dialogue as a theoretical and practical approach to comparative education, Ruth has provided our field with an invaluable response to the center–periphery dynamic of knowledge, which comparativists often criticize but rarely act to reverse. In this sense, Ruth has shown us an excellent example of seeking a unity of knowledge and action, a notion sitting at the core of the Confucian scholarly tradition.

Perhaps one piece, "A Chinese Puzzle" (Hayhoe 1989), can best illustrate Ruth's unique scholarship. This wonderful and inspiring essay encapsulates Ruth's unique ability to combine humility, expertise, wisdom and curiosity into a prompting and propelling call for our field of comparative education. It traces Ruth's intellectual journey into the comparative study of Chinese higher education, and in parallel presents our field not only as one of world historical and theoretical significance, but as an arena for intellectual and spiritual delight. In this piece, Ruth probes and constructs an ideal type of the Chinese knowledge tradition "that would crystallize its points of difference from the medieval European tradition" (ibid., 160). From there, Ruth suggests the need to pay attention to fundamental knowledge assumptions and patterns, which might in turn create opportunities for new scholarly contributions from different cultural lifeworlds, in particular from indigenous cultures in the developing world. Drawing on Habermas's concept of "communicative action," Ruth sees it "as a process within which the system is reconnected to its cultural life-world," which "might be extended to a concept of international interaction among systems" (ibid., 173). "The interaction then consists not merely of a transfer of technology and knowledge from an advanced to a less advanced region, but mutual critical reflection on the dilemmas of modernity in both contexts. Such dialogue has transformative possibilities and could be a significant part of democratic process on the level of international society" (Hayhoe 1992, 171). Ruth emphasizes that the "rationalization of these life-worlds in an international milieu could provide a vision of the redemption of Western modernity that comes not only through the internal critiques of its own scholars but also through the contribution of other sociocultural values and aesthetic sensitivities" (Hayhoe 1989, 173).

Without doubt, Ruth has brought such sentiments into her teaching and mentoring. It is no secret that Ruth is a deeply loved and trusted colleague, mentor, advisor, and teacher in our field. Over the years, Ruth has enjoyed a legendary reputation among her students and colleagues for her brilliance, warmth, sensitivity, and generosity, and her ability to "push students beyond the level of quality they had originally imagined for themselves" (Farrell 2009). How could she manage to achieve all this? The answer is perhaps hinted at in a self-reflexive piece, in which she compares the lives and careers of two great teacher—mentors in human history across the East and the West, Confucius and St. Paul. In this piece, composed exclusively for the May 6 conference, Ruth unveils the important values common to both: a strong sense of both humility and social responsibility, values which in turn have had the most bearing and influence on her own career and scholarship. She asserts that a "profound understanding of one's own emptiness and indebtedness to grace can thus be seen as a value that bridges the Christian West and the Confucian East" (Hayhoe 2012). Perhaps the words below best illustrate how Ruth draws sustenence from cultural and scholarly traditions in both the East and the West, and embodies these important values in her teaching and scholarship:

> And my sense is that....the greatest gift we can give is the gift of ourselves, including gifts of time lavished upon those whom we can encourage, guide and support. Then we can celebrate, in turn, the ways in which their scholarship and service rises above and beyond our own....The call for a scholarship that is socially responsible, and indeed seeks to be socially transformative, is thus common to both traditions. It gives all of us cause for reflection on smaller and larger issues in our teaching and scholarship.

In sum, to quote Robert F. Arnove in this volume, Ruth's scholarship "illustrates the possibilities of a dialogue among civilizations that enriches scholarly perspectives and ways of understanding differences as well as common interests across cultures and societies—the elements of continuity and change that need to be taken into account in formulating education policies reflective of local realities, even as they are buffeted by global forces....These, after all, are the very worthy goals of comparative education, to which she has contributed so much over a glorious career."

Moving Forward with Ruth Hayhoe's Legacy

Ruth's publications have influenced multiple generations of students and scholars in the field of comparative education in both the East and the West. Her scholarship is deeply treasured by many comparativists, and such sentiments are strongly echoed in the chapters included in this volume. Structurally, there are three sections in this volume, which cover three complementary subthemes: "Comparative Education, International Relations and Dialogue across Cultures," "Chinese Higher Education and the World," and "Inquiries into Chinese Education Inspired by Ruth Hayhoe."

Essays in the first section of the book, "Comparative Education, International Relations and Dialogue across Cultures," are united by a common interest in comparative education as a field of study and the role that different embodiments of a dialogue across cultures might play in our understanding of educational phenomena. In her opening chapter in this section, Karen Mundy pays tribute to Ruth's modeling of the scholar as a "listening intellect." She reflects on the impact that her first graduate course with Ruth in 1989 had on the development of her own research on international organizations and global collective action in education. She argues that Ruth's course foreshadowed a whole field of research focused on global governance; and shows how Ruth encouraged students to use wide-ranging normative and critical theories to generate evaluative frameworks for a type of scholarship that reaches forward toward more effective global institutions. Wing On Lee's Chapter 2 explores the lessons he has learned from Ruth's approach to the study of education, illustrating how these have helped him to make sense of his own experiences of teaching and learning in three countries: Singapore, Hong Kong, and Australia. In particular, he highlights Ruth's dedication to understanding the normative schema that underlie whole educational systems and her practice of looking at her own life, and the life of other influential educators, as fundamentally the story of a human quest for moral and normative sense making. He concludes that Ruth "has fully regarded herself as the research instrument, and her own experience is a source for interpretation of her times and the people around her, and in return they have provided meaning in her life." Joseph P. Farrell, Ruth's longtime colleague at the University of Toronto, explores in his Chapter 3 the cultural and spiritual role that one organization, the International Scouting Movement, has made to the construction of global cultural dialogue. He shows how the scouting movement extended a constructivist approach to learning that drove its rapid, almost viral uptake around the world. In Chapter 4, Yeow-Tong Chia examines the evolution of two academic discourse communities in education: comparative education and the history of education, drawing on his own research to highlight the need to build stronger bridges between them. He argues that Ruth's scholarship and her emphasis on cultural and intercivilizational dialogue provides the epistemological and discursive space to move one step further by bringing non-Western histories and cultures into the discussion on both fields of study. Finally, Heidi Ross and her student Yimin Wang (Chapter 5) pay tribute to Ruth by telling a dialogic story of six scholars and their engagement with education in China. This essay explores three layers of dialogue: in time, in relational space, and finally, dialogue as "humanizing globalization" to explore the overlapping scholarly contributions of six prominent China scholars: Ruth Hayhoe, Heidi Ross, Suzanne Pepper, Lynn Paine, Jing Lin, and Gerry Postiglione.

The second section "Chinese Higher Education and the World" depicts the evolving and increasing interactions between Chinese higher education and the world community. The chapters included in this section make an insightful call for a more critical interaction between the Chinese cultural and knowledge system and the world community, on the one hand, and a more rigorous exploration into the rich Chinese cultural and knowledge tradition, on the other. In this process, the Chinese university will not only play a key role, but also enjoy a unique opportunity for self-transcendence. Qiang Zha's Chapter 6 sheds some light on the pitfalls and fallacies of transnational higher education establishments and arrangements on Chinese soil, and warns that the seemingly booming transnational higher education activities in China may now be confronting a looming crisis. As a possible solution, he suggests a critical culturalist agenda that emphasizes the principle of pursuing complementary strengths/interests and synergies in developing transnational higher education arrangements, rather than simply focusing on commercial benefits. In Chapter 7, Rui Yang studies more broadly the Chinese faculty members of Western universities as a kind of Chinese knowledge diaspora, and argues that they are a modern kind of cosmopolitan literati, who could contribute actively to higher education internationalization in both China and their host systems (Canada in his case study). Drawing on Ruth Hayhoe's hypothesis that China's rich traditional culture could bring forth a Chinese model of the university, Hongcai Wang (Chapter 8) envisions "a fusion of the soul of the Western university system and the spirit of Chinese culture into one body" in a conscious effort to take a first step in defining a Chinese model of the university. Robert F. Arnove, on the other hand, insightfully observes in Chapter 9 that China now has a unique opportunity to address the mounting tensions among the competing demands of equity, quality, and efficiency, of institutional autonomy, academic freedom, and public accountability, and between the instrumental and intrinsic goals and purposes of education, as it strengthens its system in the face of the pressures of a neoliberal globalization. At the end of this section in Chapter 10, Ningsha Zhong traces the cultural adaptation of the idea of university autonomy in the process of knowledge transfer from the West to China. She argues that Chinese universities, with their evolving focus on the unity of knowledge and action in the exercise of autonomy within government policies, have shown innovativeness and zeal for change. She suggests this may, in turn, become a resource in terms of new forms of knowledge and action for generations to come in the international arena. To a large extent, these chapters exemplify Ruth's self-reflexive approach to educational issues and problems, which places an emphasis on a philosophical exploration of historical and cultural milieu.

The last section "Inquiries into Chinese Education Inspired by Ruth Hayhoe" includes four chapters that carry forward Ruth's pioneering work in the study of Chinese education. Through her work, Ruth has offered us a compelling alternative narrative that calls for reexamining the traditional paradigms that marginalize the power and influence of local and indigenous knowledge and knowledge agents. Inspired by Ruth's insight into how indigenous knowledge and practice can be used as a way of reshaping educational policy and intellectual thought within contemporary China, Irving Epstein (Chapter 11) examines the struggles of Chinese children and youth when confronting global capitalism, and maintains that the persistence of their own cultural values and norms have allowed at least some of them to negotiate the neoliberal principles of global capitalism according to their own terms. In Chapter 12, Vilma Seeberg and Haiyan Qiang present a vivid narrative that describes how the collegial circles of three women scholars (with Ruth being one of them) intersected during a Canada–China higher education development project, and how their private efforts helped build locally controlled, appropriate projects that are having a far-reaching, transgenerational, beneficial impact both locally and internationally, also over the long term. David Post discusses Ruth's engagement with Hong Kong over 30 years in Chapter 13, from her arrival in a Hong Kong Christian community to her return as the president of the Hong Kong Institute of Education, a "full-circle" in Ruth's own words. In fact, David Post poses the challenging question of whether or not the "circle" metaphor can fully describe the growth in complexity of Hong Kong and Ruth Hayhoe, both having shown an amazing capacity for absorbing cultural and societal changes, and both having spiraled their developmental paths over a long time period. Finally, we have left the last word to Ruth in her own chapter, which challenges educators of Hong Kong to root their reforms in the richness of China's educational traditions and thereby bring a new spiritual and cultural energy into global education discourse. Based on a synthesis of Song neo-Confucian and English Renaissance values, she suggests the concept of humane talent in place of human capital. A parallel synthesis between Ming neo-Confucianism and Deweyan pragmatism could give birth to a notion of inclusive individuality, she proposes. Furthermore, a radical creativity rooted in Daoist naturalism could undergird the courageous reforms that are underway in Hong Kong schools, enabling them to model significant Chinese values for the world.

Last but not the least, we would like to take this opportunity to thank all who were involved in preparing for and organizing the conference on May 6, 2011. Yeow-Tong Chia was one of its co-organizers, and provided enormous support to forming the conference program and liaising with the presenters. Grace Karram Stephenson played a key role in coordinating all the activities relating to the conference, from registration to reception arrangements. Many of Ruth's colleagues at OISE/UT joined in the conference and chaired many of the sessions. Among them were Eric Bredo, Tony Chambers, Michael Connelly, Grace Feuerverger, Glen Jones, Sarfaroz Niyozov, Julia Pan, Tricia Seifert, and Njoki Wane. Two of Ruth's longtime colleagues and mentors, Cicely Watson and Vandra Masemann, were with us the whole day. In addition, many OISE/UT students helped as volunteers that day, assisting in each and every session. They include Jack Lee, Jian Liu, Carly Manion, Meggan Madden, Francine Menashy, Yuxin Tu, Julian Weinrib, Naxin Zhao, and others. Yueh-Shun Chang, a design program student at York University, designed the conference poster. To make a long story short, we truly appreciate their generous support, without which this conference could not possibly have happened, let alone have been such a huge success. This book is a proud outcome of the efforts of many.

References

Bray, Mark. 2009. Taken from Mark Bray's supporting letter for Ruth's nomination for the CIES Honorary Fellow.

Cook, Bradley J., Steven J. Hite, and Erwin H. Epstein. 2004. "Discerning Trends, Contours, and Boundaries in Comparative Education: A Survey of Comparativists and Their Literature." *Comparative Education Review* 48 (2): 123–149.

Farrell, Joseph. 2009. Taken from Joseph Farrell's supporting letter for Ruth's nomination for the CIES Honorary Fellow.

Gu, Mingyuan. 2009. Taken from Gu Mingyuan's supporting letter for Ruth's nomination for the CIES Honorary Fellow.

Hayhoe, Ruth. 1989. "A Chinese Puzzle." *Comparative Education Review* 33 (2): 155–175.

Hayhoe, Ruth. 1992. "Universities, Cultural Identity, and Democracy: Some Canada-China Comparisons." *Interchange* 23 (1 and 2): 165–180.

Hayhoe, Ruth. 2004. *Full Circle: A Life with Hong Kong and China*. Hong Kong: Comparative Education Research Center, The University of Hong Kong.

Hayhoe, Ruth. 2012. "A Bridge too Far? Comparative Reflections on St Paul and Confucius." *Frontiers of Education in China* 7 (3): 338–346.

Hayhoe, Ruth, and Julia Pan. 2001a. "A Contribution to Dialogue among Civilizations." In *Knowledge across Cultures: A Contribution to Dialogue among Civilizations*, ed. Ruth Hayhoe and Julia Pan (pp. 1–21). Hong Kong: Comparative Education Research Centre, The University of Hong Kong.

Hayhoe, Ruth, and Julia Pan, eds. 2001b. *Knowledge across Cultures: A Contribution to Dialogue among Civilizations*. Hong Kong: Comparative Education Research Centre, The University of Hong Kong.

Ross, Heidi. 2009. Taken from Heidi Ross' supporting letter for Ruth's nomination for the CIES Honorary Fellow.

Yang, Rui. 2009. Taken from Rui Yang's supporting letter for Ruth's nomination for the CIES Honorary Fellow.

Part I

Comparative Education, International Relations, and Dialogue across Cultures

Chapter 1

From International Relations to Global Governance in Education: A Tribute to Ruth

Karen Mundy

Introduction

In January 1989, I was fresh from three years of work as a secondary-school teacher in rural Zimbabwe and from a round-the-world trip home that had culminated in a six-week, cross-country visit through pre–Tiananmen Square China. I was returning to graduate school at the University of Toronto and had enrolled in my first course, titled "International Academic Relations," offered by Professor Ruth Hayhoe. There I arrived dressed in baggy jeans and clunky boots bought at the new tourist market in Beijing, with self-cut hair and no particular career aspiration. I viewed the masters degree as a short period of respite, providing space for my reintroduction to Canada and time to make sense of the experience I had had of being a volunteer expatriate educator, working for a foreign government in a part of the world that was scarred by colonialism, civil war, and many iterations of "development."

My first course with Ruth left an indelible mark on me. While other students took Ruth's lead and pushed into research on globalization in higher education or more particularly on transformations in Chinese higher education, the intellectual starting point that Ruth's course provided led me in a different direction—toward the study of "global governance" in education, and more specifically, the intricacies of bilateral, multilateral, and nongovernmental efforts to support a universal entitlement for education as part of a more globally just world order. This journey—and the important role Ruth's mentorship and intellectual acumen have played in it—is the topic of this short reflection.

Ruth's Framing of International Relations in Education: "A Listening Intellect"

I can still remember aspects of my first course with Ruth in minute detail. Each week, new intellectual windows would fly open, and the rapid flows of conversation and ideas were such that at times I was left in a speechless vertigo. In the opening weeks, not only Marx and Max Weber, but Habermas, Rajni Kothari, Ashis Nandi, Ali Mazrui, and Johan Galtung were covered, as students were guided to think about and to compare different paradigms for understanding world order and the place of education and knowledge within this order.

Readers of Ruth's articles, "A Chinese Puzzle" (Hayhoe 1989b) and "Redeeming Modernity" (Hayhoe 2000), will already have an introduction of the major themes of this course, and will be familiar with the questions that lay behind it. For, in 1989, Ruth had finished her initial work on the rocky evolution of higher education in China, from the early twentieth century, through to the Cultural Revolution and the beginning of China's open-door policies. Her attention was now focused on understanding the opportunities and challenges of achieving a culturally and politically appropriate transformation of higher education in China, in a context of rapid and expanding educational influence from Western countries and West-dominated multilateral organizations.

Ruth began her survey of "International Academic Relations" by introducing us to the field of international relations (IR) in political science. This field, long dominated by scholars whose central concern was the problem of war, was at that time in a period of profound disarray. The Cold War had solidified an approach to understanding world order that was dominated by a concern with interstate relations (Holsti 1985). However, contending groups of scholars had begun to challenge the dominance of this agenda. Led by scholars like Johan Galtung, Ali Mazrui, and James Rosenau, these scholars demanded that the field of IR be opened up to other concerns, the concerns of common citizens (Galtung 1973,

1980, 1989; Mazrui 1975; Rosenau 2005). They called for a new kind of modeling of alternatives in global society and new attention to the issues of global social inequality and global environmental degradation. They returned to the essentially Kantian project of thinking of world society as a community of people, not states, for whom issues of peace and war, while important, were not of singular concern. And, in contrast to the behavioral and positivistic mainstream in the field of IR, this group of scholars did not shy away from idealism and the notion that academic research should be undertaken with an eye to its ability to model better global institutions and political processes.

The course provided me with my first introduction to neo-Marxist world system theories, and to the profound critiques of Western modernity found in the work of the Frankfurt school critical theorists and other critical scholars from the non-Western world, like Ashis Nandy and Rajni Kothari (Habermas 1984; Wallerstein 1984; Kothari 1987; Nandy 1987). For me at that time, these were the ideas that I found most powerful and persuasive, and I identified my own intellectual work almost immediately under the world systems banner in comparative education. However, Ruth's course had a profound pedagogical structure that did not allow us to jump easily onto any intellectual bandwagon. Thus, she asked us to consider not only the limitations and potential for domination in Western notions of science and rationality, but also the potential risks involved in accepting more radical notions of "de-linkage" from the world community. Using Habermas's (1984) theory of communicative action as a foil for our conversations, Ruth gently led us to answer for ourselves the question: Are there aspects of the Western knowledge tradition worth preserving? Only many years later did I understand how profoundly this question derived from Ruth's own research on the brutal suppression of intellectual knowledge during China's Cultural Revolution and from her efforts to carve out an approach to the opening of Chinese universities that might bring Chinese knowledge traditions into a sustained, mutually beneficial dialogue with certain aspects of Western knowledge. Though I cannot recall having any sustained discussion about China in the course, I can now see that, in its essence, we were being offered an opportunity to learn from Ruth's own encounter with the "puzzle" of China's educational development as that country entered more directly into a new phase in its relations with the wider world.

In one of Ruth's selected course readings, Rajni Kothari (1987, 290), utilizes the term "a listening intellect" to describe the important role that intellectuals must play in the creation of humane governance in world society. Beyond the substantive intellectual components of Ruth's course, I still marvel at the way, in one 12-week session, Ruth was able to embody this ideal. Her course guided us toward the habit of "listening" deeply to alternative ideas; juxtaposing different constellations of knowledge as a way to puzzle out alternative approaches to our specific interests—which in that year ranged from the global dominance of the English language, through to the workings of bilateral aid agencies, the politics of foreign student flows, and the impact of the World Bank. She encouraged us to draw on the widest range of ideas and scholarship available when seeking out answers to our intellectual encounters with the "puzzles" of international educational relations, and did not allow us to shy away from the profound need for new ideas that bridge competing paradigms about knowledge, power, and interests in world society (Hayhoe 1986).

Contemporary Debates: From IR to Global Governance

Today, educational policy research continues to frame education as primarily the domain of sovereign states. Comparative education—a field of scholarship in which both Ruth and I have made our central contributions—continues to operate fundamentally as an arena for sharing knowledge about "other" educational systems. However, in my work and in the work of a growing group of scholars, questions raised in Ruth Hayhoe's course about the role of education in the development of a world system or world society have become increasingly prominent. In my case, I can trace an intellectual path from the conversations about IR and world order that began in Ruth's class, through to my overarching interest in global governance in education, and to my more particular interest in the potentially emancipatory (as well as harmful) roles that can be played by international organizations and global civil society actors through their efforts to extend universal and equitable access to education.

A growing interest in the study and practice of "global governance" and "global social policy," in the fields of political science, IR, and public administration, has supported this journey (Barnett and Duval 2005; Koenig-Archibugi 2010)—something that Ruth's course foreshadowed. Over the last two decades, three things seem to have contributed to this rising interest in global governance as a topic or theme for mainstream IR scholarship. First, after decades in which bipolar power politics lay at the core of IR, the end of the Cold War opened up the field of IR and made the practical potential for international cooperation seem less limited. The fact that the relatively peaceful collapse of the Soviet Union had been unanticipated highlighted the failure of then contemporary, state-centric IR theory, which had focused on the power of states but missed the crucial role that citizens themselves could play in bringing about larger changes in the world system. Second, processes of "globalization," not only of economic relations but in terms of the rising magnitude of interregional and de-territorialized flows of all kinds of social interaction, suggested a further need to look beyond the state to understand the determinants of world order (Ruggie 2004; Rosenau 2005). Processes of economic integration and liberalization not only undermined the sovereignty and capacity of the postwar Keynesian welfare state in the West, while enhancing the power of emergent economies, they also created new forms of transnational private authority (both corporate and nongovernmental) whose roles had not been adequately captured in earlier IR paradigms.

Finally, new attention to global governance was predicated upon the presence of a generation of IR scholars ready to step into the theoretical void created by globalization and the end of the Cold War. In what later came to be described as a "constructivist turn," these scholars argued that normative or ideational structures had always mattered at least as much as material factors in the world polity, primarily because systems of meaning define how actors interpret and work on their material environment (Ruggie 1982; Finnemore 1996a, 1996b; Price and Reus-Smit 1998). Such changes could not be attributed solely to a change in the material/strategic interests of states; instead, they depended on the ability of nonstate actors to assert normative agendas that states later adopted in order to preserve domestic and international legitimacy (Finnemore and Sikkink 1998; Keck and Sikkink 1998). By emphasizing examples of norm-driven change in the international system, empirical research by constructivists opened the way to a new discussion about global governance that would have seemed purely idealistic two decades earlier.

In my view, a global governance frame for understanding IR in education pushes us (as my first course with Ruth had done) to look beyond what had become rather stale arguments about dependency and the hegemony of the West, and about centrality of states and governments. Returning to the Habermasian notions of communicative action and Ruth's own emphasis on dialogue across cultures, we might utilize the framework of global governance to look at the possibilities and potential for global institutions to function as arenas for an expanded dialogue among states and other collective actors in world society. For, as Inis Claude (1966) asserted in his early writing, global institutions are more than the simple pawns of self-interested states: They are also the sites of "collective legitimation," the process whereby we lay out common aspirational horizons for human well-being on a global scale.

The Real Worlds of International Organization in Education

To understand the prospects for better global governance in education, we need to start with a clear account of how we came to our current situation. In Ruth's scholarship and in her courses, a heavy emphasis was placed on historical reasoning, and using in particular the Weberian methodology of ideal types as an opportunity for understanding the contexts, interests, and ideas that have driven the development of specific configurations of educational actors. In my work, this emphasis has been picked up not only through historical case studies of multilateral organizations and other transnational actors active in education, but also through comparing their theories of action and modes of operation in the context of changing patterns of power in the world system (Mundy 1998).

At the global scale, today we have a range of global institutions whose activities in education are profoundly problematic. On the one hand, we have those institutions whose work has grown primarily in answer to the post–World War II challenges of "development" in postcolonial societies—United Nations Educational, Scientific, and Cultural Organization (UNESCO), United Nations Children's Fund (UNICEF), and the World Bank—but even more importantly (in terms of resource flows), national (bilateral) development agencies and a wide range international nongovernmental organizations. These institutions, over time, have provided an agenda for global collective action in education, first focused on the creation of skilled elites, and gradually shifting to the universalization of access to basic education as their raison d'etre (Severino and Ray 2010). However we may view them, they play a potentially crucial role in a world system that is crisis prone and increasingly integrated economically. In these organizations, we may see the first inklings of a global "social safety net" for children, and an opportunity to speak across the boundaries of the nation state about inequality in educational opportunities and outcomes. Yet, they are a fragmented and competitive brotherhood with little coherence in their programming and operations. They are predominantly rooted in Western contexts and traditions, and have to date been deeply marred by the geopolitical and strategic interests of the Western world. Today, among this first group of actors, the dominant sibling is the World Bank, which acts as a sort of "global credit union" for development projects in low- and middle-income countries, and increasingly stands at the helm of global technical and intellectual efforts to frame a standardized educational reform agenda (Carnoy 1999). The World Bank relies on a nomothetic science of the economic man, thus framing the purposes of education in narrow terms, primarily as a means of human capital forma-tion for economic development (Mundy 2002, 2010; Mundy and Menashy 2012). To use the lexicon from Hayhoe's course on international academic relations, our central global institutions in education-for-development operate in ways that are deeply at odds with the notions of a "listening" intellect and a dialogue across cultures. When imagined as an arena for communicative action among citizens in an emergent global order (to use the Habermasian ideal), the World Bank is woefully inadequate.

A second cluster of global and regional educational institutions—quite different in character from the education-for-development cluster—has emerged among like-minded governments seeking policy solutions to simi-lar domestic problems. Initially, the task of international information shar-ing about educational policy was mandated to UNESCO, and was directly related to the liberal postwar ideals of creating equality of opportunity through enhanced provision of education (Mundy 1999). Later, competi-tion between the Soviet Union and the United States helped to produce strong regional-level interests in information sharing and standard setting in education. Shared approaches to policy–problem solving have gradually developed in the work of many other regional intergovernmental organiza-tions (Dale and Robertson 2002).

The Organisation for Economic Co-operation and Development (OECD), for example, has become an increasingly influential policy actor, perhaps most notably through its work in the area of cross-national testing and comparison. OECD has been rightly criticized for "teaching" member governments to "think" about the relationship between education and the economy in a neoliberal register (Henry et al. 2001; Resnik 2006). However, it also seems to me a persuasive alternative model for our global institu-tions, when compared to the central actor in the education-for-development regime, the World Bank. At the level of communicative action, the OECD's ways of working have tended to more directly engage member countries in substantive dialogue about education, drawing their differ-ent visions of the public good in education into conversation by inviting them to partake in self-reflexive reviews of their own practices and experi-ences. Perhaps as a result, the OECD's education agenda has consistently highlighted the important redistributive functions of education, focusing more on equity (rather than absolute poverty), and keeping the problem of social cohesion front and centre in its agenda (Mahon 2010). As just one small example, from the Programme for International Student Assessment (PISA) data, the OECD has developed a secondary analysis that suggests that learning systems that offer more highly equitable access to education (in which education is typically publicly provided) are also those that pro-duce the highest learning outcomes. Using the same data set, secondary analyses sponsored by the World Bank conclude that higher-quality learning is being produced in educational systems where services are delivered by private providers—a policy it has advocated for many years, but has been unable to "sell" in its loan packages to developing countries (Mundy and Menashy 2012). We need models like the OECD's work in education, which is more dialogic and less didactic, in any reconfiguration of global institutions in education.

There is, of course, a burgeoning of other significant global- and regional-level actors in the educational policy space that needs to be more deeply explored. Among them is the World Trade Organization, for example, which has played a part in the liberalization of trade in educational services (Verger 2009), and a new generation of transnational corporate ventures, whose activities straddle commercial self-interest and global philanthropy (Bhanji 2008). In my own work, I have in particular highlighted transnational civil society—comprised of various social movements, voluntary organizations, and other organized forms of collective action (such as unions and faith-based bodies). To assess these groups, which now have entered into the mainstream of global policy setting, I feel it is important that we try to establish a framework that draws from competing paradigms of civil society in political theory, so that we remain aware of the normative frames through which they make their contributions, whether through contestation, holding governments to account, or building the fundamental habits of engagement and civility among citizens. It seems to me that civil society actors may build deeper dialogue across different knowledge and cultural traditions in ways that states cannot. Yet, they are political actors too, rife with self-interest and intellectual biases. Only through empirical investigation into their theories of change and their real world practices can we assess their potential to contribute to a common aspirational horizon for collective action in our globalizing world system (Mundy and Murphy 2002; Mundy 2008).

One area of interest for future research is the role of emergent economic powers, like China, in the evolution of global collective action. In an important way, the rise of China as a key political actor on the world stage brings me full circle, back to my initial encounter with Ruth's work in 1989. Most recent research has focused on self-interest as the driving force behind Chinese relations with the broader world, following the traditional emphasis on nations and their sovereign interests as key drivers of IR. However, taking a page from Ruth's analysis, I believe we should look more carefully at the new wave of Chinese activism in international development and other global institutions as a fundamental opportunity for China to shape a global cultural dialogue, a dialogue to which China and other emergent powers will bring not only national self-interest, but also moral and aspirational maps for human well-being different from those of the Western world (Li 2012). Our aim must be to understand these aspirational maps, the particular historical contexts, interests, ideas, and limits that shape them, in terms that allow us to explore, in dialogic ways, their potential to contribute to a stronger and more thoroughly "humane" form of global governance.

Conclusion

This chapter began as a reflection on my first course as a graduate student in 1989, titled "International Academic Relations," which I took up with my dear friend and teacher, Ruth Hayhoe. I have tried to capture briefly the content and pedagogical structure of the course, which proved so generative for my own future scholarship. I have also described the new field of global governance research, which alerts us to the need for increasing attention to new kinds of international actors and the need for better empirical research into the causes of variation in the influence of global actors and institutions on education. More importantly, I have tried to suggest how Ruth helped me to place my own understanding of global institutions within an explicit normative framework, seeing in these institutions not only patterns of Western hegemony and the limits of Western forms of bureaucratic rationality, but also their possibilities as dialogic arenas within which collective aspirations for human society and its well-being may be forged. I remain convinced that the expansion of transnational relations in education must be understood, empirically, historically, and critically, through careful studies of the internal cultures and external political interests that shape them. I am also convinced that we should never forget that such institutions will shape and mediate our insertion into an ever-enlarging "global public domain" (Barnett and Finnemore 2004; Held 2005). Global governance research in education thus challenges us to use our empirical research about transnational and international policy processes in education as the foundation for a richer normative debate about the "limits of the possible" in the evolution of collective educational purposes on a global scale.

REFERENCES

Barnett, Mark, and Martha Finnemore. 2004. *Rules for the World: International Organizations and Global Politics.* Ithaca, NY: Cornell University Press.
Barnett, Mark, and Raymond Duvall, eds. 2005. *Power in Global Governance.* Cambridge, UK: Cambridge University Press.

Bhanji, Zahra. 2008. "Transnational Corporations in Education: Filling the Governance Gap through New Social Norms and Market Multilateralism?" *Globalisation, Societies and Education* 6 (1): 55–73.

Carnoy, Martin. 1999. *Globalization and Educational Reform: What Planners Need to Know*. Paris: UNESCO International Institute for Education Planning.

Claude, Inis, Jr. 1966. "Collective Legitimization as a Political Function of the United Nations." *International Organization* 20 (3): 367–379.

Dale, Roger, and Susan Lee Robertson. 2002. "The Varying Effects of Regional Organizations as Subjects of Globalization of Education." *Comparative Education Review* 46 (1): 10–36.

Finnemore, Martha. 1996a. *National Interests in International Society*. Ithaca, NY: Cornell University Press.

Finnemore, Martha. 1996b. "Norms, Culture and World Politics: Insights from Sociology's Institutionalism." *International Organization* 50 (2): 325–347.

Finnemore, Martha, and Kathryn Sikkink. 1998. "International Norm Dynamics and Political Change." *International Organization* 52 (4): 887–917.

Galtung, Johan. 1973. "A Structural Theory of Imperialism." *Journal of Peace Research* 10: 319–340.

Galtung, Johan. 1980. *The True Worlds: A Transnational Perspective*. New York: The Free Press.

Habermas, Jurgen. 1984. "Modernisation as Societal Rationalisation." In *The Theory of Communicative Action*, Vol. 1. Boston: Beacon Press.

Hayhoe, Ruth. 1986. "Penetration or Mutuality? China's Educational Cooperation with Europe, Japan, and North America." *Comparative Education Review* 30 (4): 532–559.

Hayhoe, Ruth. 1989a. *China's Universities and the Open Door*. Toronto: OISE Press.

Hayhoe, Ruth. 1989b. "A Chinese Puzzle." *Comparative Education Review* 33 (2): 155–175.

Hayhoe, Ruth. 2000. "Redeeming Modernity." *Comparative Education Review* 44 (4): 423–439.

Held, David. 2005 "At the Global Crossroads: The End of the Washington Consensus and the Rise of Global Social Democracy?" *Globalizations* 2 (1): 95–113.

Henry, Miriam, Robert Lingard, Fazal Rizvi, and Sandra Taylor. 2001. *The OECD, Globalisation and Education Policy*. Oxford: Pergamon Press.

Holsti, Kal. 1985. *The Dividing Discipline*. Boston: Allen and Unwin.

Keck, Margaret, and Kathryn Sikkink. 1998. *Activists beyond Borders*. New York: Cornell University Press.

Koenig-Archibugi, Mathias. 2010. "Understanding the Global Dimensions of Policy." *Global Policy* 1 (1): 16–28.

Kothari, Rajni. 1987. "On Humane Governance." *Alternatives* XII: 277–290.

Li, Sharon. 2012. "How China Views Its Role in Global Governance and Its Education Initiatives." *Frontiers of Education in China* 7 (1): 103–123.

Mahon, Rianne. 2010. "After Neo-Liberalism? The OECD, the World Bank and the Child." *Global Social Policy* 10: 172–192.

Mazrui, Ali. 1975. "World Culture and the Search for Human Consensus." In *On the Creation of a Just World Order: Preferred Worlds for the 1980s*, ed. Saul Mendlovitz (pp. 1–37). New York: Free Press.

Mundy, Karen. 1998. "Educational Multilateralism and World (Dis)order." *Comparative Education Review* 42 (4): 448–478.

Mundy, Karen. 1999. "UNESCO and the Limits of the Possible." *International Journal of Educational Development* 19 (1): 27–52.

Mundy, Karen. 2002. "Education in a Reformed World Bank." *International Journal of Educational Development* 22 (5): 483–508.

Mundy, Karen. 2008. "From NGOs to CSOs: Social Citizenship, Civil Society and 'Education for All'—An Agenda for Further Research." *Current Issues in Comparative Education* 10 (2). Available online at: www.tc.columbia.edu/cice/.

Mundy, Karen. 2010. "Education for All and the Global Governors." In *Who Governs the Globe?*, ed. Martha Finnemore, Deborah Avant, and Susan K. Sell (pp. 333–355). Cambridge, UK: Cambridge University Press.

Mundy, Karen, and Francine Menashy. 2012. "The World Bank, the International Finance Corporation, and Private Sector Participation in Basic Education: Examining the Education Sector Strategy 2020." In *Education Strategy in the Developing World: A Conversation about the World Bank's Education Policy Development and Revision*, ed. Alexander Wiseman and Christopher Collins (pp. 113–131). Bingley, UK: Emerald Publishing.

Mundy, Karen, and Lynn Murphy. 2002. "Transnational Advocacy, Global Civil Society: Emerging Evidence from the Field of Education." *Comparative Education Review* 45 (1): 85–126.

Nandy, Ashis. 1987. "The Traditions of Technology." In *Traditions, Tyranny and Utopias: Essays in the Politics of Awareness,* ed. Ashis Nandy. Delhi: Oxford University Press.

Price, Richard, and Christian Reus-Smit. 1998. "Dangerous Liaisons: Critical International Theory and Constructivism." *European Journal of International Relations* 4 (3): 259–294.

Resnik, Julia. 2006. "International Organizations, the 'Education-Economic Growth' Black Box and the Development of World Education Culture." *Comparative Education Review* 50 (2): 173–195.

Rosenau, James N. 2005. "Governance in the Twenty-First Century." In *The Global Governance Reader*, ed. R. Wilkinson (pp. 45–67). New York: Routledge.

Ruggie, John Gerard. 1982. "International Regimes, Transactions, and Change: Embedded Liberalism in the Postwar Economic Order." *International Organization* 36 (2): 379–415.

Ruggie, John Gerard. 2004. "Reconstituting the Global Public Domain: Issues, Actors and Practices." *European Journal of International Relations* 10 (4): 499–531.

Severino, Jean-Michel, and Olivier Ray. 2010. The End of ODA: The Death and Rebirth of Global Public Policy. Working Paper 167. Washington DC: Centre for Global Development.

Verger, Antoni. 2009. "The Merchants of Education: Global Politics and the Uneven Education Liberalization Process in the WTO." *Comparative Education Review* 53 (3): 379–401.

Wallerstein, Immanuel. 1984. *The Politics of the World Economy: The States, the Movements and the Civilizations.* Cambridge: Cambridge University Press.

Chapter 2

Meaning Making in Cultural Experience: Insights from Ruth Hayhoe for Interpreting Internationalization and Localization in Australia, Hong Kong, and Singapore

Wing On Lee

Introduction

It is my great honour to contribute a chapter for this book organized in the honour of Ruth Hayhoe to express our thanks to her for all the contributions she has made as a scholar, as a professional, as a friend to many of us, and as a humane person to everyone. I started to read Ruth Hayhoe's work while I was studying for my PhD at the University of Durham. I read more of her works later when more publications came along. However, I only started to understand her scholarship more when I had an opportunity to work closely with her for three years during the time she served as Director at the Hong Kong Institute of Education. It was a very rich three years of learning for me, as I not only read her works, but I was also able to see how she finds meaning and creates meaning in life, and for me, this is the crux of her scholarship and professionality. I was particularly impressed with the way she wrote, as she researched and wrote in a style ahead of her time, a time when comparative education was significantly influenced by system analysis, patterns of development, policy transfer, and as she describes about what she learned from Brian Holmes, a problem-oriented, rationalistic, and scientific approach. While Hayhoe has been influenced by those approaches, she decided to go her way, while she grew in her scholarship and obtained a diversified personal experience, able to understand deeply another culture: Chinese culture.

The purpose of this chapter is to analyze Ruth Hayhoe's scholarship. She is a prolific writer, and has published volumes of work with a vast coverage of areas and topics. It would not be an easy task to analyze all her publications. Instead, I would like to focus on what is underneath her scholarship: her approach to life, to friendship, to knowledge, and human understanding. What I would like to show in this chapter is that Hayhoe's scholarship cannot be fully understood without a totality of these considerations. As a paper to celebrate her scholarship, and in return to her contribution, I would conduct a meaning-making exercise of my own as my academic dialogue with her, and an illustration of how her approaches can be applied in my meaning-making process in the course of my cultural experience in Australia, Hong Kong, and Singapore.

Significance of the Context

Ruth Hayhoe always writes in context. Contextual analysis penetrates her works, and is characteristic of her writings. The diverse topics notwithstanding, I always find the introductory chapters to be the most fascinating part of her books. For example, in her introduction to the book *Education and Modernization: The Chinese Experience* (Hayhoe 1992), she particularly mentions that context is important in understanding the concept of modernization in China:

> Much of the conceptual terminology used to explore issues of education and modernization has been drawn from Western experience. Its application to China is thus almost inevitably a process of measuring Chinese experience against that of the West. We have tried, therefore, to be consciously theoretical in our use of the key concept "modernization," weighing its meaning for the Chinese context. (xiii-xiv)

The significance of the cultural context is beyond being a background for understanding. Hayhoe describes it as a kind of resource—cultural resource—a source for understanding, and a source for insight and wisdom (Hayhoe 2011). Because the cultural context is an epistemological resource, dialogue across cultures is therefore an important means of enriching human knowledge and understanding. Amidst her works, a penetrating academic agenda of Hayhoe's is *Knowledge across Cultures* (Hayhoe 1993; Hayhoe and Pan 2001), and in her writings, she variably called this "dialogue among cultures," "dialogue among civilizations," "East–West dialogue," "cultural interchange," "civilizational interaction," and "international interaction."

One of Hayhoe's most impressive contextual analyses is Gu Mingyuan's *Education in China and Abroad: Perspectives from a Lifetime in Comparative Education* (with an introduction by Ruth Hayhoe) (Hayhoe 2001). The introduction to this book demonstrates her mastery of comparative education in China, and amazingly, her mastery of the works of Professor Gu Mingyuan, the most eminent comparativist in China. The book is a collection of Professor Gu's articles, selected for translation into English. The selection of the articles in this book was done on her recommendation. The introduction shows the details that Hayhoe has mastered about the development of the field of comparative education in China, how this field started as a means to learn from the West, how the attention was turned to the former Soviet Union as a target of learning, how the Cultural Revolution became a testing time for Gu, and how new learning opportunities surrounding progressive learning opened up for him during this period. The introduction shows how Hayhoe can not only discuss the educational changes in the context of political changes, but also how all these changes become meaningful to a person's life, and how the professional growth of an influential person like Gu can further create impact into the system. This is the beauty of Hayhoe's scholarship. She manages to integrate the situational and contextual aspects of an issue, the time, and/or the person to create meanings and insights.

Another book showing a similar approach, but the further breadth of her scholarship is *Portraits of Influential Chinese Educators* (Hayhoe 2006). Her first chapter, "Creating the portraits—an interpretive framework," provides an artful summary of Confucian, Neo-Confucian, and Daoist philosophies of education, particularly the thoughts that would help to understand features of education in contemporary China. This summary does not only provide an "interpretive framework," but also, to quote, "a context for the educator's life" (38). The wonder of this book is that Hayhoe was able to identify the most influential Chinese educators. "The influential Chinese Educators" is a topic of difficult choice, as it all depends on what grounds she takes to judge that these educators being selected are *the* "influential educators." There is no doubt a "personal experience" dimension in her judgment, particularly how Hayhoe's life came across the lives of these educators, and the specific and significant impacts they have made in their times and their localities. For the influential educators she chose to write about, she even called them "ten lives in mine" (Hayhoe 2005). A common thread in these people's lives is how they worked ahead of their time or how they have preceded their time in what they said, what they did, and what they foresaw, and how these educators persisted over time and against oppositions and difficulties, particularly over the period of the Cultural Revolution. In summary, they are all progressive educators in one way or another, and the choice of these educators to be portrayed also reflects Ruth Hayhoe as a progressive educator herself. It is the life-touching-life process that has made her choose these progressive educators.

Research Methodology: The Researcher as the Instrument

The *Portraits of Influential Chinese Educators* offers a deliberate section on Hayhoe's research methodology, and I think this represents the culmination of the methodology she has adopted all along. She criticizes the shortcoming of the "secular rationality" and objectivist research as it only focuses on what could be observed, measured, and patterned, and because of this, philosophy is losing its cultural role, and the inner meaning of human lives tends to be ignored. The narrative approach allows Hayhoe to fill the gap of empirical research, and more importantly presents the researcher as the focal point in the process of research and discovery, which would both allow and require the researcher to interact with the environment, with the subjects, and even develop a relationship between the researcher and the participants. This is crucial to Hayhoe's research methodology, as all along, she has been a very engaging "participant observer" and her writings are records and narratives of what has happened in her life and to the people around her. It not only shows her intellectual interpretation of her surroundings and the people around her, but it is a process of sense making, and she has found meaning and created meaning about herself, about those people she chose to narrate, and about the broader intellectual and cultural frameworks that have created the context for those meanings. Ruth Hayhoe has fully regarded herself as the research instrument, and her own experience is a source for interpretation of her times and the people around her, and in return, they have provided meaning in her life. It is in this context that I see her motivation in writing *Full Circle: A Life with Hong Kong and China* (Hayhoe 2004). And this is a record of meaning making in her life, a life that integrates her experience into research, and a life that generates insights from the experience, which further provides insights for her research into her surroundings and the people around her. *Full Circle* also provides insight into how Hayhoe finds meaning in her life, how she finds life meaningful, how she makes others' lives meaningful, and how she creates meaning in life. It is through her interactive engagement with others in the course of life that she has conducted her research not only through cultural dialogues but also personal dialogues.

A Storytelling Approach to Comparative Education

One striking feature of Ruth Hayhoe's academic writing approach is storytelling. Two of her books are titled *Portraits*, namely *Portraits of Influential Chinese Educators* (Hayhoe 2006) and *Portraits of 21st Century Chinese Universities* (Hayhoe et al. 2011). Her *Full Circle* (Hayhoe 2004), although not named portrait, is actually a self-portrait. However, explaining and defending storytelling as an academic-writing approach was most elaborately discussed in her early work *China's Universities: 1895–1995* (Hayhoe 1999), a book developed from her PhD thesis. The introductory chapter of this book is called "A Story, Not a History." In this chapter, she explains in detail why she adopts a storytelling approach. She identifies a couple of dilemmas among comparative researchers. First is the dilemma between universality and particularity, and second is the dilemma between objectivism and holism or monism. The former dilemma creates a dualism between factual knowledge and moral imperatives but the latter goes beyond factual knowledge to moral imperatives (Hayhoe 1999). In sum, she regards the dichotomy between fact and values in European dualism as unnecessary (Hayhoe 2006).

Hayhoe feels that there is a need to bridge these polarizations, and she has found a way that would attend to the demands of scientific objectivism and cultural/personal particularism, by using an integral storytelling approach. Thus, "telling the story" is a particular approach she has adopted to share her academic analyses and insights. As indicated from the title of the introductory chapter, her storytelling is more than a historical account or a narrative—she has something more to achieve. She not only wants to tell what has been and what is, but she also wants to probe what should be and what might be in the future, but not in a prescriptive way. In her words:

> Thus my intention is to go beyond the kinds of explanation associated with the modernization narrative, which traditionally tried to discover contextual "causes" of particular phenomenon or make predictions on the basis of deductive theory and then test them in a carefully defined context. It is not, however, to offer a prescription for the next stage, derived from socialist narrative. Rather, I hope to tell the story in such a way that there is an integral link between understanding what is, or what has been, and reaching forward toward what should be, or what might be, the case in the future. There should be a room for openness, and a sense of responsibility, a recognition that moral direction can be derived from a logical working out of a preferred future within the university community. (Hayhoe 1999, xiii)

Her storytelling is more than a historical account, as the stories she tells are interwoven with her personal experience. In this way, her scholarship is developed from her personal experience, and the breadth of the stories shows the breadth of her exposure and experience. Furthermore, because of her wide exposure and experience, she has an inner urge to share these stories with others. This is how she explains her drive to write *Full Circle*: "Part of the explanation is a kind of inner compulsion" (Hayhoe 2004, 17).

To some extent, Hayhoe feels that there is no better approach than storytelling in expounding on the academic insight that has to be understood in cultural contexts. This is particularly so when she pondered about the approaches to write an introduction for Gu Mingyan's book:

> In reflecting on what this introduction might contribute to this volume, I have wrestled with different possible approaches. I decided on one that is simple, but which I hope will provide a helpful background for readers of the volume. That is to use a narrative approach, outlining highlights of Gu's own life story which were important in his development into a scholar of such distinction and national influence. (Hayhoe 2001, 8)

Hayhoe has extended this approach in crafting the book on influential Chinese educators. By writing their stories, she was "opening up the story of their lives to an international readership." In writing their stories, she was also "sketching out the story of their institution" (Hayhoe 2006, 12).

A Progressive Educator

One important reason for Hayhoe adopting a storytelling approach in her academic writing is that she attempts to integrate diversities and cultural particularities. This is what she explains she wants to do, for example, in portraying the 11 Chinese educators:

> Each of the educators was a unique individual, who had made remarkable contributions in both educational thought and action. They had grown up in different time periods and different regions of China, and had served within different institutions in all the major regions in China. Their lives and educational ideals were quite diverse, yet there were certain threads that bound them together, reflecting their educational heritage. (Hayhoe 2011, 15)

Hayhoe's writings have covered quite a wide array of topics, such as Chinese universities, cultures, philosophies, epistemology, and individual educators and scholars. Yet, there is also a thread in her academic analyses. She has tried to bridge cross-cultural understanding about progressivism in the Chinese contexts, to make it understandable to international readers.

The concluding chapter of *China's Universities* reveals her fundamental concern about the progressive contribution of higher education in China:

> Hopefully, China's universities will play an important role in the future, not only as channels of new knowledge and technology for needed arrears of economic and social development within China, but also in introducing to a wider world progressive dimensions of Chinese culture and lessons learned from China's social development over a dramatic century of change. (Hayhoe 1999, 272)

She has taken efforts to look for insights from traditional Chinese thoughts and contemporary Chinese educators. She points out the progressive tradition of China through her discussion of Neo-Confucianism, particularly through analyzing the thoughts of Wang Yangming:

> Why have I told his [Yangming's] story in such detail here? Largely because I believe his life provides a picture of the patterns of life that are seen less as personal choices, than as the way life is to be lived by Chinese intellectuals steeped in the Confucian tradition. The first point is that a Confucian philosophy by no means commits one to a life of conformity and stereotype, but to a life of creative thought, writing and teaching, combined with social responsibility, that may come at a very high cost. (Hayhoe 2006, 34)

In portraying the 11 influential Chinese educators, the descriptors for these educators are: visionary leader, independent thinker and educator, pioneer, a life that bridged China and the Anglopone world, new directions, new career, new disciplines, integration of heritage, a vision for science and internationalism, a vision for transformation, and an open and committed heart and mind. Commenting on the individuals, she highlights that "one is struck by the remarkable degree of autonomy he

[Zhu Jiusi] was able to exercise" (139); "Its [Pan Maoyuan's theory] ultimate purpose is to enable human beings to realize their full humanity"
(168); "The nurturing of the self, of individualism and of a strong subjective awareness, is important [Wang Fengxian]" (221); "What he [Wang
Yongquan] values most about the Beida spirit is its openness and the
way in which their lively debates on all kinds of topics are always taking
place" (260); "Gu Mingyuan has probably done more than any other
Chinese educator to lay a foundation that will enable Chinese thinkers
to articulate a global vision for education and culture" (291); "Chinese
education thus has a complex dual role in the present period—'it must
establish the independent individual personality, and stimulate the rich
and varied development of the individual, while at the same time function as a kind of antidote to the unlimited development of individualism'
[Lu Jie]" (319).

Overall, Hayhoe concludes that her portraits of the 11 influential
Chinese educators show that "most of the educators had come across
Deweyan progressivism in one way and another" and that:

> The lives and ideas of these educators do not conform to either of the ste-
> reotypes of Confucianism that have been dominant in Western educational
> thought—that of a closed hierarchical social order that encouraged sub-
> ordination and conformity and was antithetical to modernization, on the
> one hand, or that of an instrumentalist ethos of self-discipline, community
> cohesion and nationalist loyalty which produced the "East Asian economic
> miracle" on the other. (359)

Hayhoe tries to clarify that we also need to adopt a cultural lens to
understand progressive concepts in China. In her latest book, *Portraits
of 21st Century Chinese Universities*, she explains the contextual meaning
of such concepts as "university autonomy" and "academic freedom" in
China. The Chinese term for university autonomy is autonomy as "self
mastery" (*zizhu*) rather than autonomy as "self governance" (*zizhi*) that
has the connotation of legal and political independence. With regard to
"academic freedom," Western epistemology is dominant with rationalism and dualism in the Western context. In the Chinese context, academic freedom is more often expressed through the degree of "intellectual
authority" (*sixiangquanwei*) that Chinese scholars enjoy. Moreover, the
meaning of "intellectual freedom," quite different from European rationalism, requires knowledge to be demonstrated through action for the
public good, and that knowledge be seen as holistic and interconnected,
rather than organized into narrowly defined separate disciplines (Hayhoe
2011, 17).

Crossing with Ruth Hayhoe: Meaning Making of Cultural Experiences in Australia, Hong Kong, and Singapore

The above elaboration on the scholarship of Ruth Hayhoe is more a retrospective retrieval of what I have learned from her, rather than an objective analysis of her works. I regard the opportunity of working closely with her during 1998–2001 a very privileged experience for me both academically and spiritually. In the process of working with her, I observed her way of life, and learned from her in the process. I observed how a university president was driven by her inherent humanitarian concerns and academic inquiry as the foundation for all her works—her life experience, interpersonal interaction, and academic pursuit are all integrated. Her life is the foundation for her academic insights, and her academic insights provide a yardstick for her judgment and action. I saw the integration of cultures in her, and how she explains the East to the West and vice versa. Below, I would like to share how I learned from her in interpreting my comparative pathways in life; luckily, I later got an opportunity to live across cultures, and I also learned to interpret my cultural experiences based upon my training in comparative education. I grew up in Hong Kong, but in 1984, for the first time, I left my own country to study comparative education at Durham in the United Kingdom. Furthermore, for the first time, I became aware that I knew so little about Hong Kong, when I began to study Hong Kong from afar. At the same time, I developed my interest in Singapore and Japan, in the process of comparing Hong Kong with these two countries. In 2005, I obtained a privilege to work at the University of Sydney in Australia. It was a cultural shock to me, but because of my training in comparative education, and after working with Ruth Hayhoe for three years, I took the perspective of integrating life experience with academic understanding. I worked in Australia for only two years, but it was a very rich time for me in terms of cultural experience and understanding. In 2010, I got another opportunity of working outside Hong Kong, now at the National Institute of Education in Singapore. At the time this paper has been written, I have lived in Singapore for just more than two years. These experiences are nothing comparable to Hayhoe's rich experiences of living in different cultures, but the principle of integrating cultural experience and academic understanding has provided me a perspective of continuous interpretation of the diverse discourses taking place in different cultures. I have also found that being actively engaged in the discourses while working in different cultures is an essential part

of participant observation, and the background of comparative education training in general and having lived in different cultural contexts
are also essential for meaning making academically. Below, I will share
how I draw meanings through my active participation as an insider and
how I reflect about the unique perspectives that can be drawn out as an
outsider analyst. The thread of analysis below mainly stems from the
interaction between internationalization[1] and localization in the three
places.

From Internationalization to Intercultural Education in Australia

Internationalization is a very significant agenda of Australia, especially
in higher education. With many universities setting internationalization
on their development agenda, Australia has become particularly known
for its recent expansion in overseas enrollment and export of educational
services. In 2002, Australian public higher institutions enrolled 185,000
international students as compared to 29,000 12 years ago, leading to 21
percent of the total student enrolment in higher education, and one-third
of these international students were studying in offshore programs. For
example, the international students contributed US$2 billion to Australian
universities. In addition, further substantial amounts were spent by these
students and their families on living expenses when residing in Australia
(Harmon 2005). In 2010, 227,230 international students enrolled in
Higher Education in Australia.

Internationalization of higher education is a means to many ends, and
thus represents broad interests and varied perceptions in Australia. First,
internationalization is a means of raising revenue for the higher-educational
institutions. Internationalization is in this sense a commercial export of
higher-education services, reflecting Australia's policy shift from aid to
trade since the mid-1980s. The commercial basis of internationalization
leads to the expansion of international students in the higher-education
system. Second, internationalization of higher education functions as a
means of enhancing the international outlook of the exporting country,
international impact, and international relations. The second function is
closely related to the first one. On the one hand, the commercialization of
education is established as a means of sensitizing the nation to global competition. On the other hand, the expansion of higher-education exports is
also a means of enhancing the international impact of Australia. Third,
internationalization is also a means of enriching cultural understanding.

This leads to the awareness among Australian academics to internationalize the higher-education curricula (Lee 2008).

From a cultural perspective, the investigation of the different natures of the internationalization of higher education in Asia has been regarded as significant for the understanding of localization and contextual impacts in globalization, and advancing understanding across cultures. In the context of contemporary taxonomies of globalization, for example that of Sklair (1999), which distinguishes among the World Systems model, Global Society, Global Culture, and Global Capitalism, it is the latter two that stand out. Economic and cultural globalization form key elements of the changing context of international relations in education.

While teaching at the University of Sydney during 2005–2007, I came across intense criticisms among the academics about the recruitment of international students for economic reasons, without attention to their learning needs. As alleged by Park (2009), taking an internationalization perspective, there is far more demand for integrating Australian students and international students than internationalizing learning content and context. There has not been much discussion and effort to understand the practice of internationalizing the learning context with respect to international students' cultural background and internationalized learning environment. There are many factors which interfere with internationalization in the learning context such as English proficiency, culture difference, and the lack of awareness of these issues both in the wider public and among the academics. This kind of question is important to address, as this will have significant epistemological implications. For example, Welch (2004) challenged the basis of knowledge in Western traditions, and called for the need to examine the development of knowledge from various cultural perspectives.

Shortly after joining the University of Sydney, my colleagues (D. O'Connor and L. Napier) and I were funded by the University to work on a project titled "Transformation towards internationalization: The individual and the classroom," and the project led to a publication edited by Waugh and Napier (2009). We surveyed and interviewed the students in the Faculty of Education and Social Work, and we invited students to come together to share their learning experience. The process enhanced our awareness that there were times when the students found it difficult to understand our teaching, not because of their language proficiency or their academic abilities but because of their cultural backgrounds. University of Sydney academics gained much in the process of realizing that we needed to reconstruct epistemologies that take into account students' cultural backgrounds, and when we started to think this way, the international students became cultural assets for us to achieve these goals. We also realized that teaching international students is a valuable opportunity to learn for ourselves, at least to understand how students from different cultural backgrounds differ in their reactions to an academic issue.

In this way, the discussion on internationalization shifts toward intercultural education. This echoes Stier's (2006) assertion that internationalization is about intercultural communication and intercultural competence. He concedes that internationalization requires the teaching of six "i-Characteristics":

- intercultural (themes and perspectives),
- interdisciplinary,
- investigative (curiosity and passion for new cultural experiences and knowledge),
- integrated (national and international students),
- interactive (teacher–student; student–student), and
- integrative (theory–practice).

Thus, internationalization is not "complete" without getting across cultural boundaries, and leading toward intercultural learning. The base of knowledge will be redefined, and there will be cultural appreciation in the process of learning, and this will eventually enhance the intercultural perspectives of globalization. In this way, internationalization, intercultural education, and globalization will have an integral effect upon one another.

The Emergence of the Chinese Learner Discourse in Hong Kong

It is well established in the literature that localization occurs in the process of globalization and that this will balance out the dominance of globalization effects. The dichotomy implies conflicts and polemic tensions between what is supposed to be global and what is supposed to be local. However, my observations from working in Hong Kong suggest that localization and globalization may not necessarily be in conflict with, but on the contrary, can be complementary to each other.

Hong Kong had been a British colony for over 150 years, during which Hong Kong was totally subjected to British and international influence both culturally and politically, and was autonomous in international trade as an independent polity. The British influence notwithstanding, Hong Kong during the period of colonialization has gone through significant waves of sinicization in politics, culture, and language. The 1973 Chinese language movement was a political movement to force the British–Hong Kong government to recognize Chinese as an official language in parallel with English. The movement signifies the striving of Hong Kongers to maintain the official status of local language vis-à-vis the value of English as an international language that has already been ingrained in the territory. The university student movement taking place in the mid-1970s was a record of the enthusiasm of the university students in identifying the political and cultural root of the people, and obviously the political root was grounded in the Chinese cultural root. Yan Wing Leung (2003) in his PhD thesis has identified a variety of types of patriotism, including cultural patriotism. I have conducted an intercity comparative study on teachers' perception of citizenship education in three Chinese cities, namely Hangzhou, Guangzhou, and Hong Kong. To my surprise, Hong Kong teachers placed more emphasis on the Chinese traditions than their counterparts in the other two Chinese cities in the mainland (Lee 2005). The Hong Kong case further shows that cultural traditions may not be easily eroded by globalization and internationalization, but could on the contrary be reinforced instead. In an Oxfam study about globalization and citizenship education in Shanghai and Hong Kong, it was also found that Shanghai teachers are more concerned about globalization and more enthusiastic to know more about the international world than the Hong Kong teachers, except that the former's major interests are focused on knowledge and skills, and the latter's on values (Lee and Leung 2006).

In 1996, as Director of the Comparative Education Research Centre, I made a decision to publish a manuscript produced by John Biggs and David Watkins, entitled *The Chinese Learner: Cultural, Psychological and Contextual Influences* (Biggs and Watkins 1996). The book, now regarded as a seminal work in the field, was based upon observations from two educational expatriates from Australia and New Zealand, about the process of learning among Chinese students in Hong Kong. Biggs and Watkins highlighted two aspects of the so-called paradox of the Chinese learner: (1) Chinese learners are often taught in conditions not conducive to good learning according to Western standards, such as large classes, expository methods, relentless norm-referenced assessment, and harsh classroom climate, yet they outperform Western students, at least in science and mathematics and have deeper, meaning-oriented, approaches to learning and (2) Chinese learners are generally perceived as passive rote learners, yet they show high levels of understanding. Five years later, the paradox of the Chinese learner was extended to the Chinese teachers in a follow-up volume entitled *Teaching the Chinese Learners: Psychological and Pedagogical Perspectives* (Watkins and Biggs 2001). Here, the authors found that the tightly orchestrated teacher-centred teaching allowed students to be active, even in large classes. Moreover, Western teaching innovations such as constructivist teaching methods and problem-based learning were found to work well with the Chinese learners if carefully implemented by the Chinese teachers concerned (Watkins and Biggs 2001, 18). This led to the conclusion that Western assumptions about poor teaching in a Chinese context with large classes; strict, expository teaching; and passive learners can be challenged. The two volumes of Biggs and Watkins established that there were features specific to the Chinese learners that need to be addressed in pedagogical examination.

Following up on these observations, Mok and I published a special journal issue, entitled *Construction and Deconstruction of the Chinese Learner: Implications for Learning Theories* (Lee and Mok 2008). Analyzing the articles, we found diverse approaches in the study of pedagogies for the Chinese learners. Some authors adopted the notion of paradoxes of the Chinese learners in further understanding the East–West divide in teaching and learning, such as the different approaches to mathematics teaching and learning (Callingham 2008; Wang and Lin 2008). Others extended the investigation of the Chinese learners beyond the cognitive aspects to uncover the emotive and social aspects of learning. For example, Mok et al. (2008) described the social reasons underlying the help-seeking behaviour of the Chinese learners that might make outsiders mistakenly regard the Chinese learners as passive learners. Harbon (2008) depicted how the deepening of teacher–student relationships could enhance learning. Mak moved further to demystify the concepts of the Chinese learners, arguing that the Chinese learners, even though they may be different from those of other cultures, still needed to resolve problems common to all learners (Mak 2008). Moreover, Chinese pedagogies were not easily stereotyped. Rather, they emerged in response to changing educational contexts and to changing demands on teaching and learning (Chan 2008). In sum, the articles solicited for the special journal issue argued that studying pedagogies for Chinese learners made a special contribution to a more general understanding of teaching and learning theories. In particular, cross-cultural studies can show how self-concept theories can be revisited or reconstructed, as Wang and Lin (2008) found that students of some high-performing countries in mathematics could have relatively low self-concepts, and vice versa, whereas within country, that is, intra-culturally, students' self-concepts and learning achievements are positively correlated (cf. Lee and Mok 2008). Moreover, Chan (2008) argues that there might not be such thing as "Chinese learners." Considerations among her sample teachers included adaptation and integration of various learning strategies. Even within a Chinese cultural context, teachers need to adopt a transformational approach in teacher development and/or teaching strategy development that integrates a cultural orientation with the changing educational demands and expectation that a society like Hong Kong undergoes.

Internationalization as an Overarching Influence over Plurality in Singapore

While living and working in Singapore, I have observed that internationalization is also a very important agenda in the country. The nature of internationalization is quite different from that of Australia. While Australia's internationalization was initially a means of attracting income and expanding Australia's political and cultural influence, internationalization in Singapore is a means of positioning the country as a cosmopolitan city-state. Interestingly, it is also a means of balancing diverse cultural interests within the country. The adoption of globalization or internationalization as an anecdotal development direction in Singapore is a two-edged sword: enhancing both internal harmonization and international outlook. The experience in Singapore has given me surprise after surprise, especially in terms of how an Asian city deliberately adopts an "external agenda," such as globalization and the institutionalization of English as a language in public life (Tham 1989). These external agendas were acting as an overarching framework that supersedes internal diversities, potential conflicts, and issues, such as ethnic and language differences. Building a nation upon a plurality of racial backgrounds—with 75 percent of the population being Chinese, and the rest comprised of Malay, Tamil, and the others—multiracialism, multilingualism, and multiculturalism have been propounded as the main tenets of integrative strategy since the founding of the nation (Chan 1989), with the externality of the English language being adopted in public life not only as a precondition for survival, but paradoxically also as a justification for multilingualism and multiculturalism (Tham 1989). English is regarded as a bridge language that can break down ethnolinguistic communal barriers, and as a neutral language acceptable to all ethnic groups (Shotam 1989; Gopinathan 2011). Because of the need to balance a diversity of interest, the government attempts to give equal attention to the diverse ethnic/cultural groups residing in Singapore, but at the end, no specific cultural agenda prevails. When elaborating upon Singapore's meritocracy, Tan points out that ethnic cultural practices are encouraged in Singapore in the private sphere, but in the public realm, the government has made it deliberate that no racial community is disadvantaged in decisions and selections:

> "Multiracialism" celebrates a harmonious society made up of distinct "racial" groups...These ethnic identities and their respective practices encouraged to flourish in the private sphere. In the public realm, decisions, selections, and promotions are made in ways that officially do not disadvantage any particular racial community. (K. Tan 2010, 275)

In Singapore, the transcending factors become more prominent. For example, the nation-building agenda calls for shared values in terms of tolerance, cooperation, mutual understanding, and common endeavour among Singaporean citizens. The government's stress on achieving economic goals through education and the ideology of meritocracy has provided the public with common social goals in societal terms and the sense of fairness and justice in individual terms that would transcend ethnic differences (Tham 1989). Moreover, the pursuit of an internationalization agenda in equipping the country to meet twenty-first-century needs also provides future-oriented goals for the whole populace to focus on establishing a more promising future for the nation (Singapore 21 Committee 1999).

While Singapore's education agenda is always without doubt national, the development tactic or strategy is by and large "global." As Koh (2007, 186) puts it: "The Singapore way of participating in global capitalism is tactical because it uses a range of social, economic and education policies and translate them into national imperatives or into discourses of crisis." In the area of citizenship education, the agenda of civic, moral, and national education has been balanced by personal development, such as "being and becoming," social–emotional learning, and character education. Moreover, the notion of "consumer citizenship" has also evolved, which reflects the significance of marketization in the midst of globalization among Singapore citizenry (Baildon and Sim 2010). Tan remarks that "Globalization is recognized as a double-edged sword that is seen as being beneficial to the well-educated and mobile Singaporeans. They were labelled the 'cosmopolitans' for their relative adaptability and receptivity to globalization and their English language proficiency" (E. Tan 2010, 85). According to Koh (2007), this is the "metapragmatics of globalization in Singapore." Part of the features of the cosmopolitan Singaporeans depicted in the *Singapore 21 Report* is the possession of a "culture of internationalization" (Singapore 21 Committee 1999). In school, Singapore's citizenship pedagogies are diversified, well informed by the international literature, with the national focus being mixed with choices of various instructional approaches by teachers. Sim's (2010) study of social studies teachers in Singapore has identified four pedagogical typologies, namely expository and highly controlled, rationalistic and persuasive, interactive and participative, and constructive and experiential. In my study of Asian citizenship pedagogies, I have argued that the Asian educators are by and large familiar with the international literature on pedagogies, but making informed choices of their own in its application and implementation (Lee 2010). This seems to fit the situation of Singapore quite well.

What I have experienced over two years, as a participant observer, led me to observe some stark contrasts between Hong Kong and Singapore in terms of research agenda. While the cultural agenda of the "Chinese Learner" has grown to be a significant agenda, with a predominantly Chinese population, this cannot be applied to the Singapore context, as this is obviously one racial agenda within the ethnically mixed populace. Being Dean of Education Research at the National Institute of Education, I am in charge of managing research projects in the Institute. Looking into many of the projects, I have found that the academic dialogue and policy discussions in Singapore reflect a clear demand for empirical evidence base in both academic and pedagogical research and policy making, and both in the Institute of Education and Ministry of Education. There is repeated mention that Singapore is a small state, and it must live up to international standards in order to survive, and to achieve and sustain its competitiveness internationally. This seems to resonate with the bigger picture of the Singapore society, somewhat de-emphasizing cultural differences to minimize cultural conflicts and maximize social harmony. Likewise, in research on schools and the classrooms in Singapore, despite having addressed the significance of the context, there is an underplaying of cultural specificities in relation to particular ethnic groups, and the schools and classrooms are treated contextually, but this does not necessarily mean "culturally."

While the Chinese learner is a deliberate research focus in Hong Kong, and the study on citizenship identity has a focus on cultural identity (versus political identity), there is relatively little exploration of the Singapore learner or Asian learner that would appeal to the cultural roots of the educational features in the society, compatible to the Chinese learner. This does not mean that the education system in Singapore is a direct knowledge transfer from the West. The Singapore education system has indeed outstanding uniqueness—a strong belief in the examination system that would function as a meritocracy, which is essential for achieving educational equality; a strong belief in streaming but working hard to bring the best for the students in different streams; a flexible approach emerging out of a centralized and rather rigid school system (such as the introduction of independent schools, schools specializing in art and physical education), integrated programmes, a government-supported International Baccalaureate programme, and the allowance for the top 10 percent and bottom 10 percent students not to take O-Level examinations, and so on. However, the research in education and the development of these unique systems are regarded as the outcome of rationalized analyses, and thus empirically oriented, rather than an option based upon the cultural features, given the existence of diverse cultures within the nation.

Singapore has positioned itself as the education hub of Asia, and the internationalization of education has been an explicit policy agenda of the country. However, the kind of education hub that Singapore positions itself is a "secondary hub" rather than a "primary hub" according to Cribbin (2008), meaning that the country facilitates overseas students "coming through" Singapore for higher studies, rather than "coming to" Singapore as an end destination. The way Singapore "internationalizes" education is also quite unique—by inviting major and prestigious universities from the United States and Australia to establish branch campuses, rather than expanding its own education system. Thus, while there are increasing discussions in Australia about intercultural education that come out of internationalization, the "cultural" talks in Singapore, in terms of indigenous cultural background as foundation of generalizable knowledge, are relatively insignificant or perhaps as mentioned above, mainly appearing in the private sphere. Rather, Singapore students and teachers would demonstrate themselves to be masters of international knowledge and skills (that is regarded and challenged by my Australian colleagues as Western based).

Conclusion: Significance of the Researcher's Personal Experience in Academic Meaning Making

This chapter is written to celebrate Ruth Hayhoe's scholarship, and how her academic approaches have influenced other academics like me. What I would like to demonstrate is that this approach of scholarship, especially the approach of combining life experience with academic understanding, is a significant way of generating insights that can be developed through an interaction between the researcher and the research environment. The analysis of my cultural experience in Australia, Hong Kong, and Singapore is also attributed to my Australian colleagues Felicity Rawlings-Sanaei and

Colina Mason from Macquarrie University and University of New South Wales, who specifically requested an analysis of my own cultural experiences, knowing that I have lived and worked in three countries. Their suggestion of this particular approach has encouraged me to combine my training in comparative education with the research I have conducted while living and working in the three countries, and recall seriously how the interplay of insider–outsider perspectives inform my understanding of the interplay of globalization and localization, as well as internationalization and nationalization.

The thinking process in shaping this chapter has also led me to think about how a culture-based epistemology and intercultural education agenda could emerge in the process of internationalization of education in Australia; and how the search for cultural roots and the Chinese learner agenda have emerged during the 150 years of British colonization in Hong Kong. Moreover, it has prompted me to consider how the globalization and internationalization agenda, on top of nation-building, gradually becomes an overarching national goal that is pragmatically seen as an advantage for Singapore to enhance its immersion in the global arena, on the one hand, and an indirect way to achieve harmonization in an ethnically diverse population, on the other. Furthermore, what I have learned while working in the three cultural settings has provided invaluable insights as an insider–outsider researcher to note how the emphasis on internationalization in Australia has led to growing awareness of intercultural education; how the search of cultural roots in Hong Kong as a British colony has led to the reinforcement of the localization and cultural agenda in an international city; and as a city state, how Singapore has chosen to adopt globalization and internationalization agendas that would balance out ethnic diversities.

A few decades ago, the economic miracles of Hong Kong, Taiwan, Korea, and Japan have caught the world's attention as East Asia's Four Little Dragons. Tremendous amounts of research and analyses appeared over the years trying to understand the common success factors of the four economies. Interestingly, the findings were mixed, and no commonly accepted growth formulae have been developed. The general conclusion was that these successful economies were able to make use of the opportunities available in the world market, and develop economic strategies that particularly fit their own social, cultural, and political settings and economies, and they all achieved their own successes.

My observation about the development of scholarship and teaching in Australia, Hong Kong, and Singapore has arrived at similar findings—all the three countries have different approaches in developing epistemology and pedagogies that are relevant to their own contexts. However, the interesting observation is that universalism and particularism in the three countries interact in their own ways to arrive at different emphases, with all three having differing combinations of the two: namely, a culturalist agenda is developed from an international agenda in Australia; a cultural approach to learning is developed in an international city, Hong Kong; and an internationalized agenda is developed due to the existence of cultural diversities in Singapore. Having said that, this observation by no means implies that internationalization is not important in Australia and Hong Kong, nor that culturalism is not important in Singapore. The reflection upon the three places concludes with the thoughts on universalism and particularism—a research agenda that spans Ruth Hayhoe's academic life. Here is where our common interests in comparative education cross over, and because of this, her scholarship has brought insights to me, whereby I can conduct my own cultural analysis.

Note

1. The terms globalization and internationalization are used interchangeably in the context of this chapter.

References

Baildon, Mark, and Jasmine Boon Yee Sim. 2010. "The Dilemmas of Singapore's National Education in the Global Society." In *Globalization, the Nation-state and the Citizen: Dilemmas and Directions for Civics and Citizenship Education*, ed. Alan D. Reid, Alan Sears, and Judith Gill (pp. 80–96). New York: Routledge.

Biggs, John, and David Watkins. 1996. *The Chinese Learner: Cultural, Psychological and Contextual Influences*. Hong Kong: Comparative Education Research Centre, University of Hong Kong/Canberra: Australian Council for Educational Research.

Callingham, Rosemary. 2008. "Perspectives Gained from Different Assessment Tasks on Chinese and Australian School Students Learning Mathematics." In *Construction and Deconstruction of the Chinese Learners*, ed. Wing On Lee and Magdalena Mok, special issue of *Evaluation and Research in Education* 21 (3): 175–187.

Chan, Carol. 2008. "Pedagogical Transformation and Knowledge-Building for the Chinese Learner." In *Construction and Deconstruction of the Chinese Learners*, ed. Wing On Lee and Magdalena Mok, special issue of *Evaluation and Research in Education* 21 (3): 235–251.

Chan, Heng Chee. 1989. "PAP and the Structuring of the Political System." In *Management of Success: The Moulding of Modern Singapore*, ed. Kernial Singh Sandhu and Paul Wheatley (pp. 70–89). Singapore: Institute of Southeast Asian Studies.

Cribbin, John. 2008. *The Lifelong Learning Sector and the Development of Hong Kong as a Regional Education Hub: Is Government Policy Rhetoric or Reality?* Nottingham: Unpublished doctoral thesis, University of Nottingham.

Gopinathan, Saravanan. 2011. "Are We All Global Citizens Now? Reflections on Citizenship and Citizenship Education in a Globalizing World (With Special Reference to Singapore)." Seminar paper presented at the Centre for Governance and Citizenship, Hong Kong Institute of Education, January 20, 2011.

Gu, Mingyuan 2001. *Education in China and Abroad: Perspectives from a Lifetime in Comparative Education*. With an Introduction by Ruth Hayhoe. Hong Kong: Comparative Education Research Centre, the University of Hong Kong.

Harbon, Lesley. 2008. "Chinese Students in a 'Sea' of Change: One Teacher's Discoveries about Chinese Students' Learning and Emotions through Use of Song." In *Construction and Deconstruction of the Chinese Learners*, ed. Wing On Lee and Magdalena Mok, special issue of *Evaluation and Research in Education* 21 (3): 214–134.

Harmon, Grant. 2005. "Internationalization of Australian Higher Education: A Critical Review of Literature and Research." In *Internationalizing Higher Education: Critical Explorations of Pedagogy and Policy*, ed. Peter Ninnies and Meeri Hellstén (pp. 119–140). Hong Kong and Dordrecht, The Netherlands: Comparative Education Research Centre, University of Hong Kong and Springer.

Hayhoe, Ruth, ed. 1992. *Education and Modernization: The Chinese Experience*. Oxford: Pergamon Press.

Hayhoe, Ruth, ed. 1993. *Knowledge Across Cultures: Universities East and West*. Toronto: OISE Press/Wuhan: Hubei Education Press.

Hayhoe, Ruth. 1999. *China's Universities 1895–1995: A Century of Cultural Conflict*. Hong Kong: Comparative Education Research Centre, University of Hong Kong. (First published in 1996 by Garland Publishing, Inc. New York.)

Hayhoe, Ruth. 2001. "Introduction." In *Education in China and Abroad: Perspectives from a Lifetime in Comparative Education*, ed. Gu Mingyuan (pp. 5–24). Hong Kong: Comparative Education Research Centre, The University of Hong Kong.

Hayhoe, Ruth. 2004. *Full Circle: A Life with Hong Kong and China*. Hong Kong: Comparative Education Research Centre, The University of Hong Kong.

Hayhoe, Ruth. 2005. "Ten Lives in Mine: Creating Portraits of Influential Chinese Educators." *International Journal of Educational Research* 41 (4–5): 324–338.

Hayhoe, Ruth. 2006. *Portraits of Influential Chinese Educators*. Hong Kong and Dordrecht, The Netherlands: Comparative Education Research Centre, University of Hong Kong and Springer.

Hayhoe, Ruth. 2011. "Introduction and Acknowledgements." In *Portraits of 21st Century Chinese Universities: In the Move to Mass Higher Education*, ed. Ruth Hayhoe, Jun Li, Jing Lin, and Qiang Zha (pp. 1–17). Hong Kong and

Dordrecht, The Netherlands: Comparative Education Research Centre, University of Hong Kong and Springer.

Hayhoe, Ruth, and Julia Pan, eds. 2001. *Knowledge across Cultures: A Contribution to the Dialogue of Civilizations*. Hong Kong: Comparative Education Research Centre, University of Hong Kong.

Hayhoe, Ruth, Jun Li, Jing Lin, and Qiang Zha, eds. 2011. *Portraits of 21st Century Chinese Universities: In the Move to Mass Higher Education*. Hong Kong and Dordrecht, The Netherlands: Comparative Education Research Centre, University of Hong Kong and Springer.

Koh, Aaron. 2007. "Living with Globalization Tactically: The Metapragmatics of Globalization in Singapore." *Journal of Social Issues in Asia* 22 (2): 179–201.

Lee, Wing On. 2005. "Teachers' Perceptions of Citizenship in China." In *Education and Social Citizenship: Perception of Teachers in USA, Australia, England, Russia and China*, ed. Wing On Lee and Jeffrey Fouts (pp. 209–246). Hong Kong: Hong Kong University Press.

Lee, Wing On. 2008. "The Repositioning of Higher Education from Its Expanded Visions: Lifelong Learning, Entrepreneurship, Internationalization and Integration." *Educational Research for Policy and Practice* 7 (2): 73–83.

Lee, Wing On. 2010. "Multiple Modalities of Asia-Pacific Citizenship Pedagogies: Eclectic Concepts, Hybridized Approaches and Teachers' Preferences." In *Citizenship Pedagogies in Asia and the Pacific*, ed. Kerry Kennedy, Wing On Lee, and David Grossman (pp. 335–356). Hong Kong and Dordrecht, The Netherlands: Comparative Education Research Centre, University of Hong Kong and Springer.

Lee, Wing On, and Sai Wing Leung. 2006. "Global Citizenship Education in Hong Kong and Shanghai Secondary Schools: Ideals, Realities and Expectations." *Citizenship Teaching and Learning* 2 (2): 68–84.

Lee, Wing On, and Magdalena Mok. 2008. "Editors' Introduction." In *Construction and Deconstruction of the Chinese Learners*, ed. Wing On Lee and Magdalena Mok, special issue of *Evaluation and Research in Education* 21 (3): 147–153.

Leung, Yan Wing. 2003. *Harmony or Conflict: The Role of Nationalistic Education within Civic Education in Hong Kong*. Unpublished doctoral dissertation, University of Sydney.

Mak, Grace. 2008. "Diversity in the Chinese Classroom in Changing Contexts." In *Construction and Deconstruction of the Chinese Learners*, ed. Wing On Lee and Magdalena Mok, special issue of *Evaluation and Research in Education* 21 (3): 252–266.

Mok, Magdalena et al. 2008. "Help-seeking by Chinese Secondary School Students: Challenging the Myth of 'The Chinese Learner.'" In *Construction and Deconstruction of the Chinese Learners*, ed. Wing On Lee and Magdalena Mok, special issue of *Evaluation and Research in Education* 21 (3): 188–213.

Park, Ji Yong. 2009. "Internationalization and International Students: Creating an Internationalized Learning Context for International Students' Study Preparation via CMC." *International Journal of Diversity in Organizations, Communities and Nations* 9 (1): 75–86.

Shotam, Nirmala Puru. 1989. "Language and Linguistic Policies." In *Management of Success: The Moulding of Modern Singapore*, ed. Kernial Singh Sandhu and Paul Wheatley (pp. 503–522). Singapore: Institute of Southeast Asian Studies.

Sim, Jasmine Boon-Yee. 2010. " 'Simple Ideological "Dupes" of National Governments'? Teacher Agency and Citizenship Education in Singapore." In *Citizenship Pedagogies in Asia and the Pacific*, ed. Kerry Kennedy, Wing On Lee, and David Grossman (pp. 221–242). Hong Kong and Dordrecht, The Netherlands: Comparative Education Research Centre, The University of Hong Kong and Springer.

Singapore 21 Committee 1999. *Singapore 21: Together, We Make the Difference*. Singapore: Singapore 21 Committee.

Sklair, Leslie. 1999. "Competing Concepts of Globalization." *Journal of World-Systems of Research* 2 (5): 143–163.

Stier, Jonas. 2006. "Internationalization, Intercultural Communication and Intercultural Competence." *Journal of Intercultural Communication* 11: 1–12.

Tan, Eugene Khen Boon. 2010. "The Evolving Social Compact and the Transformation of Singapore: Going Beyond *Quid Pro Quo* in Governance." In *Management of Success: Singapore Revisited*, ed. Terence Chong (pp. 80–99). Singapore: Institute of Southeast Asian Studies.

Tan, Kenneth Paul. 2010. "The Transformation of Meritocracy." In *Management of Success: Singapore Revisited*, ed. Terence Chong (pp. 272–287). Singapore: Institute of Southeast Asian Studies.

Tham, Seong Chee. 1989. "The Perception and Practice of Education." In *Management of Success: The Moulding of Modern Singapore*, ed. Kernial Singh Sandhu and Paul Wheatley (pp. 477–502). Singapore: Institute of Southeast Asian Studies.

Wang, Jian, and Emily Lin. 2008. "An Alternative Interpretation of the Relationship between Self-Concept and Mathematics Achievement: Comparison of Chinese and US Students as a Context." In *Construction and Deconstruction of the Chinese Learners*, ed. Wing On Lee and Magdalena Mok, special issue of *Evaluation and Research in Education* 21 (3): 154–174.

Watkins, David, and Biggs, John. 2001. *Teaching the Chinese Learners: Psychological and Pedagogical Perspectives*. Hong Kong: Comparative Education Research Centre, University of Hong Kong.

Waugh, Fran, and Lindsey Napier, eds. 2009. *Internationalizing Learning and Teaching in Academic Settings*. Sydney: University of Sydney Faculty of Education and Social Work.

Welch, Anthony. 2004. BICA 2003/4 report booklet 7: *Educational Services in Southeast Asia*. Sydney: The University of Sydney Faculty of Education and Social Work.

Chapter 3

And the Boys Took It Up for Themselves: Scouting, Learning, and Dialogue across Cultures

Joseph P. Farrell

Prologue

This chapter is a response to that aspect of the agenda for this celebration of Ruth Hayhoe's work, which asks: "What kind of cultural and spiritual role is being played by non-governmental organizations that make education and schooling a key focus of their work, yet do not have a specific nationalist agenda?" I argue that World Scouting is the oldest, broadest, and most successful such organization.

Introduction

In his last public speech, to the World Scouting Movement at the ninth International Scout Conference, in the Hague in 1939, just before he retired to Kenya where he died four years later, Lord Robert Baden-Powell, the "founder" of Scouting, made the following observation: "You can remember that it was not I who urged Scouting to the boys. It was only suggested to me to write a book, and the boys took it up for themselves" (Wilson 1959, 102). In most parts of the world to which Scouting has spread, and that is most parts of the world, its growth has been very much a matter of the boys, and with the spread of Girl Guiding, Girl Scouts, and coeducational Scouting, the girls as well, "taking it up for themselves." The objective here is to try to understand the growth of a voluntary nonformal educational movement, which started in 1907 with an experimental camp for 20 English boys in Brownsea Island in Dorset, England, and which now has roughly 30 million members in 166 countries. These are in locations where the Scouting program has been formally recognized by the World Organization of the Scouting Movement (WOSM)—there are about 30 other nations where the Scouting movement exists in nascent or well-developed form but has not yet been "recognized." As of February, 2011, there were exactly six nations in the world in which there was no recognized, or nascent but not formally recognized, Scouting presence (Scout. org 2011a).

This is a movement that began with a nationalistic flavor in England, responding (at least in the view of the early leaders there) to a perceived need to "improve the quality" and self-reliance and resourcefulness of English boys who would in the future be needed to counter the then-rising power of Germany and other competitor nations, and to maintain the British Empire. However, it subsequently became such a force for learning about and practicing international understanding and democratic living together that in 1981, the WOSM was the first organization ever to receive a newly established international United Nations Educational, Scientific and Cultural Organization (UNESCO) Prize for Peace Education. It has also been several times among the finalists for the Nobel Peace Prize, and has received many other international awards and recognitions for its work in, for example, environmental learning.

The popular perception, at least in North America and other rich areas of the world, is of a predominantly recreational activity aimed at middle-class youngsters in richer nations. In reality, Scouting understands and identifies itself as a nonformal *educational* movement (although since the "method" is based on learning through games and fun and adventure wise leaders at the local level do not ordinarily mention "education" to the young members!), with most (roughly two-thirds) of its worldwide membership in poor nations among poorer young people.

Since the distinction between "formal" and "nonformal" education was introduced into the educational literature in the 1960s, there has been a widespread tendency in that literature to associate "formal" education with the schooling of *young people* (from preprimary through university), and "nonformal" education with the provision of organized opportunities to learn for *adults*. Thomas LaBelle in his 1981 presidential address to the Comparative and International Education Society urged comparative educators to turn their attention to the study of nonformal education of *children and youth*, arguing that it is much more widespread, and much more important to the overall development of young people, than is commonly assumed by educational researchers. After reviewing the role that nonformal educational programs for young people play in the United States, he concluded that "educators might be better off looking at schools as only one locus for education, as many youngsters and parents apparently do" (LaBelle 1981, 329). This chapter is in part a response to that challenge.

Scouting is a particularly interesting case for the comparative study of nonformal education for young people. It is the most internationally widespread of such programs, covering almost all of the world's peoples and cultures and faith/spiritual traditions. It has also proven to be very successful at adapting a common set of core ideals and principles, a common set of practices, and a common teaching/learning methodology to very different cultural settings. It is also entirely *voluntary*; young people and their adult leaders become involved and stay involved only because they *want to*. What is it that attracts some 30 million young people to become involved and stay involved in this program across almost all of our world? What is the "magic" here? How has this movement managed to spread literally around the world, adapting to vastly different cultures and histories and spiritual traditions, while maintaining a core identity, a common set of basic values and beliefs, pedagogical practices and methods, and, if you will, a core curriculum?

A Personal Note

Scouting has been a fundamentally formative and integral part of my own life. I have been involved in Scouting, as boy and man, for almost my entire life. My connection started when I first walked into a Cub Scout meeting in 1948, as a hesitant and somewhat wonderstruck eight-year-old (that being the entry age for Cub Scouts in the United States). Throughout my boyhood and youth, I was a thoroughly committed scout. The movement provided me with vast amounts of fun and challenge, opportunities to learn, close friends, and wise mentors; it quite literally saved me from disaster during a particularly dangerous time in a turbulent adolescence. It was in Scouting that I first learned that I was good at, and thoroughly enjoyed, helping other people to learn. My lifelong vocation as an educator was formed in Scout meeting rooms and as a staff member, and eventually

Director, of Scout summer camps. My association with comparative and international education has its roots in my participation at age 15 years in a world scout Jamboree, living and camping with thousands of other young people from scores of different nations. I was profoundly moved by that experience and returned home with a burning desire to learn more about other cultures, how people lived and learned in them—a desire that has never left me. In 1958, I became a formally "certified" adult scout troop leader in the United States, a role I played thereafter in several states in that nation, in Chile, and in Toronto, where I led a mid-city scout troop from 1971 until 1997, when I formally "retired" from frontline leadership to pursue more background and support roles. In my extensive international professional travel, I usually wear my international scout identification lapel pin. Very commonly, within a day or two in a town or city where I have never been before, someone will notice that pin, flash me the universal "scout sign," and I find myself invited to a local scout or guide meeting, or to a weekend camp or some other Scouting activity. Thus, I have had the opportunity to see Scouting "in operation" in many different cultures. Beyond that from 1986 to 1995, I served as a member of the International Relations Committee of Scouts Canada, where I had the opportunity to see the operation of the movement at the formal international level, and converse with the then secretary general of the WOSM and his senior staff.

This personal background clearly inclines me toward a positive view of Scouting, but not an uncritical one. In an organization, especially, as we shall see, a loosely structured one, as large and sprawling as Scouting, there are bound to be difficulties, disagreements, problems, and tensions, many of which I have seen firsthand.

The Growth of Scouting as a Worldwide Movement

Table 3.1 provides estimates of total world membership in Scouting from 1907 to the present. It should be emphasized that these are *estimates*. We are familiar with the problems involved in getting accurate counts of formal school enrollments, particularly in poor nations. Such problems are even more complex in a nonformal educational movement, which is, as noted, rather loosely structured. Some nations have organizational infrastructures, and membership registration procedures, which permit quite accurate counts. Others do not. These numbers then should be taken as indicative of orders of magnitude rather than exact figures. It should be noted that these

Table 3.1 Worldwide Scouting membership growth estimated

Year	Estimated worldwide membership
1907	First experimental camp for 20 boys at Brownsea Island UK membership
1910	100,000
1922	1 million
1930	2 million
1939	3.3 million
1946	4.4 million
1952	5.5 million
1955	6.3 million
1958	7.5 million
1962	9.3 million
1964	10 million
1970	12 million
1972	13.1 million
1980	15 million
1989	16 million
2003	26.7 million
2010	30 million

Sources: *Through 1980: 75 Years of Scouting*. London: The Scout Association, 1982, pp. 51–55; 1989 and 2010. Data from the World Organization of the Scouting Movement, 2003. Vallory (2007, 175).

numbers include both boys and girls for most nations, since Scouting, while started as a boys' organization, has since become coeducational in most places in the world. What one sees overall is a pattern of long-term steady growth, decade by decade over a century and a bit, with an approximate doubling of participation during the past two decades.

That international membership is naturally spread over many different nations, 166 at last count; in some locations, the movement is very strong and large, while in others, small and sometimes fragile. The size of Scouting in any particular place is not systematically related to much of anything that can be captured by statistical series. Table 3.2 lists all nations with a Scouting population greater than 50,000 as of the end of 2010, in descending order of enrollment size, plus the year when Scouting was originally established and when it was recognized by WOSM. These 27 nations account for roughly 75 percent of the total Scouting membership, but they are a very diverse group. Eight are former British colonies and three are British offshoot societies (the United States, Canada, and Australia); thus, the historical influence of the tie through colonization or shared history/language is clear. Six are European nations. Nine are

Table 3.2 Nations with membership above 50,000 by size

Nation	Membership	Year founded	Year of joining WOSM
Indonesia	8,103,835	1912	1953
USA	5,970,203	1909	1922
India	2,423,686	1909	1938
Philippines	1,872,525	1923	1946
Thailand	1,360,869	1911	1922
Bangladesh	896, 118	1972	1974
Pakistan	526,403	1947	1948
UK	444,271#	1907	1922
Kenya	262,146	1910	1964
Korea, Rep. of	214,146	1922	1953
Japan	195,370	1913	1922
Canada	146,250	1909	1946
Germany	123,686	1910	1950
Italy	120,689	1912	1922
Hong Kong	99,591	1911	1977
Uganda	92,946	1915	1964
Tanzania, Rep. of	91,057	1929	1963
Belgium	88,307	1911	1922
Egypt	74,598	1918	1922
Australia	73,945	1908	1950
Malaysia	73,494	1911	1957
Congo, D. R.	71,486	1924	1963
Spain	65,088	1912	1923
Poland	61,394	1919	1922, 1946, 1992
Brazil	59,075	1910	1922
Sweden	59,035	1911	1922
China, Scouts of	57,039	1912	1937

Source: Reported membership at the end of 2010 by WOSM. http://scout.org/en/about scouting/facts figures/census. Downloaded 19/02/2011.

literally from all over the world, without any clear connection with the "founding nation."

For some nations, the early history, that is, how Scouting got there in the first place and how it spread, has been documented and analyzed, but not in other cases. There are many fragmentary accounts, bits and pieces, and much lore and personal histories. Many questions remain unanswered, at least in a way which might satisfy those of us who are "academics." Take as an example Indonesia, the nation with the largest scout enrollment in the world. Scouting arrived there in 1912, just two years after the movement took root in the colonizing nation, the Netherlands. It spread quickly but in a disjointed and unorganized fashion such that upon achieving independence, there were more than 60 distinct Scout Associations in the nation, affiliated with various political parties or social organizations. In 1961, the government declared that there would be only one, national, Scouting association. The central government has strongly promoted it as a means of personal and local community development throughout all the changes since independence. Community groups often sponsor and support the scout groups. In other cases, schools support them. However, noting that does not really explain *why* Scouting is so popular among young people and those who lead them.

One also notes from the "year founded" column in Table 3.2 how quickly Scouting spread internationally after its inception in England in 1907. The following section examines that history more carefully.

Early History and Development of Transfer and Institutionalization Methods

The first and most important thing to note about this history is observed in the initial paragraph of this chapter: Baden-Powell did not *intend* to start a new youth organization in England, let alone in the rest of the world. He was himself the son of an upwardly aspiring, and ultimately upwardly mobile, late-Victorian English middle-class family, and a product of the "public school" system of the time. He followed one of the standard career patterns for men of his time and social place, entering the military officer corps and serving in various parts of the Empire, especially Africa. He rose gradually through the ranks, distinguishing himself as a "scout" (read, spy), but he also acquired a reputation within the institution as something of a nonconformist, which ultimately called into question his prospects for promotion to the very highest ranks. During the Boer War in South Africa (1898–1902), which England almost lost to the "rag tag" Afrikaners of Dutch descent, Baden-Powell became a national hero for successfully leading the defense of the strategic town of Mafeking against a long siege by seemingly overwhelming Boer forces.

As an officer responsible, among other things, for training new recruits, he had become concerned with what he perceived to be the low quality—intellectually, physically, and morally—of these products of England's educational and child-upbringing systems. He contrasted this to what he had discovered during the siege of Mafeking, where he made great use of small groups of young men and older boys, who came to be labeled "patrols," for many vital tasks including communication, delivering supplies and food to the community, providing first-aid services, and other such behind-the-lines "support" services, all the while self-organizing and learning to take on new challenges. Drawing upon his own life experience, and some of the then-novel pedagogical theorists, he developed a training program for young men, and published his ideas in a book titled *Aids to Scouting* (1899). This book attracted the attention of members of the British ruling elite, among whom there was a general worry, heightened by the experience of the Boer War, about the state of the nation's youth. It was also widely read by boys much younger than its intended audience.

Baden-Powell thus returned to England after the Boer War not only as a famous war hero but also as a man with a reputation as a pedagogical innovator. He was asked to visit and observe the "on the ground" operations of several existing youth organizations, such as the Young Men's Christian Association (YMCA), The Boys' Brigades, Cadet Corps, whose leaders felt that their programs were not attracting and retaining as many boys as they hoped they would, and then to make suggestions for improvement. He concluded that there *were* fundamental problems with these programs: they were leader driven; not responsive to the needs and interests of boys and young men; too overtly moralistic and didactic; and for most of the boys and young men, basically boring. No wonder they chose not to participate! After circulating these conclusions, he was urged to develop his own ideas into a set of program suggestions for these existing organizations. He proceeded to read widely in then-fashionable "progressive" pedagogical theory, and combined his own ideas and experience with borrowings from Froebel, Johan Jahn, Ernest Thompson-Seton, and Montessori, and then tested his ideas at an experimental camp for 20 boys of varied social-class backgrounds at Brownsea Island in Dorset. Then, at the urging of a publisher friend (who apparently saw this as an economically attractive proposition), he published his program ideas in a series of fortnightly pamphlets, and then in book form, under the title *Scouting for Boys* (1908). (The title derives from the fact that he saw this work as an extension of and revision for a younger age group of the ideas he had originally published for young men under the title *Aids to Scouting*.) It quickly became apparent, however, as Springhall has noted, that

> he had over-estimated the ability of the already existing youth movements to adapt his Boy Scout scheme to their own programmes. [Rather] all over England boys collected the fortnightly parts of *Scouting for Boys* as they appeared on the bookstalls, formed troops *unaided* (emphasis added), and then persuaded favoured adults to become their Scoutmasters. (Springhall 1977, 61)

The combination of learner-centered pedagogical principles, learning by doing, emphasis on taking responsibility for one's own learning, learning at one's own pace, older boys teaching/mentoring younger boys (in the elegant world of educational theory these days we call this cross-age peer tutoring!) plus meaningful engagement with and service to their community, combined with Baden-Powell's own ideas and enthusiasm, unconventionality, and intuitive understanding of youth, produced a program which was almost instantly appealing to many thousands of British youth. As MacLoed has noted, the experimental camp in Brownsea Island had

> demonstrated that despite its sober purposes [e.g., moral and civic education, service to the community, physical growth, and so on] Scouting would also furnish exuberant fun for boys. B-P taught by practice and games...and at night he was the life of the campfire, telling stories and dancing around the flames leading traditional chants and songs. The new handbook, *Scouting for Boys*, was equally zestful. Baden-Powell called the chapters 'Campfire Yarns,' illustrated them with his own sketches, and threw in unedifying [to the 'proper' classes!] tidbits calculated to appeal to boys. (MacLeod 1983, 134)

The basic operational unit of this new program was to be the Scout Patrol, a relatively small group of boys (usually around three to eight), based on the model of the "neighborhood gang," a group of kids who would naturally "hang about together." Patrols would select their own boy leaders, choose their own activities from a long list of possibilities that the Scouting program/organization provided/suggested, but they could invent these activities for themselves. Several such patrols would together form a Scout Troop, supervised by an adult Scoutmaster. The result of all of this creative invention of Baden-Powell was a "mixture of fun, spontaneity, the outdoors, self-reliance and responsibility" (Jenkins 1990, 2).

Thus, within months of its publication, it became clear that there were tens of thousands of boys throughout the nation, and the leaders they themselves had recruited, who were "doing" Scouting on their own. As with any rapidly spreading voluntary social movement, this one attracted not only people who understood and tried to faithfully implement Baden-Powell's ideas, but some very "strange" types as well (sexual predators, religious fanatics, political activists, and others), and some who simply did not understand the program. An organizational structure was quickly cobbled together, relying mainly, in the British tradition of the gifted amateur, on voluntary labour by "gentlemen of leisure." By 1910, there were at least 100,000 boys in the nation practicing Scouting. The King requested Baden-Powell to resign his military commission to devote himself full time to this rapidly growing organization that he had not intended to start.

If Baden-Powell had not intended to start a new organization in his own country, he had even less in mind the notion that his ideas might develop into an international movement and organization.

> In his original ideas, B-P had in mind only the boys of his own country. He felt that Scouting would appeal to them and to their national characteristics. [In this he reflected the idea of "national character" which was embedded in much early academic writing in Comparative Education.] He did not anticipate that his suggestions would also appeal to men and women, boys and girls, of other nationalities. (Wilson 1959, 25)

Thus, no efforts were made by the emerging central organization in Britain to send out materials to other nations or otherwise encourage the transfer of the new program. However, as noted in Table 3.2, it did spread, and quickly. Some examples:

- In *Sweden*, a teacher at a Gothenburg boys' school found a copy of *Scouting for Boys* in the smoking room of a coastal steamer (it literally fell off a shelf in rough seas and landed on a table in front of him!). He began to read it, became interested, borrowed it from the ship's captain, and started a Scout patrol in his own school. The idea quickly spread. He translated the book into Swedish, and 20,000 copies were sold within ten days of its publication. Scout patrols and troops were quickly formed throughout the nation.
- Baden-Powell visited *Chile* in 1908 on a military mission. While there, he gave a speech on Scouting. This attracted the interest of a group of Chileans who sought more details from him, obtained materials, translated them, and formed a Scouting organization and promulgated the idea throughout the country, where troops quickly formed.
- *Scouting for Boys* was translated into *Japanese* in 1910. A few troops were formed, and there was slow and sporadic growth thereafter but "without a proper grasp of the principles and aims of Scouting" (Wilson 1959, 29). Well-publicized participation of Scouts in rescue and reconstruction after the Tokyo earthquake of 1923 captured the imagination of the Japanese public. The next year, a small contingent was sent to an international Jamboree in Copenhagen, and the contingent leader went afterward to a course at a newly established international training center (Gilwell) in England. Returning home, he developed and led training courses for Japanese leaders in the "correct" application of Scouting, and was the spark for building what quickly became a very large and popular organization.

- Scouting was brought to *India* by colonial officers who had encountered it in England or had copies of *Scouting for Boys* sent to them. At the outset, only "Anglo-Indian" or "mixed blood" boys were admitted to the Indian Boy Scouts Association, as the colonial government prohibited membership by Indian boys on the grounds that "Scouting might train them to become revolutionaries" (Wilson 1959, 20). This proscription was circumvented by colonial officers who disagreed with it through the foundation of separate ethnic or regional scout associations. By 1921, there were at least seven distinct scout associations in the colony. In that year, Baden-Powell visited for a month and managed to bring all but one of these separate groups together in the Boy Scouts Association in India. To assist in adapting Scouting to this context, Baden-Powell, with local leader collaboration, wrote *Scouting for Boys in India* (1923), using examples and anecdotes from Indian history, and with a forward framed around a quotation from the Koran: "For God we are; to God we go" (Wilson 1959, 22–23).

These early examples typify the standard pattern of the spread of Scouting in the early years. No one was "pushing" it internationally; there were no "missionaries"; in almost all cases, some adult(s) would "stumble across" Scouting, become interested in its potential for youth in their own country, get examples of the "curricular materials" that would be translated, and then it simply spread "on the ground" within each new country, as the youngsters "took it up for themselves." Early on, however, various challenges appeared in this unplanned and undirected international spread of a voluntary nonformal educational movement.

Challenges and Solutions

The Need for an Organization, but What Sort of Organization?

Just as the rapid spread of Scouting within England had required some kind of central organization, so it became quickly apparent that the rapid and unanticipated international spread of Scouting also required some sort of an organization. There were groups claiming the name "Scouting" whose ideas and activities were not even close to those intended by Baden-Powell. In some nations, there were several separate groups, divided on religious, linguistic, or ethnic/racial lines. Baden-Powell had suggested early in the 1910s the calling of an international meeting to start sorting these issues out, but World War I intervened. The terrible carnage of that war profoundly altered Baden-Powell's thinking and perception of the place of Scouting in the world.

Shortly after the war ended, plans began for the first world scout Jamboree, held in 1920 in the United Kingdom, which drew 30,000 scouts from 30 nations. In conjunction with this assembly, an "International Scout Conference" of the leaders of these various national scout associations was held. From this meeting came the establishment of the Boy Scouts International Bureau, located in London. However, this was conceived as a very loosely structured organization, more of a voluntary movement than a tightly controlled organization. As Masemann notes (1990, 28):

> The rise of the Boy Scout movement exemplifies historically the rise of a group of people with a common purpose, common outward symbolism, a shared set of rules, a shared organization, and a charismatic leader...However, if Scouting was to succeed in later years, it had to transform itself from a *movement* to an *organization* (emphasis added).

However, as Vallory (2012, 14) notes:

> Baden Powell stressed from the outset that the sense of "movement" within the organization was to be maintained, which meant that more importance was placed on principles and method than on the organization itself. And even more so internationally, since a set of standard principles determining Scout recognition was being established and great measures being taken to end the centralizing and controlling tendency of world organizations.

"Headquarters" had no real executive or command authority over the associated local scout associations. It could and did provide international leader training, publish information and materials of various sorts, organize and conduct international meetings, and in various ways promote the exchange of information and ideas. However, it had one function, as referred to above, which was and is crucial: "recognition." *Headquarters* controls the "brand" of Scouting. Only the international organization can recognize a national organization or association as legitimately referring to itself, and being recognized internationally as "Scouting."

This is of profound importance. As it has turned out, the "pedagogical method" of Scouting, as briefly referenced above, has turned out to be so popular among boys (and since 1909, girls) that there have been constant and regular attempts over the last century to appropriate it, and the associated name "Scouting," to all sorts of organizations with aims ranging from not completely consistent with, to fundamentally contrary to, the original and lasting values of the movement.

What are the Principles and Conditions for Membership?

According to the World Scout Bureau, which is the actual "office" of the WOSM, the Mission of Scouting is as follows:

> The mission of Scouting is to contribute to the education of young people, through a value system based on the Scout Promise and Law, to help build a better world where people are self-fulfilled as individuals and play a constructive role in society. This is achieved by: 1. involving them throughout their formative years in a *non-formal educational process* 2. using a specific method that makes each individual the principal agent of his or her development as a self-reliant, supportive, responsible and committed person, 3. assisting them to establish a value system based upon spiritual, social and personal principles as expressed in the promise and the law. (Scout.org 2011b)

It is the Scout Promise and Scout Law that translate all of these high-blown words into reality in a language understandable to a scout-age person. Every new scout must formally "pledge" the Scout Promise to become a member of the organization. In every place in the world where I have seen Scouting in action, this is done in a brief but quite formal and rather solemn ceremony, to emphasize its importance.

The Promise and Law are essential to understand the worldwide spread of Scouting.

As Vallory notes (2009, 208–209), the Scout Promise and its attendant Law, however, translated and altered across time and place, represent a social code "that benefits others rather than the person who adopts it. It is a set of rules designed to produce better citizens, with a series of principles that would later become essential for maintaining the ideological unity of the movement." Since my primary association with world Scouting has been through Canada since 1968, I note below the current English-language version of the Canadian Scout Promise, with notes regarding how each phrase is currently interpreted locally and internationally.

Scout Promise

On my honour, I promise: In my experience, this is taken very seriously by the prospective scouts. The idea of pledging "on my honour" raises this above the common and casual "promises" they make. Personal honor is a very serious matter.

That I will do my best to do my duty: "Do my best" is key here. The idea is not that one must *be best*, as in winning competitions, but rather that one should *do one's best*, according to one's own abilities. The Scouting "method" encourages collaboration and cooperation rather than competition.

To God: A sense of spiritual life and values is a fundamental part of Scouting. This has proven to be a source of regular tension in the movement, and one of its greatest strengths and reasons for its worldwide appeal. In the overwhelmingly Christian "founding" nation, the word "God" made sense, as it does generally among monotheistic religious groups. However, it is noted above that among the earliest members of world Scouting, separate associations sprang up based on confessional lines, and Scouting quickly spread to non-monotheistic nations. One solution to these patterns, which was "officialized" in the early 1920s, was that membership in World Scouting was conditional on a nation having a single umbrella association that encompassed any and all separate (on confessional or linguistic or whatever grounds) scout associations within that nation. Another solution was that in official documents, the word "God" was often over time replaced by "spiritual values." This allowed the easy inclusion of non-monotheist and non-deist religions and cosmologies. As Nagy noted in his 1967 report, just about the only folks who would be excluded are "militant atheists" (Nagy 1967, 39). A quick scan of the nations listed in Table 3.2 indicates the wide range of religious/cosmological understandings that live happily together in world Scouting. It is notable that the largest "Scouting" nation, Indonesia, is also the largest Islamic nation in the world! It was also established early on, at the third International Conference in 1924, that "the policy of the Movement forbids any kind of sectarian propaganda at gatherings of mixed faiths." At that same conference, it was declared "that the World Movement shall have as its unalterable foundation the recognition of Scout Brotherhood, regardless of race, creed or class" (Wilson 1959, 66).

And the Queen: In non-monarchial nations, this is translated as "my country." This is meant to be active, contributing citizenship, not passive citizenship. In 1919, Baden-Powell wrote, in a guidebook for scoutmasters: "A Scout is active in doing good, not passive in being good" (Baden-Powell 1919, 34). After reflecting on the carnage of World War I, and the increasing spontaneous growth internationally of the Scout Movement, he broadened the conception of citizenship from "the local" to "the global," or rather to both simultaneously (an early capturing of what we now refer to in comparative education terms as "The Dialectic of the Global and the Local" (Arnove and Torres 2007). In a speech in 1922, he noted the dream that

> Where the young citizens, male and female, in all countries are brought up to look upon their neighbours as brothers and sisters in the human family allied together with the common aim of service and sympathetic helpfulness towards each other, they will no longer think as heretofore in terms of war as against rivals, but in terms of peace and goodwill towards one another...This spirit is the soul that is needed to make the League of Nations a living force instead of a mere formal pact.

He also noted that he dreamed of making the Scout Movement the League of Nations' youth movement (Amalvy 2007, 4).

To help other people at all times: This is the operationalization of the notion of active local and international citizenship discussed above.

And to carry out the spirit of the Scout Law: The Law can be seen essentially as a further detailing of the everyday meanings of the lofty ideals of spiritual values and active citizenship discussed above. The Canadian version reads as follows: **A Scout is helpful and trustworthy, kind and cheerful, considerate and clean, and wise in the use of all resources.**

As the WOSM evaluates applications for membership, it considers whether the proposed wording of the Promise and Law, and the governing statutes of the new national organization, reflect these core values and beliefs. In cases of clear conflict, the application is rejected out of hand. (Also, existing national associations may be, and have been, "de-certified" if they stray too far from those principles.) In cases where it appears that an agreed compromise can be found, further conversations are proposed. And the world organization is prepared to be flexible to take into account particular national situations. As Vallory (2012, 220) notes: "The position adopted by the World Scouting organization on these issues is that they depend on the situation of each national association."

In this mid-portion of the chapter, I have briefly outlined the approach taken by the WOSM to protect, we might say, the "purity of the brand" of Scouting internationally. This has been of key importance because it is such a popular "brand" that many groups and regimes, who have nothing at all to do with the principles noted above, have wanted to adapt it to their own purposes, including inter alia the Nazi regime in Germany, where Scouting was not formally recognized internationally in the years prior to World War II because of its nationalist and racist content and which eventually morphed into the Hitler Jugend; or the Ballilas in Fascist Italy in the same period (Mussolini tried personally to convince Baden-Powell that his was a superior form of Scouting—Baden-Powell was not impressed!); or the Pioneers in the Soviet Union, which was a clear takeoff of the attractive parts of Scouting while violating the fundamental principles of voluntarism, personal–individual and spiritual development, and internationalism (see Farrell 2001 and Vallory 2012 for extended commentaries on this).

Why Does Scouting as a Voluntary Organization Attract So Many Members?

The Anthropologist E. T. Hall has noted the following:

> It is a common assumption among Western educators that children must be 'motivated' to learn, that is, offered inducements and bribes to learn. In this the educators are patently wrong, otherwise how is it possible to explain the universal acquisition of both language and microculture with enthusiasm and alacrity? As a matter of fact, while it is not uncommon to find children who do not always like school, children as a whole love to learn, young people love to learn, and when the drive to learn ceases, that is a message that one should take seriously, because it signifies that there is little left in life to hold one on this earth. My own view on this matter is that the learning drive is on a par with the sexual drive. (Hall 1986, 159)

David Olson, a leading cognitive scientist who has spent his career trying to understand how people learn, has noted the following contrast between what cognitive science "says" and what schooling does (Olson 2003, ix):

What Cognitive Science Says	What Schooling Does
What people learn depends on what they already know	What they learn depends on what the school mandates.
People learn because they are intrinsically interested or because they love learning	They pursue knowledge because they "need the credit"
Learning is inspired by the search for meaning and growth and understanding	What they learn depends upon what books, chapters, or pages they are responsible for
The growth of mind is spontaneous and continuous.	It is a matter of obligation and duty

The "Method" of Scouting reflects "what cognitive science says," and Hall's understanding of learning as well. It is also heavily rooted in the work of Maria Montessori. In 1914, Baden-Powell observed that

Dr. Montessori has proved that by encouraging a child in its natural desires, instead of instructing it in what you think it ought to do, you can educate it on a far more solid and far-reaching basis. It is only tradition and custom that ordains that education should be a labour…One of the original objects of *Scouting for Boys* was to break through this tradition. (Jeal 1991, 412; see also Farrell 1990)

Montessori later wrote of Scouting as freeing children "from the narrow limits to which they have been confined" (Jeal 1989, 413). Both appear to have seen Scouting as a way to extend Montessori's ideas about early childhood learning to older young people (Farrell 2007). However, the question remains: Why do the young folks from so many nations of the world join and stay?

Here there is something that our various "grand theories" seem to have "grand trouble" in dealing with. If you ask a scout, as I have done in many cultures around our world, why they are in Scouting, the most common response is (translated directly by me, or by a local translator): "It's fun. We get to do neat stuff that other kids can't, or won't!" There is always, insofar as I can detect, a strong sense of personal pride and accomplishment. A bit over a decade ago, I had the quite surprising experience of having one of my former scouts as a student in one of my graduate courses, which focused on how teachers, as adult learners, actually learn to teach in various cultures. In one of his "personal reflection papers," he summarized neatly much of what I had been observing around the world for so many years. He noted that as a scout, he had no idea that he was learning anything:

I was in scouts [he joined our troop at age 11 and stayed on as a junior leader] simply because it was fun. All of my friends were there, and we did neat stuff together, adventures, canoe trips, summer camps, hikes on the Bruce Trail, service projects like laying in a garden for a seniors home, and we had to deal with difficult stuff and get on with it. And we had to deal with some difficult other kids, so we learned how to do that. It's only now when I think back on it as a grad student that I realize that we were actually *learning* so much. If you'd said then we were going to be learning, we would have fled. Learning is what we did in school, and it definitely wasn't fun. Fun was what happened in Scouts.

As Jenkins (1990, 1) put it: "Obviously, masses of children and their homely [British meaning] adult leaders would not have become Scouts simply because an elite leadership thought it would be good for them; they enjoyed what they made Scouting mean for themselves."

My sense of all of this experience is that the "genius" of the Scouting "Method" is that it does not try directly to "teach." Rather, it is designed to "enable learning," which, as I argued in 1997, is the way all of educational planning must go if it imagines itself ever to be successful (Farrell 1997). And Scouting does this by subterfuge in a way. Fun, adventure, and challenge are the attraction; learning is the outcome. In a series of small essays in the journal *Curriculum Inquiry*, I have provided further examples and analyses of how this "Method" works out in areas such as Moral Learning (Farrell 2003), Democratic Citizenship Learning (Farrell 1998), and Identity Development (Farrell 1996). To close, I repeat that this learning power is everywhere identifiably "local" while also identifiably "global." This is perhaps the greatest strength.

Thus, the Scouting Movement is an exemplar of a century-long ongoing "dialogue across cultures" of the sort which Ruth Hayhoe has long called for among more formal educational institutions.

REFERENCES

Amalvy, Richard. 2007. *Baden Powell's Third Life: Peace and Love Rather than Fear. Introduction to: Baden-Powell, Robert: "Education in Love Instead of Fear" (Re-edition of the report presented to the 3rd International Congress of Moral Education). Geneva, August 1, 1922.* Geneva: World Scout Bureau.

Arnove, Robert F., and Carlos A. Torres, eds. 2007. *Comparative Education: The Dialectic of the Global and the Local.* 3rd ed. Lanham, MD: Roman and Littlefield Publishers.

Baden-Powell, Robert. 1899. *Aids to Scouting.* London: Gale and Poldan Ltd.

Baden-Powell, Robert. 1908. *Scouting for Boys.* London: Herbert Jenkins Ltd.

Baden-Powell, Robert. 1919, 1943. *Aids to Scoutmastership [World Brotherhood Edition].* London: Herbert Jenkins Ltd.

Baden-Powell, Robert. 1923. *Scouting for Boys in India.* New Delhi: Boy Scouts Association in India.

Farrell, Joseph P. 1990. "Learning as Work or Learning as Play." *Curriculum Inquiry* 29 (3): 243–247

Farrell, Joseph P. 1996. "Narratives of Identity: The Voices of Youth." *Curriculum Inquiry* 26 (3): 235–243.

Farrell, Joseph P. 1997. "A Retrospective on Educational Planning in Comparative Education." *Comparative Education Review* 41 (3): 277–313

Farrell, Joseph P. 1998. "Democracy and Education: Who Gets to Speak and Who Gets Listened To?" *Curriculum Inquiry* 28 (1): 1–7

Farrell, Joseph P. 2001. "On Learning Civic Virtue: Can Schooling Really Play a Role?" *Curriculum Inquiry* 31 (2): 125–135.

Farrell, Joseph P. 2003. "Hey Joe...? Moral Education, Moral Learning, and How Could We Ever Know If and When the First Produces the Second?" *Curriculum Inquiry* 33 (2): 105–115.

Farrell, Joseph P. 2007. "Education in the Years to Come: What We Can Learn from Alternative Education." In *Changing Education: Leadership, Innovation and Development in a Globalizing Asia Pacific*, ed. Peter D. Hershock (pp. 199–224). Hong Kong and Dordrecht, The Netherlands: Comparative Education Research Centre, University of Hong Kong and Springer.

Hall, Edward T. 1986. "Unstated Features of the Cultural Context of Learning." In *Learning and Development: A Global Perspective*, ed. Alan Thomas and Edward Ploman (pp. 157–176). Toronto: OISE Press.

Jeal, Tim. 1989. *Baden Powell*. London: Pimlico.

Jenkins, Elwyn. 1990. *Boy Scouts and the Colonial Heritage in South Africa*. Unpublished paper. Pretoria, South Africa: Vista University.

LaBelle, Thomas J. 1981. "An Introduction to the Nonformal Education of Children and Youth." *Comparative Education Review* 25 (3): 313–329.

MacLeod, David I. 1983. *Building Character in the American Boy. The Boy Scouts, YMCA and Their Forerunners 1870–1920*. Madison, WI: University of Wisconsin Press.

Masemann, Vandra. 1990. *The Culture of Scouting: Institutional Transfer in Short Pants*. Paper presented at the annual meeting of the Comparative and International Education Society, Anaheim, CA.

Nagy, Laszlo. 1967. *Report on World Scouting/Etude sur le Scoutisme Mondial*. Geneva: Graduate Institute of International Studies/Institut Universitaire de Hautes Etudes Internationales.

Olson, David. 2003. *Psychological Theory and Educational Reform: How School Remakes Mind and Society*. Cambridge, UK: Cambridge University Press.

Scout.org. 2011a. *Facts and Figures*. Geneva: World Organization of the Scout Movement. Available online at: www.scout.org.

Scout.org. 2011b. *Mission and Values*. Geneva: World Organization of the Scout Movement. Available online at: www.scout.org.

Springhall, John. 1977. *Youth, Empire and Society: British Youth Movements, 1883–1940*. London: Croom Helm.

Vallory, Eduard. 2009. "Status Quo Keeper or Social Change Promoter? The Double Side of World Scouting's Citizenship Education." In *Scouting Frontiers: Youth and the Scout Movement's First Century*, ed. Nicholas R. Block and Thomas M. Proctor (pp. 205–220). Cambridge, UK: Cambridge Scholars Press.

Vallory, Eduard. 2012. *World Scouting: Educating for Global Citizenship*. New York: Palgrave Macmillan.

Wilson, John S. 1959. *Scouting Round the World*. London: Blandford Press.

Chapter 4

Historicizing Comparative and International Education, and Internationalizing History of Education: A Personal Reflection on Ruth Hayhoe's Call for Cultural Dialogue

Yeow Tong Chia

A key focus of Ruth Hayhoe's scholarship has been the call for cultural dialogue and mutual understanding between the East and the West. Inspired by her lifelong passion for global cultural dialogue and understanding, this chapter proposes a deep dialogue between two academic discourse "cultures"[1] in education—history of education, and comparative and international education—both of which I consider to be my intellectual "home." This is a reflective, and, in part, personal piece on my own intellectual journey in both fields of study, and the impact of Ruth's work on my thinking and scholarship. A deep dialogue and conversation, not only between scholars, but also between the professional institutions representing these two fields of study would result, I hope, in a renewed emphasis on history in comparative and international education, and a reawakened global and international consciousness in the field of history of education.[2] In other words, we need to go beyond ad hoc conversations to more systematic and intentional dialogue.

Nonetheless, my chapter will lay a greater emphasis on history of education, as I am deeply concerned with the future of this field. More specifically, I focus on history of education in Anglo-Saxon societies, particularly in North America. The spark for my reflections came from the announcement in October 2009 by the School of Graduate Studies at the University of Toronto that the intake of doctoral students for the Ontario Institute for Studies in Education's (OISE) History and Philosophy of Education program would be suspended. At the same time, the program was granted a two-year conditional approval. When the graduate students in the History and Philosophy of Education program heard this news, they organized online petitions, town-hall meetings, and other protests, including soliciting letters from academics all over the world in support of the program, but it was to be of no avail.

This de facto killing of the history of education program at OISE is the most recent illustration of the crisis facing educational history in North America and globally. I organized a panel at the 2010 Canadian History of Education Association annual meeting to address this issue. Provocatively titled *The Death of History of Education?*, the panel sought to discuss the intellectual, institutional, and identity dimensions of the crisis facing the role and place of history in the study of education. The first two essays presented a bleak picture of history of education and foundations of education. As Roland Sintos Coloma (2010) argued in his presentation, we are witnessing "the decreasing significance of history as disciplinary knowledge and as integral to social foundations." And that is the case in much of Canada, the United States, and the world today, as psychology and sociology of education have gained importance in teacher-education programs, often at the expense of the historical and philosophical foundations of education. However, that was not the case half a century ago—History of Education was one of the key courses and programs in Schools and Colleges of Education (at least in the Anglo-Saxon world).

Nonetheless, the intellectual roots of educational history are separate from those of mainstream history. Leopold von Ranke was considered by most mainstream historians as the founder of modern historiography, since his view and approach to history marked a departure from the teleological and "lessons-from-the-past" views manifested in medieval and Enlightenment histories. Ranke established history as a discipline separate from philosophy or literature. And he stressed the use of primary sources in the study of history, in order to study the past *wie es eigentlich gewesen*— as it really was.[3] G. R. Elton (1967), a twentieth-century proponent of Rankean historiography, sums it up as follows:

> The task of history is to understand the past, and if the past is to be understood it must be given full respect in its own right. And unless it is properly understood, any use of it in the present must be suspect and can be dangerous. (47, 48)

He further believes that "the study of history is a search for truth" (ibid., 51) and that it is tied in with the effort at making history scientific.

In his seminal piece, *What is History?*, E. H. Carr (1987) challenges the conception of history as objective fact, calling it a "fetishism of facts…completed and justified by a fetishism of documents" (16). He thus questions the "solidity, rigidity and accessibility of the historical fact," remarking "that the cult of facts prevailing at this time may have had something to do with the fact that the facts appeared in those years to smile so propitiously upon the universe of expansionist Western culture, where of course history was being written" (Thompson 2000, 11). Carr (1987) regards history as "a continuous process of interaction between the historian and his facts, an unending dialogue between the present and the past" (30). In addition, he sees of the historian as crucial to the historical enterprise, arguing that "the function of the historian is neither to love the past nor to emancipate himself from the past, but to master and understand it as the key to the understanding of the present" (ibid., 26). With regard to objectivity, "the historian had to find objectivity not by virtue of some moral or religious criterion outside history, nor by eschewing any wider generalizations and sticking to a mere recital of facts, but by looking for a larger meaning within history itself, an ongoing history moving from past through present to future" (Evans 2000, 225). That is not to say that Carr has completely repudiated the historical method established by Ranke: According to Evans, Carr affirms the "[h]istorical method…based on the rules of verification laid down by Ranke and elaborated in numerous ways since his time. It is common to all historians working in…various theoretical modes" (ibid., 127).

Besides having a more relativistic view of historical objectivity, Carr (1987) believes that history should be viewed from the present, and we can learn lessons from the past:

> Learning from history is never a one-way process. To learn about the present in the light of the past means also to learn about the past in the light of the present. The function of history is to promote a profounder understanding of both past and present through the interrelation between them. (68)

This would resonate well with the aims of education history. Even so, there was no mention of any historians of education by Carr.

Unlike mainstream history, history of education arose out of the field of education studies, and the advent of modern school systems provided the impetus in the study of educational history:

> The rise of modern state school systems, the variations in types found today in different lands, the new conceptions of the educational purpose, the rise of science study, the new functions which the school has recently assumed, the worldwide sweep of modern educational ideas, the rise of many entirely new types of schools and training within the past century; these and many

other features of modern educational practice in progressive nations are better understood if viewed in the light of their proper historical setting. Standing as we are today on the threshold of a new era, and with a strong tendency manifest to look only to the future and to ignore the past, the need for sound educational perspective on the part of leaders in both school and state is given new emphasis. (Clubberley 1920, ix)

Indeed, Campbell and Sherington (2002), two noted historians of education at the University of Sydney, state that "the history of education as an organized discipline is clearly associated with the rise of the modern teachers college, the modern department, school or faculty of education within universities" (49). History of education was almost synonymous with the history of schooling.

Due to its origins, as well as its location within the field of education, history of education remains "an underdeveloped theme in academic history and mainstream historians continued to avoid a field tarred with the educationists' brush" (McCulloch and Richardson 2000, 32). The assumption that historical studies of education actually have something to contribute to present-day and future education serves to marginalize the field from mainstream history:

> Much of the history of education in the early to mid-twentieth century had been written in isolation from the mainstream discipline of history. Academics in university departments of history often held the sub-discipline in disdain, principally because of the way it had come to celebrate and justify the educational past. (Campbell and Sherrington 2002, 52)

The education histories written in the period up to the 1960s were within the "Whig" tradition, which emphasized the development of teachers and portrayed "the history of education unproblematically as a story of continual improvement and refinement led by a partnership between the education profession and the benign nation state" (McCulloch and Richardson 2000, 37). These were mostly written by educationalists, and the quote by Clubberley in the previous paragraph epitomized this kind of historiography. As Bowles and Gintis (1976) commented, "looking backward, one might—as many educational historians do—see an inexorable march along a single line of ascent" (152). In the meantime, the Whig interpretation of history had been discredited in mainstream historiography by the 1930s, most notably by Sir Herbert Butterfield's *The Whig Interpretation of History* (1931) and Sir Lewis Namier's *The Structure of Politics at the Accession of George III* (1929).

The Whig argument posits that religion, in the form of the Reformation, the Enlightenment, and the idea of liberal democracy, accounts for the origins of public schooling in Europe and North America. The Reformation leaders saw education as a means to spread their ideas. Martin Luther, the "father" of the Reformation "considered popular education to be crucial to the success of the Reformation, and exhorted secular authorities to establish schools for their subjects" (Melton 1998, 4). Indeed the Reformation's emphasis on *sola scriptura* necessitated the spread of mass literary in order for the Bible to be read and understood by the laypeople. The Enlightenment philosophy, on the other hand, focuses on education as a universal right of man. These two ideas provided the backdrop for liberal democracy as one of the factors accounting for the rise of public schooling. As Ken Osborne (1999) argues, with regard to democracy:

> Citizens were entitled to rights, not the least was the right to vote. This made education important...if working men, and eventually, women, were to be allowed to vote and take part in public affairs, then they should be at least be able to do so intelligently. Education was necessary if democratic citizenship was to be a reality. (7)

In sum, the liberal notion of education emphasizes the emancipatory nature of schooling, something that signalled a march toward progress. This came under attack from the 1960s.

In the book *Education in the Forming of American Society* by Harvard historian Bernard Bailyn (1960), he "pointed to the narrowness of the discipline and the questions asked within it" and argued that education history "was waiting to be discovered in many places other than schools" (Campbell and Sherrington 2002, 52). This resulted in a fundamental shift in the historiography of education, in which "the stimulus to change came initially from the new interest of historians in social and intellectual aspects of the past" (ibid.). The upshot of these changes and historical revisionism meant that the notion of progress in educational history could no longer be taken for granted. With the discrediting of Whig historiography in the history of education, and with the recognition that education is more than schooling alone, the stage was set for a fundamental shift in the historiography of education, in which "the stimulus to change came initially from the new interest of historians in social and intellectual aspects of the past" (ibid.). The upshot of these changes was that:

> Revisionism, whether benign or radical, had linked education history to the new social history. But it had also broken the close bond between educational history and the teacher education curriculum. The new educational history began to look like the new educational sociology. The questions it asked were not necessarily comfortable for existing educational practice. It could be accused of undermining the confidence of beginning teachers. As

a discipline, the history of education had flowered. The number of historical works of insight and depth in the field of education were extraordinary.
Oral historical and quantitative methods, as well as new discoveries and
theories about how to read the documentary evidence of the past had led
the historian's gaze into areas barely touched previously. (ibid., 56)

The notion of progress in educational history could no longer be taken
for granted. History of education broke out of the narrow confines of
school (institutional) history, to explore the culture and society that had
an impact on education, broadly defined. OISE's History of Education
program is a good example, with scholars working on rural and family
history, industrialization, gender history, immigration, and ethnicity. The
proliferation of books and journal articles (especially in history of education in the English-speaking world) that go beyond seeing educational
history as confined to schools is a testament of Bailyn's legacy (Urban
2011).

I would like to point out one caveat here. Bailyn was not the first to
point out that American educational history was too narrowly focused on
schools and the institutions of schooling. Educational historians, most
notably Lawrence Cremin (1960), had been calling for the same thing
about the same time as Bailyn's seminal piece.[4] Nonetheless, it seems to
me that Bailyn's critique has been seen as the turning point in the field of
educational history.

While there has been a flowering and proliferation of scholarship on
educational history, in its efforts to become more historical, the field
became increasingly marginalized and alienated from departments and
faculties of education. This resonates with Jurgen Herbst's (1999) summary of the field of educational history since the 1960s:

> In the United States this had been the turn away from a preoccupation
> with teacher training to academic history; in Europe it was the increased
> sophistication in educational historiography unaccompanied by a system-
> atic exploration of the history of the classroom. (746)

At the same time, educational history remains on the periphery of mainstream history departments.[5] What we are witnessing over the past
decades is the uprooting of history of education as a field of study in
schools of education, especially in teacher-education programs, with the
recent de facto closure of OISE's History of Education program being
the latest example (Campbell and Sherrington 2002; Coloma 2010; Kerr
et al. 2011). As a result, it seems to me that history of education and educational historians do not fit into either education or history departments
today.

Another phenomenon I observed was that despite the problematization of the nation state as the sole frame of reference by historians, the majority of historians of education still work within the confines of the nation state. A look at the programs for recent US History of Education Society meetings, Australia and New Zealand History of Education Society conferences, as well as Canadian History of Education Association meetings demonstrates my point. Why is this so? That is, why do many historians of education, especially those in North America, still work within the confines of the nation state, even though, like mainstream historians of education, they have repudiated the nation state as a frame of reference?[6] A related question would ask why most historians of education tend to study only their own country, and why there seem to be few comparative and international studies that adopt historical approaches these days.

I do not have the answers to these questions, but they are pertinent to my own dissertation research. Titled *The Loss of the "World-Soul"? Education, Culture and the Making of the Singapore Developmental State, 1955–2004*, my dissertation examines the role of education in the formation of the Singapore developmental state, through a historical study of education for citizenship in Singapore (1954–2004), in which I explore the interconnections between changes in history, civics, and social studies curricula, and the politics of nation building (Chia 2011). Building on existing scholarship on education and state formation, the dissertation goes beyond the conventional notion of seeing education as providing the skilled workforce for the economy, to mapping out cultural and ideological dimensions of the role of education in the developmental state. I argue that the story of state formation through citizenship education in Singapore is essentially the history of how Singapore's developmental state managed crises (imagined, real, or engineered), and how changes in history, civics, and social studies curricula served to legitimize the state, through educating and moulding the desired "good citizen" in the interest of nation building. Underpinning these changes has been the state's use of cultural constructs such as Confucianism and Asian values to shore up its legitimacy.

Nonetheless, because my work is situated in both history of education and comparative and international education, I struggled during my early years in the doctoral program over which discourse community I should belong to and which could be considered "home" to me. I found that I do not fully belong to the field of history of education in North America, which I find too North American centric. Neither am I fully at home with the Comparative and International Education Society, as I am more concerned with writing history than with methods. My struggle was articulated in my entry in the H-Education listserv online guest discussion "Where Do Historians of Education Live?: Disciplines and Interdisciplines in the Academe," where I shared my "identity-crisis" of not being fully at home in these two discourse communities, nor in Asian Studies, which does not focus much on education. Professor David Labaree's response to my entry was reassuring, as he pointed out the advantages of being in different discourse communities, and urged me not to be too worried about finding the right community. Reading *Full Circle* by Ruth Hayhoe (2004) helped me to better situate the discourse and intellectual communities that best suits my research interests. I have decided that I would aim to contribute to the fields of history of education, comparative and international education, and Asian Studies by virtue of my doctoral dissertation on Singapore.

While I have achieved some form of resolution, I still wonder where and how I fit in, as I seem to be at the intersections and margins of these fields of study. This appears also to parallel the field of educational history, which is at the margins and intersections of educational studies and history. And, as I mentioned earlier, much of the scholarship in history of education remains parochial, with the international and global dimensions more or less absent. In the field of comparative and international education, where the international and global are emphasized, there is "the sacrifice or almost total abandonment of the historical dimension in comparative educational research" (Kazamias 2009, 155). To support his claim, Kazamias (2009) quotes Larsen's (2001) findings that "research strategies in comparative education from 1955 to 1994 revealed that only 10.5 per cent of almost 2000 articles in the *International Journal of Educational Development, Comparative Education* and *Comparative Education Review* relied on historiography and historical research" (156). Historical scholarship in the field of comparative and international education has thus declined, as evidenced in the articles published in the key journals of the field. And amongst the current history of education doctoral students with whom I am in contact, not many are interested in the field of comparative and international education.

The current neglect of historical research in comparative and international education contrasts with the prominence and importance given to history by the key founders of the field. Back in 1900, Sir Michael Sadler emphasized the importance of history in comparative education:

> Therefore, if we propose to study foreign systems of education, we must not keep our eyes on the brick and mortar institutions, nor on the teachers and pupils only, but we must also go outside into the streets and into the homes of the people, and try to find out what is the tangible, impalpable, spiritual force which, in the case of any successful system of Education, is in reality upholding the school system and accounting for its practical efficiency... (Sadler 1900, reprinted in Bereday 1964, 309–10)

Kazamias (2009) highlights the importance of history in order to understand this "tangible, impalpable," and "spiritual force." Nicholas Hans (1958) develops Sadler's ideas even further, arguing that "the first step [to study comparative education] is to study each national system…in its historical setting and its close connection with the development of national character and culture" (7). As such, I feel a sense of dissonance with the current ahistorical trend of comparative and international education scholarship.

Nonetheless, I managed to achieve some form of resolution to my struggle as I discovered two articles by R. Freeman Butts, "Civilization-Building and the Modernization Process: A Framework for the Reinterpretation of the History of Education" (1967a) and "Civilization as Historical Process: Meeting Ground for Comparative and International Education" (1967b). The former article was written for historians of education and the audience of the latter article was comparative and international education scholars. While I disagree with R. Freeman Butts's view of a universal march toward civilizations and modernization, we should not be too quick to repudiate both concepts. In her presidential address to the Comparative and International Education Society in 1999, Ruth Hayhoe (2000) asks the pertinent question: "Are we so busy throwing out new theories, constructing new terminologies, and hastening into new arenas of discourse that we are unable to learn…lessons from other civilizations?" (425).[7] She suggests that we should fully understand the current modernist discourses, and the responses of non-Western civilizations to modernity. Instead of rejecting modernity altogether, Hayhoe proposes the redeeming of modernity through dialogue among different civilizations:

> [Habermas] depicts a jagged profile of modernity that has resulted from a selective rationalization in the area of instrumental technical knowledge. Redemption is possible, he suggests, through reinvigorating the life world of moral values and aesthetic understanding. The concept of rationality itself can be enriched and transformed in this process. The unconstrained dialogue…he proposed can be realized in intent efforts to hear voices coming from other civilizations…we often take for granted benefits of modernity that have become as natural as breathing and lack appreciation of the intense efforts in other societies to carry forward their own modernity projects. (ibid., 424)

Ruth Hayhoe's call for dialogue among civilizations was in part a response to Samuel Huntington's "clash of civilizations" thesis. Hence, the late R. Freeman Butts is, in a way, a forerunner in calling for a "civilizations" approach as a bridge to both comparative and international education, and history of education. The civilizations approach that Ruth Hayhoe adopts is what she refers to as a culture explicit framework, which is historically transmitted, and manifest through worldviews, epistemologies, and unquestioned "ways of life" in her work on China. This differs from how "civilization" is commonly viewed by scholars in North America and Europe. Scholars in the West often conflate civilization with imperialism and colonialism, which is not the case among Asian scholars (Duara 2001). One can even put forward a case that China is more of a civilization state than a nation state (Jacques 2009).

With this renewed and reinvigorated concept of civilization from scholars studying Asia, I found the key to bridge my interests in the field of educational history, comparative and international education, and Asian Studies. Additionally, Ruth Hayhoe's scholarship demonstrates a deep understanding of China's culture and history. Indeed, the historical method and perspective were a key approach adopted by such founders of the field of comparative and international education as Michael Sadler and Nicholas Hans.

I would therefore like to propose a reconsideration of the idea of civilizational dialogue as the "meeting-place" (using Butts's words) for history and comparative education. To study the multicultural without the historical and the global/international (history) narrows our understanding of any nation's history, and by its extension its educational history. This would better reflect the increasing multicultural nature of the countries in which we live today. A dialogue among civilizations framework also has its pedagogic implications, in countering the "national security" discourse and motivation (post-9/11) behind the study of other civilizations, evident in the "clash of civilizations" approach. Dialoguing, and respecting differences, is a start of the journey of learning to live with people and cultures that are different from our own.

Professor Ruth Hayhoe's many publications demonstrate just that—calling for and promoting intercultural dialogue between the East and West, making an invaluable contribution to scholarship in comparative education, as well as higher education. At the same time, her seminal works, such as *China's Universities and the Open Door* (1989) and *China's Universities 1895–1995: A Century of Cultural Conflict* (1996), demonstrate a deep understanding of the historian's craft and a deep knowledge of Chinese history, even though she never considered herself to be a historian. As such, she embodies the spirit of historicizing comparative education, and moving beyond the parochial confines of educational history, particularly in North America and Australia. She is of course not the only comparative education scholar who is deeply historical. I particularly acknowledge the legacy of William Brickman (1977), cofounder and first president of the US Comparative and International Education Society in laying the foundations for historical study in comparative and international education in the United States, Robert Ulich (1967), R. Freeman Butts, as well as the scholarship of Noah Sobe (2007) and Andy Green (1990). However, many of these historical works in comparative and international education are Eurocentric. More can be done to include other historical traditions such as Asia.

In this regard, Ruth Hayhoe's scholarship and her emphasis on cultural dialogue provides the epistemological and discursive space and link not only between history of education and comparative education, but more importantly, bringing the non-Western histories and cultures into the discussion on both fields of study.[8] Her research and scholarship therefore exemplify the vision of historicizing comparative and international education, and internationalizing and globalizing history of education. However, even though individual scholars like Ruth and others in the field of comparative and international education, history of education, and even mainstream history have been engaging in dialogue and conversations in their scholarly work, such efforts are insufficient. Beyond dialogue among individual scholars, more collective and institutional dialogue, involving such professional organizations as the Comparative International Education Society (CIES) and History of Education Society, would help to deepen, broaden, and potentially sustain the existing conversation between these two discourse communities.

NOTES

1. This draws loosely from Jerome Kagan's (2009) conceptualization of the humanities, social sciences, and science as different intellectual "cultures."
2. I recognize that there have been conversations and dialogue among the scholars in the fields of history of education and comparative education both in the past and today. Deceased scholars, such as Claude Eggertsen, William Brickman, Robert Ulich, and R. Freeman Butts, had published in history of education and comparative education. Current comparative education scholars who also publish in history of education include Andy Green, Nobe Sobe, and Joel Spring. However, Joel Spring's history publications are neither comparative nor international, as they focus on American educational history.
3. Richard Evans feels that this phrase has been widely misunderstood, and should instead be translated as "how it essentially was" (Evans 2000, 17).
4. Lawrence Cremin was instrumental in the setting up of the US History of Education Society in 1960, and was its first president (Urban 2011).
5. Nonetheless, historians in mainstream history departments continue to publish good educational histories. Examples include Thomas H. C. Lee's (2000) *Education in Traditional China: A History* and Fritz Ringer's (1979) *Education and Society in Modern Europe*.

6. Gaither (2001) argues that the repudiation of Whig historiography is one reason why historians of education focus less on global histories of education and more on national and local educational histories.
7. Hayhoe calls the Chinese response as "humanizing modernity," and the Japanese response as "harmonizing modernity."
8. Ruth Hayhoe is not the only scholar who is doing this important "linking" work. See Thomas H. C. Lee's (2000) *Education in Traditional China: A History*. However, Lee does not belong to the discourse community of history of education or comparative and international education.

REFERENCES

Bailyn, Bernard. 1960. *Education in the Forming of American Society: Needs and Opportunities for Study*. New York: Vintage Books.

Bowles, Samuel, and Hebert Gintis. 1976. *Schooling in Capitalist America: Educational Reform and the Contradictions of Economic Life*. New York: Basic Books.

Brickman, William W. 1977. "Comparative and International Education Society: An historical analysis." *Comparative Education Review* 21 (2–3): 396–404.

Butts, R. Freeman. 1967a. "Civilization-Building and the Modernization Process: A Framework for the Reinterpretation of the History of Education." *History of Education Quarterly* 7 (2): 147–174.

Butts, R. Freeman. 1967b. "Civilization as Historical Process: Meeting Ground for Comparative and International Education." *Comparative Education* 3 (3): 155–168.

Campbell, Craig and Geoffrey Sherington. 2002. "The History of Education: The Possibility of Survival." *Change: Transformations in Education* 5 (1): 46–64.

Carr, Edward Hallet. 1987. *What is History?* 2nd ed. London: Penguin Books.

Chia, Yeow Tong. 2011. "The Loss of the 'World-Soul'? Education, Culture, and the Making of the Singapore Developmental State, 1955–2004." PhD diss., University of Toronto.

Clubberley, Ellwood P. 1920. *The History of Education: Educational Practice and Progress Considered as a Phase of the Development and Spread of Western Civilization*. London: Constable and Company.

Coloma, Roland Sintos. 2010. "History Matters: Troubling Foundations in Teacher Education." Paper presented at Canadian History of Education Association biennial conference, Toronto, October 24, 2010.

Cremin, Lawrence. 1960. *The Transformation of the School: Progressivism and American Education, 1877–1957*. New York: Random House.

Duara, Prasenjit. 2001. "The Discourse of Civilization and Pan-Asianism." *Journal of World History* 12 (1): 99–130.

Elton, E. R. 1967. *The Practice of History*. Sydney: Sydney University Press.

Evans, Richard J. 2000. *In Defence of History*. London: Granta Books.

Gaither, Milton. 2001. "Globalization and History of Education. Some Comments on Jurgen Herbst's 'The History of Education: State of the Art at the Turn of the Century in Europe and North America.' " *Paedagogica Historica* 37 (3): 641–647.

Green, Andy. 1990. *Education and State Formation: The Rise of Education Systems in England, France, and the USA*. New York: St. Martin's Press

Hans, Nicholas. 1958. *Comparative Education: A Study of Educational Factors and Traditions*. 3rd rev. ed. London: Routledge and Kegan Paul.

Hayhoe, Ruth. 1989. *China's Universities and the Open Door*. Armonk, NY: M. E. Sharpe.

Hayhoe, Ruth. 1996. *China's Universities 1895–1995: A Century of Cultural Conflict*. New York: Garland Publishers.

Hayhoe, Ruth. 2000. "Redeeming Modernity." *Comparative Education Review* 44 (4): 423–439.

Hayhoe, Ruth. 2004. *Full Circle: A Life with Hong Kong and China*. Hong Kong: Comparative Education Research Centre, The University of Hong Kong.

Butterfield, Herbert. 1931. *The Whig Interpretation of History*. London: Bell.

Herbst, Jurgen. 1999. "The History of Education: State of the Art at the Turn of the Century in Europe and North America." *Paedagogica Historica* 35 (3): 737–747.

Jacques, Martin. 2009. *When China Rules the World: The End of the Western World and the Birth of a New Global Order*. New York: Penguin Press.

Kagan, Jerome. 2009. *The Three Cultures: Natural Sciences, Social Sciences, and the Humanities in the 21st Century*. Cambridge, MA: Harvard University Press.

Kazamias, Andreas M. 2009. "Comparative Education: Historical Reflections." In *International Handbook of Comparative Education*, ed. Robert Cowen and Andreas M. Kazamias. Dordrecht, the Netherlands: Springer.

Kerr, Donald, David Mandzuk, and Helen Raptis. 2011. "The Role of Social Foundations of Education in Programs of Teacher Preparation in Canada." *Canadian Journal of Education* 34 (4): 118–134.

Lee, Thomas H. C. 2000. *Education in Traditional China: A History*. Leiden: Brill.

McCulloch, Gary, and William Richardson. 2000. *Historical Research in Educational Settings*. Buckingham: Open University Press.

Melton, James Van Horn. 1988. *Absolutism and the Eighteenth Century Origins of Compulsory Schooling in Prussia and Austria*. Cambridge: Cambridge University Press.

Namier, Lewis. 1929. *The Structure of Politics at the Accession of George III*. London: Macmillan.

Osborne, Ken. 1999. *Education: A Guide to the Canadian School Debate—Or, Who Wants What and Why?* Toronto: Penguin/McGill Institute.

Ringer, Fritz. 1979. *Education and Society in Modern Europe*. Bloomington and London: Indiana University Press.

Sadler, Sir Michael. 1964 reprint [original 1900]. "How Can We Learn Anything of Practical Value from the Study of Foreign Systems of Education?" *Comparative Education Review* 7 (3): 307–314.

Sobe, Noah W. 2007. "An Historical Perspective on Coordinating Education
    Post-Conflict: Biopolitics, Governing at a Distance, and States of Exception."
    Current Issues in Comparative Education 9 (2): 45–54.
Thompson, Willie. 2000. *What Happened to History?* London: Pluto Press.
Ulich, Robert. 1967. *The Education of Nations: A Comparative and Historical
    Perspective.* Cambridge, MA: Harvard University Press.
Urban, Wayne J. 2011. "The Word from a Walrus: Five Decades of the History of
    Education Society." *History of Education Quarterly* 50 (4): 429–459.

Chapter 5

Humanizing Globalization: Six Scholars Bridge East and West through Comparative and International Education

Heidi Ross and Yimin Wang

A story cannot be told without words, and yet words carry with them assumptions and connotations that may hide as much as they reveal.

—*Ruth Hayhoe* 1999[1]

We know very little—or at least we do not dare to write it down—about our ways of working and of dealing with each other and about how these patterns influence the spread and acceptance of ideas in academic circles.

—*Robert Cribb* 2005

Introduction

This chapter tells a "dialogic story," whose protagonists are six scholars, storytellers, actors, and collaborators, most of whom identify professionally with the field of comparative and international education (CIE). In a sense, they/we are, save one, primarily "Western" scholars, but we are reluctant to use that unifying label, because their/our career-long engagement with Chinese schools, teachers, and students has also embedded them/us within the transforming story of Chinese education and its scholarship. Their/our professional involvement, geographical positioning, and personal experiences often overlap; however, they/we have also traveled different paths toward understanding the "puzzling[2] and unfolding" story of Chinese education.

We have chosen this chapter's "they/we" subject because the first author is also one of the actors in the story. This dual role serves to foreground the idea that no matter where we are from and currently living—be it the United States, Canada, Hong Kong, the United Kingdom, or China—what we have in common and what connects us is that China and Chinese education have become part of what Habermas (1985) would call our shared "lifeworld," or perhaps what Tu Weiming refers to as that clan of scholars of "Greater China."

For us, this shared lifeworld is constituted by both a mutual, yet individualized, commitment to China and Chinese education and also a set of fluid but shared values of collaboration, back-grounded recognition, and hope for humanizing globalization. Lifeworld, as we use it in this chapter, also encompasses what Cummings (1999) called the "intellectual substance" that brings scholars together, and what Robert Cribb (2005) has referred to as "Circles of Esteem." Cribb defines a circle of esteem as a "cluster of scholars that respects each other, cite each other's work, push each other's ideas into the academic marketplace, and, occasionally, rise to each other's defense" (Cribb 2005, 289). Cribb is compelling in his assertion that "one of the peculiarities of academic life is how seldom we turn our analytical skills on our own professional lives" (289). While we believe he is correct, Ruth Hayhoe is a powerful exception, and her unswerving respect for history and personal reflexivity throughout her career has inspired our desire in this chapter to reflect upon our space in Chinese educational research and practice. In her reflections for this project, Lynn Paine referred to this space generally as one of intersecting lives. Certainly, the intersection of scholars studying Chinese education has become more heavily trafficked and dense, yet that shared if crowded space is what makes our work both satisfying and important. Lynn concluded simply, "it's about the real people that we know." Ruth shared a very similar reflection, recalling how she was "really turned off" by scholars from the United States in the early 1980s who came to China chiefly to mine data for their scholarly careers. "They were not really interested in the local people in China."

With this in mind, we tentatively describe the "us" of this chapter as a circle of esteem, a cluster

of scholars who respect each other. These scholars may work on different topics, but they read each other's work, cite each other and help to push each other's ideas into the broader academic world. Circles of esteem are fluid entities, changing shape, size and composition as the research agenda of their members changes. They may be small or large, and many scholars may be a member of more than one circle...While they last, circles of esteem are positive and affirming to their members. (Cribb 2005, 291)

Overlapping and beyond these aspects of our lifeworld is our personal, surely normative, and even sentimental involvement or entanglement with Chinese education across time and space, ranging from our early days in the wake of the Cultural Revolution[3] to today's "globalized" China. Within this shared lifeworld, our individual localities, life experiences, and intellectual standpoints provide each of us with our own distinct "horizons" of understanding that in turn shape our perspectives on China, research on China, and our "own" cultures and societies. These different horizons and boundaries may create "friction" (Tsing 2005), but friction is generative of the diverse and multiple understandings that enrich dialogue and that is necessary for a "fusion of horizons,"[4] which in turn expands our shared lifeworld beyond the boundaries and localities of China, the United States, and Canada.

I (Heidi Ross) am positioning myself in this chapter as part of the shared lifeworld that I also hope to illuminate; this professional and often personal (at least in Cribb's sense) shared community of others comprises a continuum of people. This continuum ranges from people who are quite similar or familiar to me, to others—again borrowing from Tu Weiming—whom I must expand my "horizons" to understand, if not embrace. I am also writing about the/my self, a self that belongs to a group of scholars who are working toward transcultural understanding.

The six scholars profiled include, of course, Ruth Hayhoe, whose varied and distinguished "full circle" career is the much-deserved focus of this collection (see Hayhoe 2004). In addition, we feature Gerard Postiglione, Professor and Director of the Wah Ching Center of Research on Education in China of the University of Hong Kong, whose prolific scholarship has highlighted social change, Chinese education, and education for Chinese ethnic minorities, among many other topics.

Another Hong Kong-based scholar, Suzanne Pepper, is included in our group as an exceptionally perceptive witness and interpreter of Chinese educational history; since the late 1970s, she has used her location in Hong Kong to write on both Chinese education and Chinese politics, including issues of governance and democracy. She is also the chapter's lone political scientist—a discipline to which nearly every other scholar profiled makes reference.

Lynn Paine's comparative study of Chinese teachers, teaching, and teacher education, while ironically not her first choice for her dissertation, underscores the critical importance to the educational studies members of this community of what Gerry Postiglione called from his Hong Kong perspective the "we-feeling" of being a part of it all. Lynn's long and influential career in teaching and learning indicates that as practitioners, "You can't help but be drawn in... with the mission of national development."

Jing Lin is the only member of our group born in China, having been educated both in Guangxi and the United States. She has served as a faculty member in both Canadian and American universities and has written critically on timely topics ranging from the "Red Guards" (see Lin 1991) to the development of Chinese private education, to peace, spirituality, and environmental education. From our perspective, her local and global engagement in Chinese education tells a unique story about the power that transnational vision has to sharpen comparative thinking and enrich what we might also conceive of as a community of practice (Wenger 1998).

The final portrait is of myself: I first travelled to China as a young "tour guide" and then middle-school teacher in the early 1980s, and I have taught in and about China and Chinese education in both China and the United States since then. My personal and intellectual connections and friendships with my five counterparts have certainly shaped this story, I hope for the better, as well as my understanding of our shared lifeworld of Chinese education.

Many other fine scholars inhabit our lifeworld; we chose our six not only because we have each had a relatively long-term involvement with Chinese education and its research in multiple capacities, but also because we represent several important multidisciplinary strands of Western–China dialogue and scholarship on Chinese education, especially related to CIE; additionally, we have all had different geographical positionings and transcultural experiences in Hong Kong, Canada, and the United States.

In order to map the relational significance of the contributions of these six scholars, three layers of dialogue are used to structure and present our analysis. These layers include dialogue in time, in relational space, and finally, dialogue as "humanizing globalization." We are still in the process of analyzing the fascinating intersecting scholarly and personal trajectories—as story, not history—of our participants, and their developing research agendas that have been shaped by maturity, demands of academic and family life, changing research methodologies and approaches, and most of all the tremendous transformation of Chinese society.

One theme stands out in all but one of our stories, and that is that five of us have lived our scholarly careers primarily in professional schools of education. Gerry Postiglione suggests that those of us in China in the early 1980s were a kind of cultural ambassador. As primarily educational studies scholars and/or educators, we did not choose to study schools because they presented a politically embedded yet relatively nonsensitive site for social science research. As professionals, we were in schools to engage with real ideas and practice; as he puts it, we were there

> to take our professional knowledge and skills, to challenge them within the Chinese context to see if they could work and how they could work...Education is about human understanding [and] understanding oneself, which one learns through engagement with others. What is humanizing but human understanding? It drives our profession. This keeps me in the field, this purpose of human understanding and its diversity. I think you have to retain the enthusiasm, vitality, interest, curiosity...And drive is the most important. And that is done by a periodic reflexivity about purpose.[5]

The fact that most of us are also comparativists also allowed us a different perspective from those trained solely within the tradition of area studies, that is (possibly), a greater openness to border crossing. After all, a comparative perspective is designed to destabilize boundaries. Although we define the scope and purpose of the hard-to-define field of comparative education differently, our commitment to it provides us a particular vantage point from which to understand and try to make intelligible through our scholarship Chinese education, broadly defined. One characteristic of that vantage point is our varied level of engagement in and in some ways ambivalent commitment to area studies and their use of "a geographical metaphor to visualize and naturalize particular social spaces as well as a particular scale of analysis" (van Schendel 2002, 647).

Van Schendel (2002) concludes that the area studies configuration of scholarship has created both geographies of knowing and of ignorance through "an institutional anchoring of academic communities worldwide, which trained separately, became engaged in area specific discourses and debates, formed well-established reference circles, and developed similar mechanisms and rituals for patrolling their intellectual borders" (648). By working from the different needs and missions of professional schools of education, most of us do most of our work in different symbolic (theoretical/knowledge production) and institutional spaces. As educational studies specialists, we are, as Ruth has concluded, tasked to be multidisciplinary. Consequently, our "transnational scholarly lineages, circles of referencing, structures of authority and patronage" (van Schendel 2002, 648) are likewise multidisciplinary. We may as comparativists be less locked into geographical compartmentalization (van Schendel 2002, 658) or "Euro-US imagining." Ruth considers the possibility that disciplines as defined in nineteenth-century Europe "might hide certain elements of the Chinese scene." She considers the work by many China-focused political scientists excellent, and yet it may "have not revealed underlying cultural patterns." She concluded of her approach, "I wanted to explain in cultural terms the pieces that didn't get explained in pure political terms." From this point of view, "we" largely agree that educational studies and particularly comparative education have made a contribution to Chinese studies. Our focus on education as an institution for educating has revealed underlying patterns—even progressive ones—and in not being discipline-constrained, comparative educators' ways of seeing, according to Ruth,

> may be better attuned to China's epistemological traditions that are very integrative. They don't really adhere well to categories of the social sciences. That may give us, educators, advantages. I say this without in any way downgrading the extremely important contributions of historians, political scientists, etc. in our knowledge of contemporary China.

Layer One: Dialogue in Time

Our first layer entails *dialogue in time*, which refers to the collective and retrospective reading of each scholar's work over a time span of two to three decades. At the end of the first decade of the twenty-first century, as we are immersed in the discourse of the "rise of Asian Universities," we[6] reread the six scholars' work on China and Chinese education. This body of scholarship was written in times that range from the immediate post–Cultural Revolution period to the present era that is arguably and problematically perceived as the "time of Asia's rise."

We reread their/our scholarship along with documents that situate this scholarship within a particular sociopolitical and academic moment. We then engaged in conversation with the six scholars about the salient themes in their work, our interpretations of this work, and reflections on their own writings and work in different decades. This retrospective dialogical reading process provided us with a sense of both change and continuity, a glimpse of connectedness, and multiple levels of shared, but different, understandings of the key issues about both China and "the West," and about the simultaneously un/changing nature of cross-cultural communication in CIE.

We began our interviews by asking scholars to reflect on their decades of engagement with China and Chinese education. This question elucidated narratives of individual choice and preferences for research interests as the scholars interacted with the development of Chinese society and education, as well as educational research worldwide. These narratives immediately speak of issues of the "temporization" or "periodization" of research on CIE and Chinese education, which includes what is considered significant research on China and for China, as well as research that in a sense falls into different topics and arenas from the time of the Cultural Revolution, to the postsocialist era, to the commonly perceived time of "the rise of Asia." Meanwhile, the past several decades have also been a time in which the six scholars navigated their own interests, life, and research agendas, which forged the stories of personal histories interacting with national histories; in turn, these interactions provide a fascinating map of the trajectories of the field of CIE.

Approaching the Sense of "*Our* Time"

In the classical anthropological account "Time and the Other," Fabian (2002) decoded the binary of "my time" and "their time" by explaining how perceptions of social time define the relationship between the researcher and the researched, that is, the "politics of time" (97). Our readings and interviews with the six scholars challenged our understanding of approaching "*our* time" with a complex set of what we came to see as "our*S*" that is foregrounded and backgrounded in the scholars' works and their explanations of these works.

If the immediate "my time" can be read as the scholars' individual reflections and preferences regarding research interests and agenda, and "their time" can be read as the development of Chinese society, then "*our* time" forges the dimension of how "Western scholars read and write about Chinese education." This dimension has influenced in at least two ways the development of Chinese education, with the first layer consisting of a window through which young scholars learned from alternative perspectives especially during the early 1980s, and the other layer involving the beginning of the West–East dialogue on Chinese education. In this regard, Ruth has mentioned the effort in the early 1980s to invite the older generation of Chinese CIE scholars to the United States. In her narrative, she recalled instances such as when an insurance company was unable to insure traveling Chinese scholars and when the Chinese government had tight restrictions on students from national key universities participating in international exchange programs. Scholars like Ruth learned to navigate the systems of both countries and successfully facilitate the travel of scholars and students from China to Canada and the United States for collaboration and communication. In fact, Gerry recalls being called one of the "Kissingers of education" at the Academy of Education Development in Shanghai in the early 1980s.

In approaching the sense of "our" time, this shared dimension also entails complexity in the positionings and identities of each of the scholars, as educators/teachers, and as anthropologists or sociologists. Each of these roles has been prominent at different points of time in their personal histories. Lynn described this process in the first phase of her research, noting that "people would regularly not understand why I would be interested in something and it would take a long time to persuade people that I had a genuine interest and that it wasn't an exploitive interest." However, the second phase of her research, during which she cooperated with Chinese scholars and doctoral students, was a phase that

> has mirrored broader changes where there had been much *greater shared* discussion, some *shared* language, although I would say that language is chiefly a North American or Western language of research. That struck me as problematic, but it gave us a point of common agreement and especially working where I couldn't take a year to establish trust and relationship.

This sense of shared "our" time also reflects the negotiations and interactions of CIE as a global field of study and the emergence of CIE as a field in China. From the 1970s to the 1990s, CIE in Western academia was marked by a series of theoretical/conceptual debates, ranging from neo-Marxist, dependency, and world systems theories to postcolonialism, among many others. In a number of ways, the scholars in our interviews described these trends. For example, Gerry recalled how as a sociologist of education, who came to the field of Chinese education interested in questions of equity, access, social/cultural capital, the questions of equality and diversity for the ethnic minorities in China led him to Colonial Hong Kong and then to Guangdong and Guangxi in mainland China.

Parallel time lines between scholar and field shed light on how approaches and methods of "researching China" have differed across different stages of scholars' engagement with Chinese education, from near isolation, exacerbating "otherness," to the present, when it can be difficult to distinguish between West and East, "ours" and "theirs," both in terms of people and the field. Anthropologists read relational space in this context as involving a dimension of time (Fabian 2002; Appadurai 2005), just as our circle of esteem has been created through the process of *becoming we* over the past two to three decades. We see this process as another significant dimension of the *dialogue in time*, one that features the confluence of developing themes and concerns of Chinese education, topics of CIE, and scholars' choices and preferences regarding the issues and topics they choose to study.

Rethinking "Our Time": The Rise of Asia?

The six scholars' intense engagements with Chinese education at the personal, intellectual, and even sentimental levels represent an unfolding dialogue with Chinese education, beginning in a less-globalized time and continuing to the current globalizing era. The scholars not only witnessed the rapid post-Mao transformation of Chinese education, but also developed emotional stakes in historical or revolutionary moments. For instance, at the time of the Tian'anmen incident, Ruth served as the head of Cultural and Academic Affairs at The Canadian Embassy in Beijing. During the uncertain, emotional days that followed June 4, 1989, Heidi lived on the campus of a Shanghai high school, collecting historical narratives and researching individuals' lives.

In the current period of "the rise of Asia," the six scholars have developed diverse understandings of what that rise means and where such discourse comes from and for what purposes. Gerry noted that from a historical perspective it is a "powerful phrase"; when he began his research in China in the early 1980s, research agendas were shaped by "economic backwardness" or on a "developing country." Like those discourses, China's rise can "cloud what the real topics are that you're studying." In response to a question about how such discourse influenced his own research, Gerry said,

> If I wrote an article on the rise of China and education, the main concern would be how has education in China adjusted to China's economic rise or…, how have the aspirations changed?…I would say that one of the areas I am looking at is why some research universities develop very rapidly and others don't. How does that occur? And so, when I am looking at a place like China, I am looking at the role of the economy, the role of state subsidies…and the role of state subsidies in building world-class universities. So it does have some impact.

We conducted our interviews just as the Shanghai Programme for International Student Assessment (PISA) results were being released, which sparked another round of discussion about Chinese education in the United States. Lynn, echoing Gerry, expressed worries about discourses on the "rise of Asia" and the "rise of China," which, in her words, mean that

> if you're talking about the link between education and the economy or if you're trying to talk about education, it's far more complex than the PISA results allow us to see, but the danger is that's…as long as the attention span in the West allows.

Such "danger" has always been double-sided. On the one hand, it gives the illusion that "you always have to chase China because it's faster," which further leads to the danger of "exoticizing" and "segregating" research on education in China as a practice that is totally different from practices in the West. On the other hand, the "popularity" of Asia and/or China as an area of study makes "people feel like they should be researching...China now," which raises questions about the motivations of research and its concomitant problems. The greater concern is how such discourse may serve China's interests in problematic ways, such as when Lynn concluded that "central leaders wanted to marshal energies in a certain direction, wanting to shut off discussion in certain ways."

Suzanne Pepper, the only political scientist among our interviewees, sees "rise" discourse as

> a function of Chinese and Western media hype, which cuts two ways because the motives of the two are different. For the Chinese, it's nationalistic and legitimizing self-promotion; for the Western media it's partly commercialized sensationalism and partly milking the old fear of China.

Reflecting on the risks of "ultra-nationalism," Heidi noted how the reality and the rhetoric of the "rise of China" influenced her view that China is no longer just China, but instead part of a global society and also part of a neighborhood. This change in perception influences even the way she thinks about Chinese educational policy, such as questions about "whom they have been talking to." As a key actor in setting up cross-hemisphere collaborations, Heidi believes that the time for the "rise of Asia/China," with its concomitant problems, is "an important moment to remind the world that a rise can be a rise in power *with*, not just power *against*."

Ruth responded to discourse of the "rise" by reflecting on what she called China's "missionizing culture": "It's very exciting to me to see China consciously take up a cultural diplomacy." Referring to examples like Confucius Institutes, Ruth sees China as considering its impact well beyond the economic and expanding it to something else, something that is more humanistic.

> There is a feeling [in China] that China has a civilization, values, that are not limited to China. The Beijing Forum[7] [is an example]—it is a very important modality for taking up this responsibility of thinking ahead for the global community.

In short, in different ways, the six scholars saw their Chinese counterparts as reclaiming their own interests in the context of global dialogue or debate. They are doing so within, as Lynn put it, "a far more complex web of global relationships," where global is not just a proxy for the West.

Ruth remarked with admiration, "I know of no other country that has allowed its cultural diplomacy to be franchised out to a foreign nation."

Her point is well taken. Indeed, there is something unique about the way China is going global. As Ruth noted, we are witnessing "a very highly centralized country that cares so much about its image sharing its cultural diplomacy."[8] In this sense, it *might* be said that China is humanizing globalization through a process of creating new knowledge about China as part of the world. Jing Lin prefers to see this process in very concrete terms. It is real only when it involves people-to-people interaction—something tangible, human beings connecting through empathy, learning to see someone as a real person—what Yimin Wang has called the critical project of unnaming and renaming.

In summary, our use of the interview question "describe your scholarship related to Chinese education over two to three periods of time" was intended to gain insight into the "temporalization" or "periodization" of the development of the fields of Chinese education and CIE as they were being shaped and shaping scholars' individual (yet collective) scholarly preferences. This question also led us to reflections on the means and ends of temporalization for both the fields and for the intellectual journeys of the scholars. The sense of "our time," then, encompasses dialogue between and among the histories as individual histories and the histories of China's development, the negotiations between debates and trends of CIE as a field and the intellectual trends in China studies, and "social time" of engagement and collaborations.

Layer Two: Dialogue in Relational Space

The second layer concerns dialogue in relational space;[9] here, we reflect on scholars' intellectual commitment to and personal involvement with Chinese education, as well as to the field of CIE. In the previous section, we suggested how the six scholars traveled through and responded to "post-revolutionary China." During this time, Ruth wrote "The Changing Role of Teachers in China: Post-Mao Perspectives,"[10] Heidi wrote about modernity in *China Learns English*,[11] Lynn wrote "Women in the New China: Re-emerging Patriarchal Patterns" and "The Model and Its Consequence for Teacher Thinking and Preparation in China,"[12] Jing wrote *Education in Post-Mao* and the *Red Guards' Path to Violence*,[13] Suzanne wrote about Chinese universities and their post-Mao enrollment policies,[14] and finally, Gerry reflected on the "Implications of Modernization of Education for National Minorities."[15] Working contemporaneously, but at different stages of their academic careers and with diverse scholarly foci that flowed from different personal interests, generational experiences, and disciplinary and methodological training, all engaged in extensive and ongoing thinking and writing that influenced the knowledge production within Chinese/Asian education. Over the years, each has initiated significant collaborative projects with Chinese educators and Chinese universities and schools; each has also been invited to serve as a consulting, visiting, or advisory professor at Chinese universities, which in turn has shaped those institutions.

What highlights these scholars' contributions to Chinese education is their long-term personal involvement with and commitment to the individuals and the "field" about which they care so deeply. In Heidi's Comparative International Education Society (CIES) presidential address, she conceptualized "the 'field' of field work as more than geographical location. The field is also a field of obligation in which the researcher's identity and understanding develops as a process of negotiation" (Ross 2002). China and Chinese education as such a field eventually became each scholar's career-long commitment. After completing her volume of ten portraits of influential Chinese educators, Ruth wrote "Ten Lives in Mine: Creating Portraits of Influential Chinese Educators," in which she shared her own positioning and relationship with the Chinese educators she wrote about, along with "reflections on the dialogue of civilizations and the potential future influence of Chinese civilization in the global community" (Hayhoe 2005, 324).

Ludden (2000) once suggested that "[g]lobalization is site specific, and each part of the world constitutes the center of its own global experience." Considering how each scholar has described his or her experiences of "going in" and "returning to" the fields of China and Chinese education, we realized that each uses directional terms in varying ways. However, all evoke a sense of bilocality (or multilocality). Harvey (2006) has suggested that expanding the concept of "space" from "absolute space" to the concepts of "relative space" and "relational space" requires understanding the social meanings of a locational place in relationship to a further dimension of time.

Moments of *Entering* China

Recalling the time when "we" entered the field of China, what were once experiences of hard-won access to the field have now turned into valuable memories. Long before "China's rise" became the topic of bestsellers, the first glimmer of China's transformation propelled Ruth into her doctoral work. She recalled, "What really carried me forward was that I wanted to participate in China's opening up...It was so important for China and contributing to education would be the most valuable way of participating." She decided to travel to England to complete her Master's degree in order to be qualified to teach in a university setting because she knew China would not be hiring secondary-school teachers. Ruth remembered, "I want[ed] to contribute [to China's opening up] by teaching, but [I also wanted to] do research on the opening."

As in all aspects of life, scholarship is sometimes driven by contingency. Lynn had hoped to study workers' education; their education seemed to her to represent a nexus of arguments about politics, economics, and the good society. In the end, she had to turn to teachers as a safer topic. In a creative move, she realized teachers were intellectual workers; this necessary if prescient shift fundamentally set the trajectory of her very productive and influential career. Describing her "entering moments," Lynn recalled her experience

> as a foreigner, sort of going to China, trying to work out of ethnographic traditions, and trying to recognize my outsideness, not trying to pretend I wasn't an outsider, but thinking there was a phenomenon or a practice that I was trying to understand because it was interesting to me. I wasn't responding to some question that other people were raising, necessarily, and it certainly wasn't a question that people within China, [i.e.,] my counterparts, were raising.

The relational sense of entering and engaging with a conscious recognition of outside-ness was a powerful theme in all of our interviews.

Heidi recalled how she experienced people's rethinking of the Cultural Revolution and Mao's legacy in 1981 and 1982, as well as the Tian'anmen event in 1989 in schools. She recalled that

> for these kinds of very emotional moments for myself and for the people around me, I have always been in schools—I just have been with teachers, I've been with students and I have been literally in a school building. It's not surprising for me that when I think back to 1989, I think about Tian'anmen, but I also think about schools, because that's where I experienced it.

Experiencing historical events and the critical moments in Chinese history with real people, teachers and students significantly impacted scholars' perspectives and approaches to research. Schools, as social spaces, are not merely sites for research because they reflect politics, nor are they only sites that document history, but rather schools have become centers for scholars with genuine interests in the "black box of school," about which Heidi commented, "(back in 1981 and 1982) what I felt that I wanted to understand was more about what really went on inside, what was going on inside of a classroom."

In a similar vein, Lynn explained how she chose her site for her Zouping work,[16] which "was focused more on K-12 schooling or basic schooling, typically on *Chuzhong* (junior secondary school) and the meaning of education in a community undergoing rapid social and economic change."

Senses of "*Returning*" as Ways of Engagement

The relational sense of space also included themes of "returning" in different senses. For Jing, it involved the genuine desire to return to China for teacher training and to investigate issues of social capital and girls' schooling, as well as to set up action research for emerging private universities. She perceives her role as a "bridge" between the West and the East of education.

Gerry relates that his work on ethnicity and heritage is in part a result of growing up in New York City. Working and teaching in Hong Kong, the place that in many different senses connects the West and the East, Gerry's returning moments involve the time after his first stage of sociological and anthropological work with rural and urban schools, during which he returned to the Asian Development Bank to work on capacity building, ethnic minority policies, and educational development. He found Chinese education and people paradoxically both in the center and at the margins of development agenda. The sense of *returning* brought Heidi 11 years of engagement with girls' education in rural Shaanxi—returning to China as a field of commitment. In fact, two weeks before the first draft of this chapter was written, Heidi again returned to the field to begin a green school project that is part of an earthquake relief effort supported by a nongovernmental organization (NGO) with which she has worked for over a decade. The project involves young women, who have been scholarship recipients from the same NGO, who will be working with rural youngsters just like themselves when they began receiving their scholarships in primary school. Their "full circle" experiences underscore the sense of returning to a field of commitment, and break down the binary between outsider and insider, researcher and the researched. In contrast, for Suzanne, "returning" to the field has entailed "staying put" in Hong Kong, and continuing to research and comment on the most recent changes in China.

In varying but converging ways, our fields are not just geographical and intellectual locations, but are also socially constructed fields of lifelong obligation: obligation to students, colleagues, knowledge construction, and to professional development. These fields are the kinds of spaces that Heidi wrote about in her 2002 CIES presidential address: spaces for thinking critically about the relationships between the freedom to speak, the power to be heard and affirmed, the possibility for love, the power to silence, and the possibilities that we will be misunderstood even in the context of a space as wonderful and rare as a public home place. (Ross 2002, 431–432)

Rethinking the Spaces for Dialogue between Civilizations

China as a field is not just a site for research and scholarly engagement, but also a space with lived histories, a space for the dialogue of civilizations. Ruth summarized her first stage of engagement with China as "trying to understand the changes (in China) in terms of China," and the second stage of her research, after the collapse of the Soviet Union, as understanding the shift from a conflict over (cold war) ideology to a conflict of civilization. "But," explained Ruth, "I didn't see conflict but rather dialogue." From that standpoint, Ruth turned "to interpret for the global community some of the richness of Chinese educational experiences in Chinese civilization." As "the space then opened up in the Western world for an appreciation of Chinese civilization," a concept she explored in her book and conference Knowledge across Cultures, Ruth began her project, *China's Universities 1895–1995: A Century of Cultural Conflict* (Hayhoe 1999), in which she recounts Chinese higher education's "nationalist story (1911–1949)," "socialist story (1949–1978)," and "stories of the reform decade."

Ruth's sensibility of the importance of dialogical understanding and "privilege" of working with older Chinese scholars further led her to create her deep portraits of Chinese educators (Hayhoe 2007), one signature of her scholarship and desire to communicate the richness of Chinese heritage through their lives. Ruth sees in her work the critical importance of history in educational studies and comparative education. She explained that, "[t]he stories of institutions and of educators…are microcosms for understanding in a small setting a set of conflicts and concerns and values that were part of the wider struggle of society." Finally, Ruth describes her use of narrative as an important corrective to the objectivist tendency in much Western scholarship: This is a characteristic that exists in contrast to Chinese epistemology. "It's interpretative as [being] against the sort of imposition of theories and patterns that are so-called universal." Ruth went on to suggest that the significance of "being critical" in scholarship is exaggerated. "Being critical is not the thing that matters most to me. I think getting inside and trying to interpret and understand from *within* is [something] I have been very concerned about."

China's civilization, as a prominent topic in Ruth's writings and scholarship, also provided Jing with unique approaches. She brings a gift to peace education, which is a stream of research that has been influenced by her deep study of not just world approaches to ecology or human connection, but also her knowledge of Chinese traditions and cultures. By involving Chinese classical philosophers like Laozi and Confucius in the bigger conversations of peace and love education worldwide, and in her profound discussions of Ren (仁, loving kindness), Yi (义, selfless giving), Li (理, civility or actions of virtues), Zhi (智, acquisitions of wisdom), and Xin (信, the building of sincerity, trust and faith) as Confucian/Chinese moral ideas (Lin and Wang 2010, 4), we see another vivid example of West and East dialogue in the arena of peace and love education, and beyond.

Layer Three: Dialogue as "Humanizing Globalization"

Our third layer of dialogue is an ongoing process, transforming over the past two decades between, for example, Heidi and her students, both from the United States and from China, and our dialectical reflections on this dialogue. Ruth once wrote about the transformative power of graduate school, and Heidi's students have often quoted a famous Chinese saying about the teacher–student relationship: "a day's teacher, a life-time's father." The transformation involved in cross-cultural/national learning and in the mutual and ongoing constructions of our fields is certainly one instance of "humanizing globalization."

The other dimension of "humanizing globalization" is the genuine desire and intention of our scholars to know people (mainly teachers and students) as individuals and actors. These are reflected in specific projects by our scholars on teaching and learning, including the new publication, *Portrait of Chinese Universities*, by Hayhoe et al. (2011). In fact, the "humanizing dimension" of understanding that is reflected in this book can be traced back to Ruth's work in the early 1980s:

> [I was] trying to understand the change in terms of China: its needs, its people, its overall education system and its development, by [using and] analyzing history as a touchstone, a way to see what are the cultural underpinnings of the collaboration that had been more or less fruitful and effective, as against those that have been conflict-driven.

Ruth's comments on the differences and similarities between "human" and "humane" in English, and more importantly, the closeness in Chinese between "人" (Ren; "human") and "仁" (Ren, "humane") reminds us of Gerry's assertion that "education is about human understanding, more than education is about learning about oneself; ... one learns more about oneself by learning about others ... that keeps me rooted in the purpose of my profession, which is about human understanding." These are just a few of the examples of these expressions that shed light on our understandings of "humanizing globalization."

On the journey of humanizing globalization, it is important that we do not lose sight of complex processes of negotiations, communication, and constructive debate. China seems to offer us, in this context, the concept of "*He Er Bu Tong*" (harmonious coexistence within diversity; harmony but not conformity). Jing has reminded us of how many counties, small villages, and marginalized institutions remain left out or distanced from person-to-person global connection. Suzanne expressed concern about "the politically-motivated culture of conformity that continues to block meaningful scholarship and reform."

Friction and frustration punctuate different stages of the scholars' engagement within their fields. These not only include individual level "betrayals, " but also disagreements about what doing valid and "useful" research means, as well as the ways and methods to achieve it. Friction speaks not only of the complexities of the field and of the interactions among human actors, but also how Chinese education represents in the life of scholars and their scholarship a contested space. In this regard, Heidi pointed out that "cultivating our moral imagination requires a negotiation between hope and pain, hurt and disappointment, and care and resistance" (Ross 2002, 429). Ruth has also noted that:

[As for] challenging scholarship that it's not enough to simply objectively analyze what's going on out there, but it's important to put forward a vision of a preferred future, which is normative and which has to be based on a common humanity even though one can bring religious values in. So, common concern for the human condition, for the environment, [and] for society, and I really found that very inspiring to me ... I think China's traditions really put it in a position of when we've talked about the difference between scholarship within China and abroad. It's very difficult for anything written in China not to have an explicit moral intent, whereas we've gotten used to this sort of high value distinction and objective scholarship that doesn't even pretend to try to put forward a preferred future or a preferred direction.

Held et al. (1999) distinguished among three different stances on globalization: "Hyperglobalists," "Skeptics," and "Transformationalists."[17] Each represents a very different conception of the "dynamics and directions of global change." The salient dynamics and directions among our scholars' reflections are captured by our notion of humanization, through dialogical scholarship and practice within an expanding circle of esteem that considers cross-cultural dialogue as both a means and an end. According to Held, transformationalists' belief in globalization supersedes "hyperglobalists" and "skeptics" in their belief that globalization transforms state power and politics (10). However, our reading of the six scholars' intellectual beliefs, career paths, and life stories add a "humanized" dimension to the transformationalists' stance in interpreting the multifaceted processes of globalization, although in subtle ways, where one would hopefully define or find "a 'new frontier' " in Held's term (7).

Conclusion: Passing It on, Recreating the Circle

We conclude this chapter by sharing the advice and suggestions that our six scholars offer to new scholars in the field. Five suggested that new scholars follow their hearts, passions, and interests in selecting their research topics and in their pursuit of knowledge and development of a professional career, about which Ruth said,

> Everyone has their unique pathway and so learning how to listen to the heart and make the decision and stay with it. And I think whatever road one takes, there's going to be obstacles and difficulties along the way, but if you really know that's your calling, you'll find the strength to overcome them.

Jing, too, encourages students to talk not just from their heads but also their hearts—an example of *xin xue* (a state of mind), which is a strand of Chinese philosophy preliminarily advocated by Wang Yangming (1472–1529). Heidi and Gerry underscored the cultivation of humility and patience, about which Heidi said,

> I do stand by my field, my own personal field ethics and that's the most important thing to have is patience and humility. There's so much we don't know and patience is just required because it takes a long time to know those things and to communicate those things or to ask questions.

And Lynn approached mentoring as fundamentally dialogical –

> to help students see that they should think about their topics as leading to what they see as the most important conversations—who they want to be talking to and to what end—and what conversations they want to contribute to. To think about educational research as a conversation rather than a topic is very important.

Interestingly, and refreshingly, Suzanne brought to our more idealistic responses a critical perspective, replying,

> I don't want to give advice to the younger generation. Because I have not forgotten what it is like to be them. We rebelled against the advice of our elders. As for shared life experiences, I feel more comfortable sharing the contradictions that ultimately shape experience.

NOTES

1. Our use of the word "story" in this chapter is inspired by Ruth Hayhoe's (1999) description of her book as "a story, not a history."
2. Here we allude to Ruth Hayhoe's (1989) address "A Chinese Puzzle," in which she discusses her search through comparative education literature for concepts and tools of analysis that would illuminate issues of Chinese education.
3. The end of Cultural Revolution (1967–1977) marks the time that foreign researchers began to have access to enter mainland China for teaching and research, which is why we chose this point as the starting time of the review of this article.
4. The concept of "fusion of horizons" was used by Habermas in explaining that when we encounter cultures that differ from our own, we sometimes learn that what is objective and external to us is not so to them, and vice versa. If we then "fuse horizons" or combine lifeworlds with the other culture, we can generate new external positions that are common to both.
5. All quotes from interviewees, unless otherwise stated, are from interviews that were conducted from February 9 to March 8, 2011.
6. The word "we" thereafter refers to the authors of this chapter.
7. The Beijing Forum is "an international academic forum on humanity and social sciences co-hosted by Peking University (PKU), Beijing Municipal Commission of Education and Korea Foundation for Advanced Studies." It was "initiated in 2004 and approved by the State Council and the Ministry of Education of the People's Republic of China." The most recent event, Beijing Forum 2011, "convened from November 4 to 6, 2011, [and was] based on the theme of 'The Harmony of Civilizations and Prosperity for All: Tradition and Modernity, Transition and Transformation'." For more information, please refer to the website: http://english.pku.edu.cn/News_events/News /Outlook/8887.htm.
8. In explaining the notion of China's Cultural Diplomacy, Ruth used the example of China's effort in establishing Confucius Institutes in the world, about which Ruth further elaborated that "in this sense, I feel that China is a missionizing culture. It's a culture that has had a profound influence on the world at different periods of history. For historical reasons for the last 200 years, it kind of withdrew and now it's re-emerging. So in a way that's not surprising,

but it's been very exciting for me to see China consciously take up a cultural diplomacy. With the development of the Confucius Institute, which says to me that China is trying to respond to the challenge, [by asking and answering questions such as] 'now that you have such economic influence with the rise of your manufacturing, and the GDP becoming second in the world and so on, what kind of influence are you going to have culturally? What kind of message you are going to bring culturally?' That's been something that is very interesting to me."

9. Ross's (2002) CIES presidential address was titled "The Space between Us: The Relevance of Relational Theory to Re-imagining Comparative Education," and this conceptualization has shaped this layer of our framework.

10. See Ruth Hayhoe and Richard Jackson (1979).

11. Heidi Ross (1993).

12. Lynn Paine (1988 and 1989).

13. Jing Lin (1991 and 1992).

14. Susanne Pepper (1984).

15. Gerard Postiglione (1992).

16. *Zouping* is the name of a county in Shandong province. Lynn's "Zouping Work" refers to the project titled *Schools, Stratification and Socialization in Zouping*, funded by the Committee for Scholarly Communication with the People's Republic of China (jointly sponsored by the National Academy of Sciences, Social Science Research Council, and American Council of Learned Societies). Representative publications include Paine (1998).

17. "Hyperglobalists," "Skeptics," and "Transformationalists" represent three tendencies in understanding the role of nation state in the globalization process. In Held's definition, hyperglobalists conceptualize globalization as "a reordering of the framework of human action," which brings a "global age" that erodes the old hierarchies. "Skeptics" conceptualize the processes of globalization as both internationalization and regionalization that "depends on state acquaintance and support," and "transformationalists" thesis represents "historically unprecedented level of inter-connectedness" that was driven by "combined forces of modernity" that may "transform state power and world politics" (Held et al. 1999, 10).

References

Appadurai, Arjun. 2005. *Modernity at Large: Cultural Dimensions of Globalization.* Minneapolis, MN: University of Minnesota Press.

Cribb, Robert. 2005. "Circles of Esteem, Standard Works, and Euphoric Couplets." *Critical Asian Studies* 37 (2): 289–304.

Cummings, William K. 1999. "The Institutions of Education: Compare, Compare, Compare!" *Comparative Education Review* 43 (4): 413–437.

Fabian, Johannes. 2002. *Time and the Other: How Anthropology Makes Its Object.* New York: Columbia University Press.

Habermas, Jurgen. 1985. *Lifeworld and System: A Critique of Functionalist Reason (The Theory of Communicative Action, Vol. 2).* (Trans. Thomas McCarthy). Ypsilanti, MI: Beacon Press.

Harvey, David. 2006. *Spaces of Global Capitalism: Towards a Theory of Uneven Geographical Development.* London and New York: Verso.

Hayhoe, Ruth. 1989. "A Chinese Puzzle." *Comparative Education Review* 33 (2): 155–175.

Hayhoe, Ruth. 1999. *China's Universities 1895–1995: A Century of Cultural Conflict.* Hong Kong: Hong Kong University Press.

Hayhoe, Ruth. 2004. *Full Circle: A Life with Hong Kong and China.* Hong Kong: Comparative Education Research Centre, The University of Hong Kong.

Hayhoe, Ruth. 2007. *Portraits of Influential Chinese Scholars.* Hong Kong: Comparative Education Research Centre (CERC) and Springer.

Hayhoe, Ruth, and Ray Jackson. 1979. "The Changing Role of Teachers in China: Post-Mao Perspectives." *British Journal of Teacher Education* 5 (3): 219–229.

Hayhoe, Ruth, Jing Lin, Jun Li, and Qiang Zha. 2011. *Portraits of 21st Century Chinese Universities: In the Move to Mass Higher Education.* Hong Kong and Dordrecht, The Netherlands: Comparative Education Research Centre (CERC) and Springer.

Held, David et al. 1999. *Global Transformations: Politics, Economics and Culture.* Palo Alto, CA: Stanford University Press.

Lin, Jing. 1991. *The Red Guards' Path to Violence: Political, Educational, and Psychological Factors.* New York: Praeger Publishers.

Lin, Jing. 1992. *Education in Post-Mao China.* New York: Praeger Publishers.

Lin, Jing, and Yingjie Wang. 2010. "Confucius' Teaching of Virtues: Implications for World Peace and Peace Education." In *Spirituality, Religion, and Peace Education,* ed. Edward J. Brantmeier, Jing Lin, and John P. Miller. Charlotte, NC: Information Age Publishing.

Ludden, David. 2000. "Area Studies in the Age of Globalization." *Frontiers: The Interdisciplinary Journal of Study Abroad* 6 (1): 1–22.

Paine, Lynn. 1988. "Women in the New China: Re-emerging Patriarchal Patterns." *Re-Visions* (Spring): 1–4.

Paine, Lynn. 1989. "Teaching as Virtuoso Performance: The Model and Its Consequence for Teacher Thinking and Preparation in China." *Teacher Thinking and Professional Action,* ed. Joost Lowyck and Christopher Clark. Leuven, Belgium: University of Leuven Press.

Paine, Lynn. 1998. "Making Schools Modern: Paradoxes of Educational Reform." In *Zouping in Transition: The Process of Reform in Rural North China,* ed. A. G. Walder (pp. 205–235). Cambridge, MA: Harvard University Press.

Pepper, Susanne. 1984. *China's Universities: Post-Mao Enrollment Policies and Their Impact on the Structure of Secondary Education.* Ann Arbor, MI: University of Michigan Center for Chinese Studies.

Postiglione, Gerard. 1992. "The Implications of Modernization for the Education of China's National Minorities." In *Education and Modernization: The Chinese Experience,* ed. Ruth Hayhoe. Oxford: Pergamon Press.

Ross, Heidi. 1993. *China Learns English: Language Teaching and Social Change in the People's Republic.* New Haven: Yale University Press.

Ross, Heidi. 2002. "The Space Between Us: The Relevance of Relational Theory to Re-imagining Comparative Education." *Comparative Education Review* 46 (4): 407–432.

Tsing, Anna L. 2005. *Friction: An Ethnography of Global Connections.* Princeton, New Jersey: Princeton University Press.

van Schendel, Willem. 2002. "Geographies of Knowing, Geographies of Ignorance: Jumping Scale in Southeast Asia." *Environment and Planning D: Society and Space* 20 (6): 647–668.

Wenger, Etienne. 1998. "Communities of Practice: Learning as a Social System." *Systems Thinker* 9 (5). Waltham, MA: Pegasus Communications Inc. Available online at: www.co-i-l.com/coil/knowledge-garden/cop/lss.shtml.

Part II

Chinese Higher Education and the World

Chapter 6

Transnational Higher Education in China: Toward a Critical Culturalist Research Agenda

Qiang Zha

Introduction

With the advent of a globalization era, transnational higher education (TNHE) has become increasingly evident and constitutes a notable phenomenon in most parts of the world. TNHE is certainly a significant aspect of the internationalization of higher education and might be seen as riding the tide of internationalization. For the sake of convenience in the discussion, this chapter adopts the concepts developed by United Nations Educational, Scientific and Cultural Organization (UNESCO) and Global Alliance for Transnational Education (GATE) to narrow this term down to the particular part of postsecondary education "in which the learners are located in a country different from the one where the awarding institution is based" (UNESCO/Council of Europe 2000). Specifically, the following forms of TNHE are of greatest relevance to the Chinese context:

- Twinning: agreements between institutions in different countries to offer joint programs;

- Franchises: an institution approves provision of one or more of its programs by a foreign institution in the latter's country;
- Branch campus: a campus set up by an institution in another country to provide its educational or training programs to foreign students;
- Articulation: the systematic recognition by an institution of specified study at a foreign institution as partial credit toward completion of one or more of its programs;
- Study abroad: students from an institution travel to take courses at a foreign institution and to live in a different country for a fixed period of time. (GATE 1999)

With China being now the largest source country for internationally mobile students,[1] TNHE has also reached phenomenal proportions on Chinese soil. By April 2011, there were 579 TNHE programs or institutions licensed (by the Ministry of Education [MOE]) in China that lead to bachelor's and above degrees, operated jointly between Chinese universities and their foreign partners (MOE 2011a, 2011b). There could be even more at sub-degree level, as these are subject to approval by local education authorities and become hard to track down. Inevitably, these initiatives come with many concomitant issues and challenges, which, in turn, have stirred an increasing research interest. The research so far, however, focuses on aspects of policy or policy changes by the Chinese government and operational issues at the institutional level. There are few attempts to explore the reasons why these TNHE activities are happening on Chinese soil, whether they bring in what is needed by Chinese society and higher education, and how they may contribute to progress for the Chinese system. Put another way, the current research seems to have affirmed the value of the dominant TNHE patterns and practices, suggesting that the focus should be placed on how to improve them. This chapter challenges this judgment by proposing a critical culturalist research agenda on TNHE in China, and drawing on perspectives from neoliberalism, postcolonialism, and the culturalist approach as potential theoretical tools to underpin such a research agenda.

The Context, Characteristics, and Trends of TNHE in China

With the Shanghai–New York University having its groundbreaking ceremony in March 2011, public attention was attracted once again to the flourishing situation of TNHE in China. TNHE is actually a recent phenomenon in China. Many trace it back to the launching of the Johns Hopkins University–Nanjing University Center for Chinese and American Studies in 1986 (as the earliest non-degree TNHE program) or the Tianjin University of Finance and Economics–Oklahoma City University MBA Program in 1988 (as the first degree-conferring TNHE program). However, it is only the first decade of the twenty-first century that has witnessed TNHE programs and institutions mushroom in the country, especially since December 2001 when China became a member of the World Trade Organization (WTO). Statistics show that there were only 27 degree-conferring TNHE programs in China by June 1996 (Liu 2008). This number slowly increased to 71 by November 2001, and steadily to 164 by June 2004 and 200 by September 2007, then quickly to 579 by April 2011 (Zhang 2006; Lin and Liu 2007; Liu 2008; MOE 2011a, 2011b). If provision of sub-degree and non-degree training TNHE programs is also taken into account, it is estimated that there were 1,400 such programs and institutions by 2007 (Lin and Liu 2007). In this sense, some even argue that, given time, TNHE programs and institutions will form a third pillar in the Chinese higher education system, alongside public and private institutions (Feng and Gong 2006).

Arguably, China's embrace of TNHE is driven by its needs for capacity building (Organisation for Economic Co-operation and Development [OECD] 2004; Huang 2007), and its intention of drawing on international experience to break through some of the internal constraints of its own system. An OECD (2004) research article maintains that the "capacity building approach encourages the use of foreign post-secondary education...as a quick way to build an emerging country's capacity" (13), and "it takes on greater importance in countries whose higher education system does not meet domestic demand in terms of quantity or quality" (229). This approach thus has dimensions of quantity and quality. On the quantity side, a country that adopts this approach would wish to widen higher education accessibility and enlarge the national human resource capacity through introducing TNHE programs and institutions that can meet the country's economic and nation-building agendas; on the quality side, it would aim to improve its higher education standards through twinning and partnership arrangements with foreign universities that will facilitate knowledge transfer and raise the country's global competitiveness.

In the mid-1990s, China put forward a plan to build a well-off society by 2010, which was clearly spelled out in the *Ninth Five-Year Plan for National Economic and Social Development and the Proposal for Long-Range Objectives by 2010*. This plan set requirements both for the quantity and quality of China's human resources. Almost in parallel with its planning for a mass higher education system, the Chinese government promulgated the *Interim Provisions for Sino-Foreign Cooperation in the Running of Schools* in 1995. This essentially opened the door, in the legal sense, to TNHE arrangements on Chinese soil, requiring compulsory partnership with local institutions in China. The *Interim Provisions* evolved into the *Regulations of the People's Republic of China on Sino-Foreign Cooperation in the Running of Schools* in 2003, when China had already managed to achieve mass higher education. The new policy document stressed the aims of "attracting high-quality educational resources from overseas" and "introducing globally advanced curriculum and teaching materials, which are in urgent need in China" (*New China Newsagency* March 24, 2003, cited in OECD 2004, 229). More recently in 2007, China's MOE issued the *Notice of Strengthening the Regulatory Order of Sino-Foreign Cooperation in the Running of Schools*, which called for attention and efforts to address certain problems of TNHE in China. These include the high concentration of programs such as business, management, and information technology (IT), which operate at minimum costs and tend to have low standards, poor quality assurance resulting from the fact that there are few chances of introducing core curriculum and teaching staff from overseas, and the excessive pursuit of profit in these programs. These documents manifest the changing focus of China's policy concerning TNHE, and also hint at certain problems arising from the over-hasty growth of TNHE programs and institutions in the country.

In retrospect, TNHE programs and institutions in China feature a number of characteristics. First, the absolute majority of the Chinese institutions that are involved in TNHE are public, which is in contrast to the situation in other TNHE active countries in the region, such as Malaysia and Singapore. It is also a bit surprising, in light of the fact that all the TNHE programs and institutions function as private establishments nested within a public system. A considerable proportion of those public institutions on the Chinese side are upper echelon or elite universities, including many that were selected into the elite Projects 211 and 985, while most foreign providers are low-echelon local institutions in their own systems. The exceptions to this situation include University of Manchester and University of London from the United Kingdom, University of Michigan and University of Maryland from the United States, University of Sydney and University of Canberra from Australia, and University of British Columbia and University of Alberta from Canada. Second, a majority of the TNHE programs and institutions result from twinning or franchising arrangements and partnerships with universities and colleges in the English-speaking world, including the United Kingdom, the United States, Australia, and Canada. This homogeneity is evident in Table 6.1. Third, as mentioned earlier, there is a

Table 6.1 Top six source countries of TNHE establishments[2] in China: 2011

Source country/region	Bachelor's level	Master's level and above	Total
UK	117 (1)	13 (4)	130 (1)
Russia[3]	78 (2)		78 (4)
Australia	58 (3)	33 (2)	91 (3)
USA	55 (4)	38 (1)	93 (2)
Canada	31 (5)	9 (6)	40 (5)
Germany	25 (6)		
Hong Kong		30 (3)	30 (6)
France		12 (5)	

Sources: MOE (2011a, 2011b).

Table 6.2 MOE-licensed TNHE establishments in China: 2004 and 2011

Programs	2004 Amount	2004 %	2011 Amount	2011 %
Business (including trade, marketing, management, accounting, finance, and economics)	104	63.4	286	45.0
IT and related (including computer science, software engineering, and telecommunications)	30	18.3	99	15.6
Literature (including English, TESOL, French, German, Russian, Japanese, and Korean)	7	4.3	26	4.1
Science and engineering	6	3.7	130	20.5
Education (including kinesiology)	6	3.7	16	2.5
Health and medicine (including nursing, pharmacology)	5	3.0	32	5.0
Law	4	2.4	13	2.0
Other humanities and social sciences (including design, fine arts, music)	2	1.2	33	5.2
Total	164	100	635[4]	100

Sources: Feng and Gong (2006) and MOE (2011a, 2011b).

Table 6.3 Distribution of TNHE establishments across the three economic regions: 2011[5]

Economic development zones	Bachelor's	Master's	Doctorate	Total
East Coast Developed Region	192	116	5	313
Central Medium-Developed Region	227[6]	23	0	250
West Underdeveloped Region	5	10	1	16
Total	424	149	6	579

Sources: MOE (2011a, 2011b).

phenomenal concentration of TNHE programs in such fields as business and IT, as shown in Table 6.2, although recent years have witnessed an increase of science and engineering programs. Finally, the current TNHE programs and institutions are unevenly distributed across the country, favoring the economically prosperous coastal region, as illustrated in Table 6.3. This would inevitably enhance the currently unequal patterns of distribution of China's own universities, and therefore affect equity of access among the Chinese population.

The Challenges Facing TNHE in China: Toward a Critical Culturalist Research Agenda

Paradoxes Arising from the Proliferation of TNHE Establishments in China

Despite the contribution of TNHE institutions to increasing higher education capacity and serving as a window into Western university education on Chinese soil, as well as providing cross-cultural experience, their image seems to be turning sour. The Chinese media have recently begun to portray the TNHE status quo as being "disorderly or anarchical," while potential employers have become suspicious of the quality of the education that TNHE program graduates have received. In addition, the foreign twinning universities are now increasingly likely to reject the TNHE program students who wish to continue their education in the West (*China Youth Daily* August 3, 2010; *People's Daily* August 27, 2010). Besides, given the high concentration of TNHE programs in areas such as business and IT, the TNHE establishments and arrangements are essentially incapable of complementing the scope and breadth of program offerings in Chinese higher education. Furthermore, collaborative research that could facilitate knowledge and technology transfer has barely happened. Rather, TNHE has largely enhanced the inequality of access and regional disparity that already plagues Chinese higher education. Students from wealthy families in the economically prosperous areas dominate the TNHE enrollment, a situation which helps to enhance the social stratification and polarization that has been so troubling in recent Chinese social development.

A scrutiny of the situation of TNHE programs and institutions in China reveals more paradoxes and dilemmas. For instance, if the TNHE arrangements are meant to ease the tension between higher education supply and demand, why have they grown even faster after China completed the massification of higher education in 2003? Furthermore, given China's aim of having TNHE establishments import high-quality education resources and globally advanced curriculum and teaching materials to the Chinese system, how is it that most providers are low-echelon institutions in their own systems? Why are the courses and programs introduced largely taught by sessional teachers from the provider institutions, rather than by their regular faculty? Why is the number of Chinese students going abroad growing steadily over the years, despite the proliferation of TNHE programs and institutions in China? While the Chinese government has wished to see TNHE arrangements serve to mobilize foreign and nongovernmental investment in higher education provision in China, most of them survive on tuition fees from Chinese household sources. This has led to a resource drain on the Chinese side, in addition to the continuous brain drain. It seems that the current research on TNHE in China, which focuses predominantly on state policy and issues relating to institutional operation, may be incapable of addressing these paradoxes and dilemmas at a fundamental level.

The Emerging Conflicts of Interest behind the Scene

In this author's view, this unfortunately anarchical and paradoxical situation seems to have arisen from the mismatch between China's strategy of embracing TNHE and the real intention of most foreign providers, as well as the neoliberal response of most Chinese universities. To illustrate this point, we need to reflect on the basic approaches employed in TNHE.

An OECD (2004) research article depicts four major approaches to the internationalization of higher education:

- The mutual-understanding approach: "In this approach, countries seek openness to the world and strengthened ties between countries through the creation of international networks of political and business elites" (221). It stresses academic, political, cultural, and social rationales, rather than using transnational education "as part of a broad and articulated economic policy" (221).
- The skilled-migration approach: This approach views internationalization primarily as a means of attracting skilled students who "may become skilled immigrants in the receiving country," which is considered "as crucial for the economic growth in a knowledge economy" (223).
- The revenue-generating approach: This approach views transnational education services as an important part of export industry, and explicitly seeks export revenues in its strategic vision for transnational education arrangements, in addition to other long-term benefits (e.g., mutual understanding, skilled migration) in some cases.
- The capacity-building approach: "This is an importer perspective which views cross-border education as a means to meet unmet demand as well as to help build capacity for quality higher education" (229).

There are ample examples of employing these approaches in the real world. The mutual-understanding approach might be best exemplified in such mobility programs as European Community Action Scheme for the Mobility of University Students (ERASMUS) and SOCRATES (an educational initiative named after the Greek philosopher Socrates, encouraging mobility and promoting cooperation at European level) in Europe that pursue political, cultural, and long-term economic goals within the region. Canada tends to adopt the skilled-migration approach by explicitly connecting the goal of "facilitating the entry of students" with the "benefits of a temporary study period in Canada for prospective independent immigrant applicants" (Citizenship and Immigration Canada [CIC] 2003). Notably, the revenue-generating approach has "become important in the strategic vision of…Australia, New Zealand and the United Kingdom" (OECD 2004, 225). The capacity-building approach is "more prevalent in emerging economies" such as Malaysia, China, Singapore, and Indonesia (OECD 2004, 229 and 232). There are certainly connections and overlaps among these approaches, and therefore one can find examples of mixed use of them. For instance, the United States demonstrates a hybrid approach to

TNHE, featuring aspects of mutual understanding, skilled migration, and revenue-generating approaches.

While aspects of the mutual-understanding approach might be embedded and scattered in the other three approaches, the skilled migration and revenue-generating approaches lean toward export strategies, and the capacity-building approach aligns with import strategies, often encouraging foreign providers to come and operate twinning programs or branch campuses. The OECD (2004) research indicates "a possible conflict of interests between exporters and importers" (230). With different perceptions and approaches adopted on the two sides, "the relationships between countries exporting higher education services under the revenue-generation approach and countries importing higher education under the capacity building approach are becoming more complex" (OECD 2004, 231). This complexity may now be observed in the Chinese context, and might be seen as responsible, to a large extent, for the current disorderly TNHE situation. While the Chinese government encourages twinning arrangements and institutional partnerships between public universities in China and foreign providers, for the purpose of raising the quality of higher education, broadening the range of specializations and program offerings, and facilitating knowledge transfer, the foreign providers largely see it as the opportunity for a commercial presence in China and, more specifically, for revenue generation. This discrepancy in rationale and approach has caused the paradoxes and dilemmas depicted above.

The seemingly booming TNHE activities in China may now be confronting a looming crisis. Even worse, a vicious cycle seems to be taking shape. With the massification of Chinese higher education, and the deterioration in the reputation of TNHE programs in China, a growing number of students are now able to choose to go to regular programs in public universities, while many students who turn to TNHE programs are likely to be those who cannot meet the public university admission criteria and thus are less academically qualified. If this tendency continues, some TNHE programs and institutions might be shut down. As a matter of fact, Beijing either closed or temporarily suspended 63 such programs and institutions in the single year of 2009 (MOE 2009). Unfortunately, at a time when Chinese higher education has suffered from some deterioration in overall quality as a consequence of its move to a mass system, and has experienced a critical shortage of elements that would nurture creativity and innovation, the current TNHE arrangements and establishments on Chinese soil have failed to serve the hoped-for role. They have, in fact, made little contribution to meeting China's felt need for higher education capacity building.

Toward a Critical Culturalist Research Agenda

The notion of a discrepancy between the rationales and approaches of exporter and importer countries may help to explain the paradoxes and dilemmas outlined above, yet they do not really explain the enthusiasm of Chinese public universities for embracing TNHE arrangements. Many of these universities are aware that the foreign providers are not their match, and clearly see the overconcentration on such "marketable" programs as business and IT. Why then do they still engage in twinning or franchising arrangements to offer such programs? Perhaps, the concept of neoliberalism can shed some light on this. Neoliberalism is characterized by a market view of education, and most particularly, of higher education. "It treats education as just another service to be delivered on the market to those who can afford to buy it" (Lynch 2006, 3). Under the neoliberal regime, the internationalization of higher education is seen as driven by commercial and monetary considerations (Brandenburg and De Wit 2011; Knight 2011), and is sometimes equated with commercialization (Knight 2009). While universities in the North are increasingly seeing internationalization as a huge opportunity for profit making—through recruiting more international students, establishing offshore branches, running cross-border education programs, and expanding international networks and agreements—academic institutions in the South share the profit opportunity as well, though its dimensions are relatively small, even marginal in many cases. This is largely the situation on Chinese soil, as all the TNHE programs and institutions operate as private for-profit ventures, regardless of the public nature—in most cases—of the host and provider institutions.

More importantly, the local partners on the Chinese side see the neoliberal model also as an opportunity to raise their competitiveness and reputations. This is linked to a world culture perspective, which is often interwoven with neoliberalism and operates within its value framework. This perspective holds the premise that "all cultures are slowly integrating into a single global culture," and that "schooling based on a Western model is now a global cultural ideal that has resulted in the development of common educational structures and a common curriculum model" (Spring 2008, 334–335). World cultural theorists argue that the Western-rooted school model has become globalized because it is the best. The views of neoliberalism and world culture combine to shed light on why the number of degree-level TNHE establishments has increased two-and-a-half times since 2004, even though Chinese higher education became a mass system in 2003.

Neoliberal and world culture perspectives may help to explain the institutional agendas that drive TNHE arrangements in the Chinese context, but are unlikely to acknowledge the possible fallacies in these current TNHE patterns. For instance, many TNHE programs and institutions are essentially "selling" a transplantation approach to the introduction of foreign curriculum. They tend to proclaim proudly that most of their courses, if not all, are 100 percent imported from overseas and taught by foreign instructors (though mostly sessional). This often raises questions with respect to the quality assurance of these curriculum and courses as well as concerns over their relevance and practical value in a Chinese context. Given that most foreign provider institutions involved in the TNHE arrangements have a local status in their own systems, with curricula that are practically designed to cater to human resource needs in their localities, the concerns over relevance and value seem to be quite salient.

The key to understanding these concerns may rest with the issue of knowledge and power. To address this, a postcolonial perspective may be helpful. Postcolonial analysis considers a prevailing form of knowledge to be the result of political and economic power. The global influence of West-centric knowledge is thus viewed not as a result of its intrinsic value but the persisting political and economic power of the West. Weiler (2001) depicts the relationship between global knowledge and power as involving a hierarchy of knowledge, where a transnational system of power works through such global organizations (and agents) as universities, research institutions, professional associations, publishing corporations, and testing services, which favor and legitimate West-centric knowledge.

If colonialism focuses on explicit relationships of power, postcolonial analysis pays more attention to a hidden hegemonic power—knowledge and knowledge production, which constitutes a significant discourse in the era of the knowledge economy. Fueled by such power dynamics, knowledge flows from the colonizer to the colonized, the developed to the developing, the North to the South. In this process, knowledge is political, and transnational education must also be seen as political, in that it contains and conveys the norms and expectations of how the world is and should be structured (Arnove 2009). For instance, the graduates of TNHE business programs in China might be well trained as the labor force for multinational corporations, and their IT peers should be a good fit for the global outsourcing job market. By this token, academic colonialism or academic neocolonialism informs a universal expansion of international higher education that is based on West-centric knowledge. This results, unavoidably, in a stratification of the world academic culture and education system that reinforces the inequality and dependency relationships between the North and the South (Alatas 2003; Shih 2010). Put explicitly, in TNHE collaboration, developing countries (including China) are not operating on a level playing field with developed countries.

Nevertheless, there is little doubt that these TNHE arrangements will continue to proliferate in China and elsewhere, despite the complexity of the relationships resulting from the mismatched goals and perceptions on the two sides. Indeed, TNHE activities and arrangements should still be embraced and not feared, in this author's view. That leads to the question of what perspective might serve to guide healthy forms of TNHE development. Arguably, a culturalist approach would seem to be useful and applicable. The culturalist perspective tends to reject the simplistic view that the Western schooling model can be simply imposed on local cultures. It also questions the notion that there exists a world culture reflecting a single form of knowledge. Rather, culturalists believe that "local actors borrow from multiple models in the global flow of educational ideas" (Spring 2008, 336), and stress that there exist different knowledges and different ways of knowing this world (Hayhoe and Pan 2001; Rahnema 2001; Al Zeera 2001; Little 2003). In addition, culturalists maintain that there are other indigenous educational ideas arising from different cultures that go beyond notions of human capital, also that there are multiple forms of progressive education (Schriewer and Martinez 2004; Spring 2004). "A general political agenda among culturalists is recognition of multiple knowledges, alternative cultural frameworks for schooling, and the importance of studying the interaction between the local and the global" (Spring 2008, 337). Thus, in the planning and execution of TNHE, "of greatest importance is the readiness to listen to the narrative of the other, and to learn the lessons which can be discovered in distinctive threads of human cultural thought and experience" (Hayhoe and Pan 2001, 20). The culturalist perspective emphasizes the principle of pursuing complementary strengths/interests and synergies in developing TNHE arrangements, rather than simply focusing on the commercial and profit benefits. This is applicable in China and elsewhere in the world.

Concluding Thoughts

With the help of these theoretical tools, research on TNHE in China should explore fundamental questions that bear far-reaching significance and impact, rather than relatively short-range policy and operational issues. In other words, a critical research agenda needs to be developed to dig deep into the drivers and factors behind the scenes, and consider the possibility of different orientations. Included on this agenda should be questions such as the following:

- What are China's evolving educational needs for the sake of national capacity building? In what sense can TNHE effectively help to meet the needs?
- To what extent should the educational needs for national capacity building be met by local institutions and by foreign providers?
- In the current circumstance of Chinese higher education (where the move to a mass system has recently been accomplished, yet is hierarchically differentiated), what form or combination of forms of foreign provision (e.g., franchising, twinning, offshore campus) would suit China's needs best?
- Have the major provider countries developed explicit and different policies and patterns for executing TNHE activities in China? If so, are there any differences among those countries? Are there any ways in which their policies and patterns are linked to their previous aid-based educational collaborations with China since China opened its door to the outside world in the late 1970s or even earlier?
- Are there any complementary strengths/interests and synergies between the Chinese system and the provider systems? If yes, how have the synergies evolved over the years?
- How can TNHE help develop cross-border research collaborations that facilitate knowledge transfer and the expansion of China's intellectual and technological capacity?
- In what way can the TNHE arrangements be used effectively as China's platform for brain gain or brain circulation?
- In what sense can the TNHE arrangements help channel Chinese ideas and viewpoints to the world community?

This is certainly not an exhaustive list, but only serves as a start. The theoretical perspectives cited above may help open up a wider spectrum of research topics pertaining to TNHE in China, and take the discussion and analysis to a new depth. A further related point is that TNHE research should not be limited to the domain of educational studies (in particular, policy studies in education). Rather, it should be opened up as an interdisciplinary area, involving not only education researchers but also those from a variety of relevant fields such as globalization studies, political science, economics, sinology, cultural studies, history, philosophy, anthropology, and sociology. The proposed critical culturalist research agenda and inter-disciplinary approach may promise the possibility of investigating each and every facet or layer of TNHE phenomena in China—be it political or economic, cultural or historical—and the opportunity of identifying and disseminating good experience, which, in turn, may serve to rectify the tendencies of uniformity in curricular and operational patterns and con-formity to West-centric curricula and epistemology. First and foremost, TNHE activities and arrangements should be geared toward promot-ing cross-cultural understanding, contribute to creating complementary strengths and synergies among the world's higher education systems and institutions, and improving the diversity and breadth—in terms of func-tion and strength—of any system involved.

NOTES

1. There were 1.43 million Chinese students attending foreign universities by the end of 2011. In 2011, the number of Chinese students who went to study abroad hit a record of 339,700. This figure is expected to rise to 550,000–600,000 by 2014. Since 2000, the number of Chinese students abroad increased at an aver-age annual rate of 20 percent (*BBC News Service*, April 18, 2011; *People's Daily* April 25, 2011; MOE, 2012).
2. These establishments include both TNHE programs and institutions. On the list announced by MOE on April 15, 2011, there are 535 TNHE programs and 44 institutions that may offer multiple programs.
3. The TNHE programs with Russian partners are concentrated in the single province of Heilongjiang, which is further explained in Table 6.3.
4. Some TNHE institutions offer multiple programs, and so this figure is larger than 579 in Table 6.3.
5. There is always a consensus that China is divided into three major economic development zones, yet the groupings of provinces/autonomous districts /municipalities across the three zones may differ slightly in the literature. This study adopts the grouping proposed by Tan et al. (2002), with the East Coast Developed Region including Beijing, Tianjin, Shanghai, Liaoning, Shandong, Jiangsu, Zhejiang, Fujian, and Guangdong; the Central Medium-Developed Region consisting of Heilongjiang, Jilin, Hebei, Shanxi, Inner Mongolia, Henan, Anhui, Hubei, Hunan, Jiangxi, Guangxi, Hainan, and Chongqing; and the West Underdeveloped Region having Ningxia, Qinghai, Gansu, Shaanxi, Sichuan, Guizhou, Yunnan, Tibet, and Xinjiang.
6. Within this figure, the single province of Heilongjiang claims 156 (or 68.7 percent of total) joint programs, among which 76 are with Russian universities.

REFERENCES

Al Zeera, Zahra. 2001. "Paradigm Shifts in the Social Sciences in the East and West." In *Knowledge across Cultures: A Contribution to Dialogue among Civilizations*, ed. Ruth Hayhoe and Julia Pan (pp. 55–74). Hong Kong: Comparative Education Research Centre, The University of Hong Kong.

Alatas, Syed Farid. 2003. "Academic Dependency and the Global Division of Labour in the Social Sciences." *Current Sociology* 51 (6): 599–613.

Arnove, Robert F. 2009. "World-Systems Analysis and Comparative Education in the Age of Globalization." In *International Handbook of Comparative Education*, Vol. 1, ed. Robert Cowen and Andreas M. Kazamias (pp. 101–120). New York: Springer.

BBC News Service. April 18, 2011. "Chinese Overseas Students 'Hit Record High'." London: BBC News. Available online at: www.bbc.co.uk.

Brandenburg, Uwe, and Hans De Wit. 2011. "The End of Internationalization." *International Higher Education* 62: 15–17.

Citizenship and Immigration Canada (CIC). 2003. *Foreign Students in Canada, Strategic Research and Statistics Report.* Ottawa, Canada: CIC.

China Youth Daily. August 3, 2010. "中外合作办学为何让公众印象不佳" ["Why Does TNHE Fail to Leave a Nice Impression on the General Public"]? Beijing: Communist Youth League of China. Available online at: www.jyb.cn.

Feng, Guoping, and Sisi Gong. 2006. *Sino-Foreign Joint Education Ventures: A National, Regional and Institutional Analysis.* London, UK: Observatory on Borderless Higher Education.

Global Alliance for Transnational Education (GATE). 1999. *Trade in Transnational Education Service.* Washington, DC: GATE.

Hayhoe, Ruth, and Julia Pan. 2001. "A Contribution to Dialogue among Civilizations." In *Knowledge across Cultures: A Contribution to Dialogue among Civilizations*, ed. Ruth Hayhoe and Julia Pan (pp. 1–21). Hong Kong: Comparative Education Research Centre, The University of Hong Kong.

Huang, Futao. 2007. "Internationalization of Higher Education in the Developing and Emerging Countries: A Focus on Transnational Higher Education in Asia." *Journal of Studies in International Education* 11 (3–4): 421–432.

Knight, Jane. 2009. "Internationalization: Unintended Consequences?" *International Higher Education* 54: 8–10.

Knight, Jane. 2011. "Five Myths about Internationalization." *International Higher Education* 62: 14–15.

Lin, Jinhui, and Zhiping Liu. 2007. "论高等教育中外合作办学的规范与引导" ["On Regulation and Guidance for Transnational Higher Education in China"]. 江苏高教 [*Jiangsu higher education*] 6: 75–78.

Little, Angela. 2003. "Extended Review. Clash of Civilisations: Threat or Opportunity?" *Comparative Education* 39 (3): 391–394.

Liu, Zhiping. 2008. "高等教育中外合作办学引进优质教育资源问题研究" ["A Study on Issues Relating to Importing Higher Education Resources of High

Quality along with Transnational Higher Education"]. Master's thesis, Xiamen University, Xiamen, China.

Lynch, Kathleen. 2006. "Neo-liberalism and Marketisation: The Implications for Higher Education." *European Educational Research Journal* 5 (1): 1–17.

Ministry of Education, China. 2009. 教育部关于北京市中外合作办学机构和项目最终复核结果的通知 [*Ministry of Education Notice on the Final Appraisal Result of TNHE Programs and Institutions in Beijing*]. Beijing: Ministry of Education of the People's Republic of China. Available online at: www.cfce.cn.

Ministry of Education, China. April 15, 2011a. 本科中外合作办学机构与项目(含内地与港台地区合作办学机构与项目)名单 [*A List of TNHE Institutions and Programs at Bachelor's Level (Including Joint Institutions and Programs with Hong Kong SAR and Taiwan)*]. Beijing: Ministry of Education of the People's Republic of China. Available online at: www.crs.jsj.edu.cn.

Ministry of Education, China. April 15, 2011b. 硕士及以上中外合作办学机构与项目(含内地与港台地区合作办学机构与项目)名单 [*A List of TNHE Institutions and Programs at Master's Level or Above (Including Joint Institutions and Programs with Hong Kong SAR and Taiwan)*]. Beijing: Ministry of Education of the People's Republic of China. Available online at: www.crs.jsj.edu.cn.

Ministry of Education, China. 2012. 2011年度我国出国留学人员情况统计 [*Statistics of Chinese Students Abroad in 2011*]. Beijing: Ministry of Education of the People's Republic of China. Available online at: www.moe.gov.cn.

Organisation for Economic Co-operation and Development (OECD). 2004. *Internationalisation and Trade in Higher Education. Opportunities and Challenges.* Paris: OECD.

People's Daily. August 27, 2010. "高校中外合作办学: 别再'乱花渐欲迷人眼'" ["TNHE in China: Please Stop Confusing Us with the 'Boisterous Flowers'"]. Beijing: Communist Party of China. Available online at: www.jyb.cn.

People's Daily. April 25, 2011. "More Students Choose to Study Abroad." Beijing: Communist Party of China. Available online at: english.peopledaily.com.cn.

Rahnema, Majid. 2001. "Science, Universities and Subjugated Knowledges: A 'Third World Perspective.'" In *Knowledge across Cultures: A Contribution to Dialogue among Civilizations*, ed. Ruth Hayhoe and Julia Pan (pp. 45–54). Hong Kong: Comparative Education Research Centre, The University of Hong Kong.

Schriewer, Jurgen, and Carlos Martinez. 2004. "Constructions and Internationality in Education." In *The Global Politics of Educational Borrowing and Lending*, ed. Gita Steiner-Khamsi (pp. 29–54). New York: Teachers College Press.

Shih, Cheng Feng. 2010. "Academic Colonialism and the Struggle for Indigenous Knowledge Systems in Taiwan." *Social Alternatives* 29 (1): 44–47.

Spring, Joel. 2004. *How Educational Ideologies are Shaping Global Society.* Mahwah, NJ: Lawrence Erlbaum.

Spring, Joel. 2008. "Research on Globalization and Education." *Review of Educational Research* 78 (2): 330–363.

Tan, Songhua, Rui Wang, and Jian Wang. 2002. "中国区域教育现代化研究" ["Studies for Modernization of Regional Education in China"]. *中国教育: 研究与评论* [*China's Education: Research and Review*] 2: 1–100.

UNESCO/Council of Europe. 2000. *Code of Good Practice in the Provision of Transnational Education*. Bucharest: UNESCO-CEPES.

Weiler, Hans N. 2001. "Knowledge, Politics, and the Future of Higher Education: Critical Observations on a World Wide Transformation." In *Knowledge Across Cultures: A Contribution to Dialogue Among Civilizations*, ed. Ruth Hayhoe and Julia Pan, 25–43. Hong Kong: Comparative Education Research Centre, The University of Hong Kong.

Zhang, Guoqiang. 2006. "高等教育中外合作办学的历史与反思" ["The History of and Reflections on Transnational Higher Education in China"]. *高教发展与评估* [*Higher Education Development and Evaluation*] 22 (1): 36–38.

Chapter 7

Education and Global Cultural Dialogue: Analyses of the Chinese Knowledge Diaspora at a Major Canadian University

Rui Yang

Introduction

In an era where the knowledge economy is increasingly global in form, China is competing vigorously to strengthen its innovation system, of which its universities are a key element. Among China's strategic advantages is the huge resource represented by its own highly skilled diaspora. Recognizing the potential of this resource, and in an era of skill shortages in key arenas, countries of migration, such as Canada, have targeted their migration schemes at highly skilled individuals, many of whom are mainland Chinese (Hugo 2006). A large number of mainland Chinese intellectuals work at universities abroad, often after having obtained their PhDs abroad. As knowledge carriers and producers, they are valuable human capital and are a target of national migration and innovation policies (Kuptsch and Pang 2006). Those working in Canadian universities become important assets to both Canada and China. However, there has been little empirical research on them, especially in local contexts and in relation to broader axes of spatial relations in state and society (Cartier 2003). Based on a case study of Westcoast University (a pseudonym), this chapter examines the potential to deploy China's large and highly skilled diaspora in the service of Chinese and Canadian scientific and technological development.

Westcoast is a major research university on Canada's west coast, one of the oldest in the province of British Columbia, with the largest enrollment. Highly regarded both domestically and internationally, it attracts significant numbers of international students from 135 countries. Many of them are from the Asia-Pacific region, especially from a Chinese cultural background. Aiming to be part of a growing network of learning that encompasses the globe, the university strengthens established links and develops new ones through enhanced student mobility and study abroad programs, faculty and staff exchange opportunities, and educational consortia. It encourages research projects that link its faculty and students with their peers around the world, seeks to broaden global awareness both on and off its campus through innovative programs and educational outreach in a variety of formats, and attempts to make "global citizenship" an integral part of undergraduate learning through introducing the concept into its core programs. The university also has the largest Chinese and the second-largest Japanese programs in North America. Located in a city with a sizable Chinese community, Westcoast is often perceived by many people in the Chinese knowledge diaspora as one of the best choices of universities in which to pursue their professional career.

Globalization, Brain Circulation, and Knowledge Diaspora

Globalization has fostered greater rates of mobility and an increasing reliance on transnational networks for commerce, social interaction, and knowledge transfer. In today's global economy, intellectual capital is one of the most important factors of production, underlying a nation's ability to innovate and remain competitive (Stewart 1997). Knowledge workers are enabled to seek out education and employment opportunities in other countries and have thus become highly mobile. This is especially the case for global knowledge diasporas who are, inter alia, a form of transnational human capital in the new millennium (Welch and Zhang 2007), and become more valuable in a context of fast-increasing geographical mobility and worldwide communication linked to globalization (Zweig et al.

2004). There is an urgent need for examining the contributions they make to both their homeland and their host country, and what factors influence their knowledge work.

In a context of an unequal international knowledge system (Altbach 1998), the lack of well-trained academic personnel is a major factor in the failure of countries on the periphery moving closer to the centre. Flows of intellectuals are still very largely from the South to the North. With global inequality of knowledge creation and application, wealthy countries of the global North compete to attract research talents from poorer countries of the South (Solimano 2002), whose best and brightest then consolidate the already-strong knowledge base in the former (Hugo 2002), at the cost of the latter (Grubel 1987; Kapur and McHale 2005). Nevertheless, with the present non-unilateral globalization, the hierarchical structure in knowledge distribution and dissemination has become less fixed (Meyer et al. 2001).

As the diaspora can create networks to connect professionals and scientists around the world to promote scientific and economic development in their home countries (Solimano 2002), sending countries increasingly recognize them as a channel for technology transfer. For instance, grassroots initiatives in South Africa and Latin America have been developed to link researchers abroad to networks in their home countries. Indian professionals in the United States have been the primary driving force in the transfer of knowledge to India (Cervantes and Guellec 2002; Saxenian 2006). The global network of highly skilled Korean scientists and engineers strengthens Korea's links with key host countries (Namgung 2009). Even without permanent repatriation, the knowledge diaspora still transfer expertise and skills to their countries of origin and strengthen the connection between their host and home countries.

For China, deploying the diaspora is now a priority, representing a more nuanced response to issues of brain drain (Cai 2011). The number of Chinese students taking degrees abroad has risen significantly over the past decade, from little more than 20,000 in 1997, to 1.4 million in 2007, and 1.27 million by 2010 (*The Economic Times* 2011). While it is true that return rates have been rising of late, from around 6,000 in 1997 to almost 45,000 in 2007, as more and more opportunities open up in China's dynamically growing economy, it is still the case that a significant percentage of those who study abroad will remain overseas, and indeed there is some evidence that the very brightest are most likely to do so (Cao 2004). They are an underexploited resource, expected to be able to play a vital role in China's next stage of development and accelerate the integration of the Chinese academy into the international community.

The Study

Purposive sampling was employed to ensure adequate representation of different disciplines, ranks, and men and women. All 12 interviews were conducted by the researchers on campus in November 2008. Reflecting wider patterns among the Chinese knowledge diaspora, most interviewees were from the sciences and engineering. Among the 12 interviewees, five were from medical and health sciences, two from engineering, and one each from geography, education, and fine arts, despite the researchers' great efforts to recruit and interview those from the humanities and social sciences. Compared to our previous case studies (Yang and Welch 2010), the respondents at Westcoast concentrated much more on sciences, especially medicine. Their ages varied much less than those in Australia, with most between 40 and 50 years and one nearly 60 years old. Their ranks were equally distributed with four each at full, associate, and assistant professor levels. Due to the considerable efforts made to recruit and interview females for the study, the researchers achieved a reasonably high proportion of women, with seven male and five female interviewees. This result was quite positive compared with their previous case studies because male academics tend to dominate the Chinese knowledge diaspora community. One respondent was an established artist and an associate professor without a PhD, while the other 11 doctorates were from Canada (six), the United States (two), Australia (one), Belgium (one) and China (one). A semi-structured interview, consisting of a number of key themes, provided a degree of reliability, but also flexibility, allowing interviewees to provide more details, and authors to follow up, where required.

Major Findings

In consideration of the unique features of the Chinese knowledge diaspora and based on the data collected from the interviews, the following section presents major findings:

Advantages and Disadvantages of Pursuing an Academic Career in Canada

The Chinese knowledge diaspora mainly choose where to pursue professional careers based on perceived opportunities. Most tend to stay within the system where they complete their doctoral studies. This might be due to the network they built up during their studies. Canada, however, is relatively less the case in comparison with previous studies of Australian universities (Yang and Qiu 2010; Yang and Welch 2010). While many Chinese knowledge diaspora based at Canadian universities studied for their doctorates in the United States, their reasons for choosing Canada are similar to those for their Australian counterparts to choose Australia. The advantages are obvious: Canada's good social and natural environment for their professional development and family life. The most important reasons for them to stay are career opportunities and living and work environments, as the following quotes illustrate:

> It was hard to imagine that I gave up a good position in China and moved into a totally strange environment...Gradually, I found out that the research I pursued was quite similar to the paradigm and methodology here. (Interview-KES-1)
>
> The possibility of conducting truly independent research is very attractive...The main thing is that working in Canada allows me to concentrate on my work, the work I am interested in, not anybody else's, because from that the moment I became an assistant professor, nobody told me what I should do and what I should not do. (Interview-CCE-2)

Such comments, that Canada is a better place both materially and socio-culturally to pursue a professional career, were echoed strongly by an established artist with a tenured academic post at Westcost:

> Regarding contemporary art, the environment in China at that time was not good for creation. There were many constraints to the presentation of contemporary art. So I went out. It's been a long time since I came to Canada in 1989...In contrast, Canada is a multicultural country. There is no limit to the presentation of arts. You can present whatever you like. The main point is whether you have the capability to present...The Canadian culture endows individuals with equal opportunities. (Interview-GFA-3)

When asked about the reasons for them to come to Westcoast, many also stressed "a place for (family) life." In fact, family was one of the most-cited priorities, especially by the female respondents:

> There were two major reasons for me to choose Canada. One was for my daughter who was then seven years old. [When they were in China—ed.] She had to get up very early at six o'clock in the morning, had a quick breakfast and went to school, then came back at six in the afternoon and did her homework until 10–11 pm. I had to supervise her homework and

actually that was a pain. As a Chinese parent, I wanted the best education
for her...The second reason was for my own career. I thought Canada
would be a great place. I learned at high school the history of Canada.
(Interview-HMS-4)

The fact that Canada has the reputation for being safe and friendly was
another contributing factor. Although one male respondent (interview-
CQE-4) said that "in addition (to professional considerations), the living
environment was one of the reasons why I chose to stay here," such an
aspect was stressed much more by the female respondents:

I think the most concern for me is safety. I prefer the environment in
Canada. People are friendly. And I feel safe when going home after working
very late. The environment in Canada is more friendly, more relaxed. I just
feel more comfortable staying in Canada. (Interview-JMS-6)

Westcost's location in a major cosmopolitan city with a large Chinese community also attracted Chinese knowledge diaspora:

I think the location is very important. There are great differences between
big cities and small towns. This is particularly true for cities like XXX,
which is becoming even more multicultural. (Interview-GFA-3)

With substantial experience in Western countries, these knowledge
workers and their children have become more used to Western work and
education environments. It is therefore easier for them to move to another
Western country than return to China. For Canada, the US factor is a
prominent issue. Canadian universities have long suffered from their loss
of talent to the United States. Our study confirms this. When asked if they
would be interested in jobs in the United States, most responded positively,
although the reality is always complicated when family is taken into consideration, as illustrated by the following remarks:

I would consider any offer from the US seriously, but another concern is
my family. My husband has a stable job in Canada. Then I have to think
about his need to find a job. My son is at school. He has his friends and
has got used to the education here. If we move to the US, he has to go to
a new school. I have to consider all these. So even it is a very nice offer,
and I will consider it. But it would not be easy for the family to leave here.
(Interview-MOG-7)

The actual situation becomes even more layered in consideration of age. In
contrast to the majority of the participants who were in their late 40s and

50s and who had become established in Canada, some younger respondents expressed quite different calculations. While they were still working in Canada, they consider the option of going back to China to develop their career much more seriously. Indeed, some even said they were waiting for opportunities.

There are various disadvantages of working in Canada as well. Among them, the most reported was the English language. The fact that the academic culture is very heavily English language based at Westcoast makes a significant difference in terms of their work and communication with Canadian colleagues. As the following comment expressed:

> I suffered a lot. First is the language problem. I cannot speak English so well. Second is cultural. I didn't know that I could not practice in the US and Canada with my MD degree in China. It took me a long time to try to switch to another direction. (Interview-JMS-6)

Her difficulties with English and the corresponding Anglo-Saxon academic culture were confirmed by the aforecited successful painter:

> The biggest challenge for me is the language. No matter whether you are a new immigrant or an experienced one, if you have no problem with English, I don't think there will be many issues. (Interview-GFA-3)

It is important to point out that while both genders face all these disadvantages, female respondents clearly showed more frustration and compromises throughout the often arduous journey, as illustrated by the following remarks:

> Thinking back about my experiences, coming from China, establishing myself here and getting my career started, learning English and the culture, it is particularly tough for women to simply sit here (position). It requires a lot of energy and effort, lots of commitment. I think it is because men are much better positioned than women to communicate, to have all kinds of activities with their colleagues, watch TV, drink beer...Their social life is much better than ours. I don't know much about sports. I don't drink beer. Very hard, sometimes you want to communicate with others. I don't think they want to talk with you too much if you don't have common interests. Family matters also. Usually we need to spend much time to look after our family, children. (Interview-TMS-8)

Research Collaboration with China

Previous studies have shown that cultural and linguistic backgrounds contribute to closer scholarly communications. Among intellectual diasporas, there is a strong positive sentiment regarding cooperation with the home countries (Meyer et al. 2001). Choi (1995) also observed that many Asian academics in American higher education kept close contact with their countries of origin, maintaining scientific and academic relationships with colleagues and institutions there. Considering their Chinese background and their social and academic networks in China, the Chinese knowledge diaspora should work particularly well at research collaboration with China.

Our study, however, has found that, although all of the participants expressed an interest in research collaboration with China, and most of them have maintained contacts with their friends, family, and colleagues there, the extent of actual research collaboration varied significantly. Despite the fact that the Chinese intellectual diaspora is an ideal agent to liaise between Chinese and Western academic communities, and assist the mainland to enter into the global knowledge system by joint projects and publications in mainstream international journals, very few of them had a majority of their international research collaborations with mainland Chinese colleagues. While the reasons for such a situation vary, the profound impact of marketization of China's higher education on the attitude toward academic work, and the general morale among Chinese knowledge workers is no doubt one of them, as explained below:

> They (the Chinese academics) pay much attention to what direct benefits they can get from the collaboration, or what kind of quick results the collaboration brings to them, that is, whether there would be publications in (international) journals,[1] or the opportunity to go abroad, rather than learn from each other through collaboration. (Interview-ZIO-11)
>
> I have been invited to many Chinese universities, including Sichuan Fine Arts, the Chinese Academy of Fine Arts, Luxun Institute of Fine Arts, Southwest Normal and so on. I was just asked to give lectures there. As for substantial academic collaboration, or in terms of how I can contribute, I find they always remain silent... You have a look at China's development. Much of their attention has been paid to economic development especially since the 1990s. They focus too much on earning money. Ideals are no longer important. This is a great pity! Throughout history, there have been a great number of Chinese people striving hard for their ideals... They are always talking about the prices of their drawings. I have rarely heard their discussions about the ideology aspect of the drawings. (Interview-GFA-3)

In theory, the role of such a unique group as a knowledge bridge is strategically important for both Canadian and Chinese scientific development (Li 2005), as China is fast becoming a global player in world scholarship, as its share of world scientific publications rises (Yang 2012). Given such impressive developments, more and more mainland Chinese academics are acknowledged as experts in various fields:

> The level of research in China has improved dramatically...Previously, there was not much need to communicate with scientists in China. So, mainly they sent people here and we helped train them. Now it's a learning experience for both parties. We also learn from the Chinese side. And now I must say we are pretty much at the same level and the dynamics has changed quite a bit. (Interview-CCE-2)

Meanwhile, there is an increasing need for the Chinese knowledge diaspora to work with China. In this sense, the lack of substantial collaboration is a great pity, for individuals, their institutions, and even for the countries themselves. Some recent phenomena make collaboration even more complex, together with China's rise, as shown by the comments below:

> One important issue for those Chinese scholars is blindly self-esteemed. They are so optimistic that China is re-entering the flourishing age of the Tang Dynasty and resuming its place as number one in the world. Albeit with the largest population and the highest rate of GDP, it does not mean that China is prosperous in terms of cultural development. I think it benefits economic development when entrepreneurs have such courage. But for educators and culture scholars, it is pathetic that they are not clear-headed and sensible. Can China's education really be number one? Would you be equivalent to Western professors if you are promoted to be a professor in educational ethic, or a professor in civic education by XXX Normal University? (Interview-KES-1)

Cultural Identity

In terms of the cultural identity of the Chinese knowledge diaspora at Westcoast, most of the characteristics of diasporas such as dispersion, hypermobility and memories of the homeland were evident, while political exile was, with almost no exception, strongly rejected. As to perceptions of how settled they were in Canada, and whether they felt alienated, different responses were evident. Most respondents reported they were largely happy and comfortable with their current working and living situation, indicating they were integrating into the so-called mainstream Canadian society.

However, racial discrimination remains omnipresent, although it was widely recognized among the group that Canada has been a world leader in promoting multiculturalism and that their city had been one of the highest achievers globally. Rather than showing how little their host society had achieved in terms of multiculturalism, the situation in the city in particular and in Canada more generally indeed demonstrate the difficulty of implementing multiculturalism. According to the respondents, it is also important to have a healthy attitude toward, and strategies to deal with this, as illustrated by the following remarks with very different approaches:

> Racial discrimination is and will always be there. The key point is how much an individual can change it. For example, two of my colleagues were here (in the Canadian city). They reported racial discrimination. But I didn't think so. (Interview-GFA-3)
>   I keep contact with many Chinese here. They are migrant families. They suffer a lot here. First, it is the language. But when you come out [of China], you must have the courage to meet challenges. More importantly, they have a somewhat passive attitude towards the differences in culture and society. They complain a lot, but are not interested in participation. (Interview-ZIO-11)

Like their Australian counterparts (Yang and Welch 2010), some respondents challenged the meaning of the so-called mainstream Canadian society:

> I am part of the mainstream culture because I think what I have brought is what they don't have. If they accept me, it means they must recognize my work. I have had dozens of exhibitions here in the past decade. I participate in numerous joint exhibitions, national and international. (Interview-GFA-3)

Their responses challenge the notion that migrants from China are not able to embrace an alternative environment, due to the effects of a lack of genuine interest in their host society (Gilbert et al. 2000). Their feeling of alienation was not significant. On the contrary, they are arguably a bridge between East and West: After living and working overseas for years, with knowledge acquired from both Chinese and Western societies, they have created ways to enact individualism, and combine Chinese spiritual tradition with secular Western knowledge (Wang 2001). They are cosmopolitan, rich in international experience, and can work well in various societies and culture.

Closing Observations

The global circulation of epistemic currents, including those among diasporic communities, challenges our longstanding notion of space and place (Tsolidis 2001). Diasporic intellectuals and the transnational net-works they establish, as part of the wider phenomenon of increased global mobility undergirded by greater density and diffusion of information technology, could tilt the balance toward countries such as China and create far more complex and decentralized, two-way knowledge flows. Once seen as a permanent loss, the exodus of the highly skilled is now more often seen as both a loss and a potential gain for the country of origin (Wickramasekara 2002; Lowell and Gerova 2006).

Confirming the findings from our previous research that the Chinese knowledge diaspora group is eager to assist China's development and makes efforts to do so, almost irrespective of their family history or personal views, this case study of Westcoast University shows that they could, under the right circumstances, contribute much to both Canada and China, and are keen to do so. Undergirded by their education and experience from China, postgraduate degrees from major Western countries, and posts in a system that is better positioned in the global network (Altbach 1998), they can not only help mainland Chinese scholars enter the international knowledge system, but also maintain broad contacts with other scholars in the world and conduct various international research collaborations. As potential knowledge bridges, they can play a unique role in integrating China more closely with the international scholarly community.

In practice, however, a variety of factors have restricted successful research collaboration, although they have maintained a strong passion for China. At the same time, as China emerges as a global power, this group could contribute strategically to Canada's global positioning. With rich experiences in different cultures and intellectual traditions, such individuals are a particularly important asset in an era of intensified globalization, and thus deserve special consideration at both institutional and national levels. Sadly, however, many of our respondents reported that their qualities had been much undervalued. What makes the Chinese knowledge diaspora remarkable is their strong will to help their home country, as illustrated by the quote below:

> We do have certain cultural affinity and they (mainland Chinese) feel the same way probably. I was born and raised there. The education system was extremely good considering what the country had in the early 80s. So you can see the product of that time. Early 80s, a lot of us, people in academia graduated in those years. I think I will never forget this. I had nothing at that time, and the system and the country supported me and gave me an opportunity to study. So whenever opportunities arise, I always try to help. (Interview-CCE-2)

Note

1. Most Chinese higher-education institutions have policies to financially reward their academics with English publication. Indeed, the reward could be quite substantial in comparison with their normal income. One article published in a journal listed by the Science Citation Index, for example, could be as high as their four-to-six-month income.

References

Altbach, Philip G. 1998. *Comparative Higher Education: Knowledge, the University and Development*. London: Ablex Publishing Corporation.

Cai, Hongxing. 2011. "Deploying the Chinese Knowledge Diaspora in Chinese Research Universities: A Case Study of the 111 Project." PhD diss., Faculty of Education and Social Work, University of Sydney, Australia.

Cao, Cong. 2004. "Chinese Science and the 'Nobel Prize' Complex." *Minerva* 42 (2): 151–172.

Cartier, Carolyn. 2003. "Regions of Diaspora." In *The Chinese Diaspora: Space, Place, Mobility, and Identity*, ed. Laurence J. C. Ma and Carolyn Cartier. Lanham, MD: Rowman and Littlefield.

Cervantes, Mario, and Dominique Guellec. 2002. The Brain Drain: Old Myths New Realities. *Observer* May 7. Available online at: www.oecdobsever.org.

Choi, Hyaeweol. 1995. *An International Scientific Community: Asian Scholars in the United States*. New York: Praeger.

Gilbert, Helen, Tseen Ling Khoo, and Jacqueline May Lye Lo, eds. 2000. *Diaspora: Negotiating Asian-Australia*. St. Lucia, Queensland: University of Queensland Press.

Grubel, Hwebert G. 1987. "The Economics of the Brain Drain." In *Economics of Education Research and Studies*, ed. George Psacharopoulos. Oxford: Pergamon Press.

Hugo, Graeme. 2002. "Migration Policies Designed to Facilitate the Recruitment of Skilled Workers in Australia." In *International Mobility of the Highly Skilled*, ed. OECD. Paris: OECD.

Hugo, Graeme. 2006. "Australian Experience in Skilled Migration." In *Competing for Global Talent*, ed. Christiane Kuptsch and Eng Fong Pang. Geneva: International Institute for Labor Studies.

Kapur, Devesh, and John McHale. 2005. *Give Us Your Best and Brightest: The Global Hunt for Talent and Its Impact on the Developing World*. Washington, DC: Center for Global Development.

Kuptsch, Christiane, and Eng Fong Pang, eds. 2006. *Competing for Global Talent*. Geneva: International Institute for Labor Studies.

Li, Peter S. 2005. "Immigration from China to Canada in the Age of Globalization: Issues of Brain Drain and Brain Loss." Paper presented at the HKUST's Center on China's Transnational Relations Conference, October 20–21, 2005.

Lowell, Lindsay, and Stefka G. Gerova. 2006. *Diasporas and Economic Development: State of Knowledge*. Washington, DC: Institute for the Study of International Migration, Georgetown University.

Meyer, Jean-Baptiste, David Kaplan, and Jorge Charum. 2001. *Scientific Nomadism and the New Geopolitics of Knowledge*. Oxford: UNESCO.

Namgung, Sang Un 2009. "Returning Scholars in Korean Higher Education: A Case Study of Internationalization of Higher Education." PhD diss., Faculty of Education and Social Work, University of Sydney, Australia.

Saxenian, Annalee. 2006. *The New Argonauts. Regional Advantage in a Global Economy*. Cambridge, MA: Harvard University Press.

Solimano, Andrés. 2002. *Globalizing Talent and Human Capital: Implications for Developing Countries*. Santiago: United Nations.

Stewart, Thomas A. 1997. *Intellectual Capital: The Wealth of New Organizations*. London: Nicholas Brealey Publishing.

The Economic Times. April 18, 2011. *1.27 Million Chinese Students Studied Abroad Last Year*. http://articles.economictimes.indiatimes.com.

Tsolidis, Georgina. 2001. *Schooling, Diaspora and Gender*. Buckingham: Open University Press.

Wang, Gungwu. 2001. *Don't Leave Home: Migration and the Chinese*. Singapore: Times Academic Press.

Welch, Anthony R., and Zhang, Zen. 2007. "The Rise of the Chinese Knowledge Diaspora: Possibilities, Problems and Prospects for South and North." Paper presented at the World University Network Forum, October 9, 2007.

Wickramasekara, Piyasiri. 2002. *Policy Response to Skilled Migration: Retention, Return and Circulation*. Geneva: International labor Organization.

Yang, Rui, 2012. "Scholarly Publishing, Knowledge Mobility and Internationalization of Chinese Universities." In *Knowledge Mobilization and Educational Research: Politics, Languages and Responsibilities*, ed. Tara Fenwick and Lesley Farrell. New York: Routledge.

Yang, Rui, and Fangfang Qiu. 2010. "Globalization and Chinese Knowledge Diaspora: An Australian Case study." *The Australian Educational Researchers* 37 (3): 19–35.

Yang, Rui, and Anthony R. Welch. 2010. "Globalization, Transnational Academic Mobility and the Chinese Knowledge Diaspora: An Australian Case Study." *Discourse: Studies in the Cultural Politics of Education* 31 (5): 593–607.

Zweig, David, Changgui Chen, and Stanley Rosen. 2004. "Globalization and Transnational Human Capital: Overseas and Returnee Scholars to China." *The China Quarterly* 179: 735–757.

Chapter 8

What Are the Implications of a Chinese University Model?

Hongcai Wang

Introduction

Ruth Hayhoe's hypothesis about the emergence of Chinese university model is a brilliant and imaginative one, in that she realized that there are differences in essence between Chinese culture and Western culture, and she anticipated that if the Chinese university can succeed in a dialogue between Chinese and Western culture, a new university model will be born (H. Wang 2010a). This will, of course, be a Chinese model of the university. Implied in this hypothesis is the view that the Western model of the university expresses the essence of Western civilization, and the Chinese model should do the same for Chinese civilization. At the same time, she seemed to have a very high expectation of the Chinese model of the university—that it should absorb the spirit of the Western model and not just create a superficial imitation of it. In this process, it must take Chinese traditional culture as the foundation, which seems to imply that this new model will surpass the Western model. However, it does not mean that it will be China centered, rather that it will be one expression of a multidimensional university model and for this reason, will be effective in East–West dialogue.

What I am trying to say here is that Ruth Hayhoe's hypothesis about a Chinese model of the university has very deep implications, and is worth exploring at some length. In other words, she made the point that just imitating the Western model of the University could not result in a successful Chinese university model, since the Western university model is the product of Western civilization and has its own limitations. Therefore, if we want to learn something useful from the Western university model, we must be grounded in our own civilization. If we can have an effective dialogue, that will be a huge contribution to human civilization and a Chinese university model may successfully take shape. Obviously, her perspective emanates from a form of globalization. As a result, she greatly appreciates Tu Weiming's efforts to identify the ways in which Chinese and Western civilization complement each other, and she pins her hope on the ability of contemporary Chinese universities to develop a characteristic university model. This could happen through the support of China's 985 Project for top universities or through the process of developing Confucius Institutes, but she reminds us how important it is to absorb more of the soul of Chinese traditional culture, particularly the values of the Chinese *shuyuan* or academies. We must say that Hayhoe's hypothesis has wisdom and stimulates us to think in new ways. It is helpful in pushing us to rethink the development of world-class universities and Confucius Institutes, and also to reconsider the *shuyuan*, which are a heritage of China's rich civilization. Reflecting on this historical experience will be meaningful to the exploration of the modern university system.

There can be no doubt that the Western university model plays a leading role in contemporary world higher education. However, if we simply imitate the Western university model in a superficial way, without regard to our culture, it is certain we will not succeed. There is a very different kind of logic in Chinese traditional culture compared to that of Western culture. Western culture tends to center on rationalism and highlights the ability of humankind to control the natural world, which has resulted in a highly developed science and technology. Chinese culture, by contrast, insists on holistic understanding or intuitionism, which emphasizes the harmonization between nature and humankind. It has thus brought us an overly stable social structure, which has not led to a highly developed science and technology or a highly differentiated society.

Obviously, these two cultures have their own respective advantages and disadvantages, but Chinese culture is more tolerant, something which is greatly needed in our pluralistic world. If we can carry out an effective dialogue between Chinese and Western culture, this would have a huge value for the whole world. It would not only mean moving beyond traditional

West-centric thinking modes but also it would meet the demand of sustaining an ongoing process of human development. Of course, this cannot be for the purpose reaching a kind of Chinese cultural centralism at the end of dialogue.

If we look at this objectively, the topic of civilizational dialogue between Chinese and Western cultures has been around for a long time and Chinese scholars have been facing this topic since China was forcibly opened up to the world by firepower in the Opium Wars (D. Li 1990). Yet, we have not found a satisfactory answer till now. Now, with the progress of globalization, one of the most important themes is how we are going to move beyond a West-centric thinking mode. In fact, it is very hard to move beyond this mode of thinking, since science and technology still have a predominant role in socioeconomic development, and are supported by the West-centric thinking mode. So, if we want to develop a Chinese university model that has real meaning, we must find the path of dialogue between Chinese and Western cultures. The first step is to understand the meaning and implications of a Chinese university model.

Exploring a Chinese University Model

In China, people have paid too much attention to the building of world-class universities, because they think it is the symbol of a strong country and the criterion for judging the strength of a country's higher education. This attitude results from the complicated nature of Chinese history over the past 200 years. Before 1949, China experienced a sense of great weakness, and was bullied by various imperialist powers. Chinese territory was invaded and carved up and Chinese people had no international status. The Sick Man of East Asia was the humiliating name given to China by the imperialists. All of this made Chinese people nurture a heartfelt wish that China would become strong again. The idea of building world-class universities is thus the expression of deep feelings that had been held back for many years.[1] As we all know, in a situation of national weakness, it is an empty dream to talk about building up world-class universities. Furthermore, it was clearly unrealistic in the period before a mass higher-education system had been developed. Only now, 20 years after the policy of reform and openness was launched, as the nation has become stronger and regained a respected international status, has the time come at last. In fact, this decision was appropriate at the time when higher-education massification was underway. This is, therefore, not a coincidence, but a matter of historical readiness.

The idea of building world-class universities has been around for a long time and has gradually taken shape. At the beginning, people focused on the topic of a socialist university model and did not link it with a world-class university. In the early years of the People's Republic of China, the Soviet university model was taken as an ideal model; so we totally reorganized our higher-education system along Soviet lines. When the relation between the two countries became worse and worse, China stopped learning from the Soviet Union and tried to develop an independent model. Naturally, this effort was not successful, because we wanted to find a pure socialist model, which was impossible for us. In this process of probing, we were often interrupted by left-wing politics, whose extremism resulted in the disruption of the formal education system. Only in 1978, when the policy of reform and openness was put into practice, were normal patterns of education gradually restored, and even then the influence of left-wing politics was not entirely dispelled.[2] Although people mainly focused their attention on the relation between higher education and the economy for a fairly long time, the issue of a Chinese socialist university model still attracted many people's attention. In China, the issue of how to take the road of socialism is always important. Now, however, we have discarded the idea that there is only one correct form of socialism, and we have recognized that socialism may take different forms; so we should focus on a socialist university model that has Chinese characteristics.

After the theory of a primary stage of socialism was put forward formally, the meaning of a socialist university model with Chinese characteristics changed greatly, with a different explanation for Chinese characteristics, meaning China is in a special situation, or to be more precise, China is at a primary level of socioeconomic development. So, we can learn from the Western world, and it is not appropriate to pursue a model of pure socialism. Therefore, we should not pay as much attention to the differences as to the common features of universities among different countries, whether socialist or capitalist. That has led us to search for a suitable model which is appropriate to our country's situation. We concluded that China should open its door and learn whatever is helpful to us. This approach has enabled us to think about a university model in a better way.

How to Establish a Chinese University Model in the Real World

What I have written above is on a theoretical level rather than a practical or operational one. We should come back to the real world, and get some insight from our practical experience. For example, what does it mean to be "appropriate to China's national essence?" This is something we have never addressed explicitly, especially with reference to a university model. How can it reflect the particular characteristics of the nation? And what role do differences in ideology play in the idea of the university? Apart from the fact that different ideological positions reflect the demands of different social systems, we need to reflect on what differences there might be in the actual system of management.

In the past, we tended to think about these questions in rather simplistic ways, because we paid too much attention to differences, and emphasized the incompatibility between Chinese and Western university models. In reality, this way of thinking was a kind of escapism. After all, there are many commonalities in different systems, and it is perfectly possible to make comparisons between them. So we have had to discard the way in which we used ideology as a kind of blindfold, and analyze the effectiveness of systems and policies much more openly, in terms of their similarities and differences. This has been especially the case when we have had to analyze systems and policies related to the fostering of innovative talent. If we cannot nurture a lot of first-class talent, then how can we consider our system to be very effective? We are aware that it is important to nurture a lot of highly talented students in the age of globalization. This has made us reflect on our ideas of education. And it was this that led to the idea of building world-class universities. To put it in a different way, if a university system with Chinese characteristics is not capable of nurturing high-level talent, it is meaningless.

The motives for building world-class universities are complex. As has been discussed above, it is a necessity for national pride. After more than 100 years of national humiliation, Chinese people need something that is symbolic of the nation's strength. Undoubtedly, it is a matter of pride for a country and its people to have some world-class universities, because it symbolizes the nation's standing in the world academic community, and its ability to contribute to human civilization. Second, building world-class universities serves the cause of international competitiveness. Today's world is one of the knowledge economy, which is characterized by competition in high technology, and it has been described as a kind of international competition for talent, which must be nurtured by universities. If we had no world-class universities, then it would be impossible to nurture first-class talent. Third, building world-class universities serves to satisfy a kind of cultural and spiritual need that people have. As a result of China's reform and opening up, many people have prospered and they want their children to receive a world-class higher education. Many send their children abroad, and this would be less likely if China had some world-class universities of its own. Last but not least, building world-class universities is also a political necessity. If we can build world-class universities successfully, then we can demonstrate that the socialist system is effective and has its strong points. There is thus a multitude of meanings around the project of building world-class universities.

However, suitable infrastructure is necessary to build world-class universities. This means that we should have an advanced university system, which was indeed the starting point for building a modern higher-education system three decades ago. The logic is that only when we have an advanced university system, can a Chinese model of the university emerge, and can a genuine world-class university take shape. On this point, there have been furious debates in China. After 20 years of Chinese higher-education reform, people believe the university must have autonomy and self-government, and professors should have control over academic affairs. However, many people feel that the university still plays the role of an institution that executes orders given from above and does not respond to the demands of professors. This certainly cannot be accepted by academe. As a result of this situation, there have been calls to learn from the American university system! The reason is simple. The United States has the most developed higher-education system in the world, and the most world-class universities; so it must be beneficial to imitate the American university system. Within a short period of time, this call became the voice of the mainstream and influenced the central government decision to establish the 985 Project at the centenary of Peking University's founding in May of 1998. The Project commits China to building a number of world-class universities, with the government committing to investing a lot of money in them (Chen 2006).

Obviously, this has been a mistake. This ready-to-hand American university model is not suitable for China, because it gives little regard to the Chinese cultural context. It is here that we can see the significance of the hypothesis put forward by Ruth Hayhoe about the emergence of a Chinese model of the university. Furthermore, it is notable that this hypothesis is built on the logic of cultural dialogue, which opens up a new field of vision for university development in this era of globalization.

What a Chinese University Model Means to Me

It has been my personal dream to build a strong country through higher education. Really, the topic of a Chinese model of the university fascinates me, since I am convinced that Chinese universities cannot be successful unless they find their own way. I have little capacity for probing this problem, and I feel help from abroad is really needed at this time. I therefore felt very excited when I came upon Ruth Hayhoe's hypothesis about a Chinese model of the university and this has driven me to probe further.

Why am I so captivated by this topic? Maybe that relates to my passionate hopes for China. As Chinese, we may constantly criticize our country, yet in our hearts, we all want our motherland to become stronger and stronger. As a researcher in higher education, I have developed my own thoughts on higher education, and I want to use them to answer the question of how to build a number of world-class universities. I am convinced that only when Chinese universities can solve crucial problems in the process of China's social and economic development, can they become world-class universities in reality. And I am certain that these problems cannot be solved by foreign universities, nor can they be solved by the imitation of foreign university models. These problems can only be solved by our universities as they face the practical needs arising in the process of China's social and economic development. This is my sense of how a Chinese model of the university may gradually take shape.

Therefore, I think Chinese universities must first learn one basic lesson from the American university system: American universities' spirit of serving society. If Chinese universities want to solve real problems in the process of China's social and economic development, the learning should be at an essential level, and not take the form of a simple or superficial imitation. If any university neglects the spirit of serving society, it will not be able to learn from the American university model. Only when we have learnt this spirit of service can we be qualified to discuss the issue of how we may move beyond or surpass the American University Model, and consider the parameters of a new Chinese model of the university.

Chinese universities cannot respond to society's needs spontaneously, due to the fetters of our traditional system. It is therefore our first task to break through whatever hinders this spirit of serving society. If we want to have this kind of breakthrough, we must enable the university to respond to social needs directly. Therefore, we must break out of the constraints of our administrative system. Its centralized mode of management has prevented the university from responding directly to society's needs. So, we must have university autonomy, academic freedom, and self-mastery over the management of academic affairs. In order to attain this, we must develop new relationships between the university and the state, the university and society, the university and scholarship, and indeed, the university and students. These are all basic elements in a modern university system. Universities do not necessarily represent scholarship, especially when they function as an administrative unit of the state; in fact, they may stifle the development of scholarship. The core of the relationship between the university and the state is the relationship with the government, and the key is whether government gives universities the freedom to develop independently so that they can respond in a lively and positive way to the needs of society and create suitable conditions for students' growth. The crucial issue is whether the university genuinely respects academic freedom, and this is the first duty of university administrators. If we cannot realize this basic situation, it means our university system is not a modern one, and it will be impossible to inspire genuine creativity among professors or to nurture real talent in our students. Indeed, it will not be possible for China to even approximate a world-class university. Academic freedom is the cornerstone of any modern university system (Y. Wang 2001).

If greater academic freedom is given to university professors, this will challenge the traditional administrative system. In this system, people are accustomed to defer to established authority, which has resulted in the university functioning as a unit of administration and losing its autonomy, creativity, and ability to act independently. In this situation, universities have simply tried to use quantitative indicators to promote their position in the ranks of world universities, and are further hindered from any real response to the needs of society. Therefore, the real and difficult question for Chinese academics is how to get out of this bind.

Just at this time, Ruth Hayhoe has put forward her stimulating hypothesis about cultural dialogue. Her perspective is very clear—since cultural dialogue is her starting point, her approach is international and cross-cultural, and therefore also fair-minded. It has promoted discussion within China of a Chinese model of the university at a level where globalization and global cultural dialogue serve as a frame of reference. This has enabled us to set aside many meaningless disputes over issues such as Westernization, Americanization, or the revival of a China-centric classicism. Now the conundrum we face is what the wisdom of Chinese culture really is? How are we to identify and absorb it? This is, in fact, a much more complex question as it leads to the issue of whether China's traditional wisdom is fixed and eternal, or undergoing constant change. Is it something we have to revive and recover, or is there a continuity we can simply build upon? If we have to recover or revive it, how can we do that? These are all points we are struggling with.

How are We to Find Interlocutors for the Cultural Dialogue?

It is our premise that the cultural dialogue is going on today, and indeed every university is playing the role of an interlocutor in this dialogue, since they are all the heirs of Chinese traditional culture, and engaged in learning from Western universities. They do not need to be especially entrusted with this role, since it is a natural and necessary part of their responsibility. If this is the case, we take the position that traditional culture has been reconstructed, and a pure and unitary Chinese culture has never in fact existed (Mo 1997). Culture is simply the product of interaction between human subjectivity and circumstance. Therefore, we must accept Chinese culture in its current state in mainland China, and recognize that it is quite different from Chinese culture in other geographical areas. It has been remade by recent Chinese history, including the history of the People's Republic of China, the experience of reform and openness since the 1980s, and the volatile international circumstances of the early twenty-first century. Chinese culture is a culture that is in a ferment of change. Certainly, we can find some aspects of Chinese culture in various jurisdictions, but there is no body that can represent Chinese culture as a whole. So the dialogue can only begin in the subjective situation of China's current universities. On this premise, we have selected some representative cases, first, the elite public universities in the 985 Project; second, newly developing private universities; third, China's traditional *shuyuan* or academies; and fourth, the Confucius Institutes.

The 985 universities are the most highly regarded of Chinese universities, both in the eyes of the Chinese central government and in the hearts of the Chinese public; they are also widely recognized in the international community. Private universities are seen as representing a kind of independent authority in Chinese higher education, as they have a completely different management system from those of public universities, with a strong market mechanism. They are institutions widely seen as having the greatest hope of developing into uniquely Chinese universities (Li and Chen 2002). Academies represent the spirit of traditional Chinese culture and their teachers are closest to the intellectuals from Chinese history, because they have taken the fate of China's people as their own and played the role of public intellectuals, which is very different from the more specialized professional role of contemporary academics. To some extent, this spirit still persists in the hearts of many intellectuals today, but they find themselves troubled by the tension between the political and academic worlds that they are caught up in. Although the *shuyuan* are now history, since all of them were closed down early in the twentieth century, the spirit of the *shuyuan* will never die. We always say that the spirit of Chinese culture continues to live, although it is changing and finding new forms of expression. Civilization may be something solid, but culture is a process that is always changing. Confucius Institutes might be seen as a new starting point, which represents Chinese language and culture, and may give insights into the future of Chinese scholarship, because their mandate is to share Chinese culture and scholarship with the world community.

Our academic perspective is both a macro one and one that embraces a series of case studies. On the macro level, we take certain groupings or types of institutions as the object of research, rather than specific individual institutions. On the level of case studies, we have identified four different groupings, representing different types of academic units, and we treat each grouping as a case.

The four groupings that we have selected for our study have all been affected by the call to build a strong country through higher education and have their own independent understanding of what this means. Each group has also selected its own development model. The goal of China's 985 universities is to break into the ranks of world-class universities. The goal of private universities is to respond directly to the needs of society. The goal of Confucius Institutes is to introduce Chinese culture to the world and they also have to figure out what that means. We take the *shuyuan* as a historical point of reference, which can help us reflect on the current situation of Chinese universities to some extent, particularly in connection with the issue of relations between universities and government.

How to Carry Out Dialogue between Different Cultures?

Practically, Chinese universities have to face the need for cultural dialogue in their development. Until now, the dialogue has not been very effective. Since Chinese universities are inclined to simply imitate the Western university model, this has resulted in the loss of subjectivity. Only when Confucius Institutes have been set up have Chinese universities taken the position of hosts and asserted their views; yet, it seems they still have not managed to be effective in dialogue. This spurs us to reflect on the position and the role of Chinese universities in dialogue, and hopefully this will be helpful to the exploration of a Chinese model of the university.

Case One: What Should the 985 Universities Learn from American Universities?

In China, the 985 universities can represent the strength of Chinese universities. If we want to know how to develop a Chinese model of the university, we should begin by looking at the performance of the 985 universities. We have to say that the process of building up these universities has been one of imitation of Western universities. Why? Because many Chinese scholars are convinced that the Chinese university is falling behind, from the concern over why Chinese scientists have never won the Nobel Prize to rocket scientist Qian Xuesen's question about why China is not producing top scientists. All these reflections circle around the issue of why Chinese universities always trail behind top-ranking universities in the West. Many Chinese scholars want to find the key by studying the experiences of world-class universities. They have noted that world-class universities have certain common features, including substantial financial support, a complete array of subjects, a strong research orientation, some national centers of fundamental research, and a great emphasis on internationalism. All of these elements—the financial outlay, world-class scholars, high-class students, highly advanced facilities, and international vision—ultimately result in a world-class standing (Liu et al. 2002). These various features have attracted Chinese scholars' attention, with the result that they have suggested that our government should build Chinese flagship universities, which will become the first group to pursue world-class standing (Chen 2006).

This suggestion, in turn, was successfully transformed into a central government decision and the 985 Project was set up, with a plan to build Chinese flagship universities (Min and Wen 2010). It included a series of steps. The first was investing a huge amount of money in a few universities, in order to lessen the gap between Chinese universities and world-class universities in terms of financial resources. Thus, the central government decided to give 1.8 billion to Peking University and Tsinghua University each. The second step was to amalgamate some universities in order to overcome the problem of the narrow and highly specialized subject focus of many of the universities established under Soviet influence in 1952. The third step was to expand graduate education in order to enhance the proportion of graduate students and reach patterns close to those of American research universities. The fourth step was to build key national research bases, such as key laboratories, key subject areas, and key bases for the humanities and social sciences, in order to approximate the situation in American world-class universities as far as possible. The final step was to strengthen communication and collaboration with universities around the world in order to attract more international students and enhance the international presence on campus. This has been the logic behind the 985 Project.

Many of China's universities have been aware that this kind of learning is really a matter of imitation and does not touch upon the heart of academic excellence in the American system (Y. Wang 2001). They have come to see that the creativity of Western universities can really be attributed to the system for appointing and evaluating professors, which reflects the spirit of the Western university (Zhang 2005). On this matter, Chinese universities had bumped onto the rocks, because they faced a huge challenge from the traditional personnel system. Peking University initiated a large-scale reform of its personnel system in 2003 but soon had to step back from it, due to resistance from the traditional personnel system. Other universities tried to reform their personnel systems also, but the effect was minimal. In the end, almost every university adopted a very simple way to evaluate professors' work through a quantitative method, which would not touch the sensitive areas in the traditional personnel system. Therefore, Chinese universities are still in the phase of simple imitation in the ways they learn from Western universities, and a very long way from integrating Western culture with Chinese culture (M. Li 2003).

Only when a university has its own standard for evaluating professors can it express its core essence. If a university does not have its own academic standard, neither will it have an ideal of what it should be as a university. This in turn means that it cannot specify, in an independent way, the kind of talent it hopes to attract in its faculty, the kinds of student enrollment it envisages, and its curriculum, nor will it know how to make rational use of the money allocated to it. So, the enhancement of financial resources will not necessarily lead to high quality (Y. Wang 2001). Although the 985 universities have been conferred many privileges, such as the right to set up new subject areas, assess doctoral level disciplines on their own, recruit students, and reform the curriculum, none of these activities will enhance quality unless they have an independent academic standard. The selection of the president has the greatest influence on the behavior of a university (H. Wang 2010b). If the individual appointed as president does not understand the importance of responding to the inner will of the university, and most specially the professors' will, then the university will never establish its own academic standard. It will have no choice but to use external forms of evaluation as its standard, including program approval, the awarding of prizes, and the publishing of papers. The professoriate will not have any substantial influence. In a word, in the factors which affect the 985 universities, the first is the selection of president, the second is the system of management, the third is the operational functions, and the last and least important one is finance. If it is not possible to ensure that professors have an effective role in the governing of the university, changes in the other areas will have little effect.

The process of development of the 985 universities reflects the leading role of the government, which is in charge of planning, examining, and approving. And it is also a reflection of Chinese universities' ecosystems, with universities of science and technology taking a predominant position. At the same time, it is also a process of interaction between academia and politics, which includes interactions between provincial and central governments, different universities in the same region, universities and governments at both national and provincial levels. There is a very different meaning when local (provincial or municipal) governments support universities to gain acceptance on the list of the 985 universities, since it is not only a matter of who will get more money, but also who will get higher prestige. After amalgamation and joint development until the present, 39 universities have gained entry to the 985 list, and their financial resources and prestige have been greatly enhanced. This has provided considerable space for their development.

The biggest problem they face at present is how to set up their own academic standards. This is the expression of the independent spirit of the university, and this issue of spirit is not only something belonging to the Western university tradition, but also to traditional Chinese *shuyuan*. If there is no independent academic standard, the university will have no sense of direction and purpose. If China's 985 universities take the position that becoming world class is their purpose, and the way to get there is by imitating the Western university model, the best they could possibly achieve is becoming second-tier institutions. A world-class university must be open and able to see that responding to the demands of social and economic development at home is its major purpose—it has to be an institution that deals with the world independently. If the leader of the university cannot reflect the institution's inner vision, then the university will not have the capability to think independently. So the key is to select a suitable leader and the more fundamental issue is to change the system of appointment. It will be of no use to invest a lot of money and confer a lot of privileges, if the leader is responsible only to his or her superiors but not to the internal academic community (H. Wang 2010b).

Case Two: Why the Selection of Private Higher Institutions?

Private higher institutions have been the most active sector of Chinese higher education in the past 20 years (Yan and Wu 2005). This is seen not only in the number and speed of expansion of private higher institutions, but also in the fact that their academic level has improved very quickly, and especially that there has been great progress in developing legislation to protect them. Up to 2000, there was only one private higher institution offering programs at the undergraduate level, and all the rest were offering only sub-degree programs. Now, in less than ten years, there are 40 private higher institutions offering programs at the undergraduate level. In the future, no doubt, some private research universities will emerge.[3] Only then will the importance of private higher institutions become evident.

Why have private higher institutions developed so quickly in circumstances where public universities play the predominant role? The answer is that the management of private higher institutions is very flexible, which allows them to be more active, prompt, and precise in responding to the needs of the market, and in satisfying the demands of Chinese social and economic development, where more practical talent is urgently needed. They have also responded to a huge social demand for access to higher education. Their flexible management style enables them to set up popular subjects and disciplines very quickly, recruit teachers on a cost–benefit basis, with many part-time teachers and retired teachers serving a long term, and achieve high outputs while maintaining low levels of input. Among the leaders of these private higher institutions, there are different types of actors. One group is comprised of entrepreneurs, another of celebrities, and most of the rest come from various remedial educational institutions, such as cram schools for the higher-education self-study examinations. However, they all have some characteristics in common: They are highly conscious of the market demand, very alert to changes in the market, good at using the tools of price and industrial styles of management, and good at ensuring direct links between inputs and benefits (Guo 2003, 2004). As a result, they are very successful managers.

Nowadays, the biggest puzzle is that they do not seem to have developed their own ideas for running their institutions, with the result being that their institutions do not have stable mangement systems nor is there a long-term strategy for the future. For some reasons, they have not been able to move beyond the burst of development that characterized their early years. Moreover, they have not been able to make very clear decisions as to whether to follow a commercial line or promote higher education as a public good (L. Li 2007, 2010). So, we can say that private higher institutions have the power to operate independently, but they lack the capacity for long-term development. To put it another way, they do not yet have the capacity to run their institutions in the spirit of a real university. If they maintain their commercial orientation, they are not likely to have any real future (Jia 2002; Guo 2003).

Generally speaking, private higher institutions have not been able to move beyond the limitations of a perspective that makes profit the first consideration. In China, only very few people can accept the commercialization of education. In Chinese traditional culture, people viewed education as being something for the broad public good, and Chinese people still do not easily adapt to the idea of education as an industry; rather, they tend to think it is immoral to profit by education. However, the reality of contemporary private higher institutions is that they must profit from the education they provide, or they will die out. Furthermore, the key issue is not whether they profit or not, but what it means for them to make a profit. If they see profit as a way of sustaining their institutions for the long term, then the public will accept this. If they profit for other purposes, however, the public will say no to them. In other words, the public will not tolerate a situation in which private university leaders simply want to get a return on their investment but are not devoted to the educational cause they have undertaken. Until now, most private higher institutions have taken an approach that might be described as one of low devotion and high returns. This has had a negative influence on their prestige and quality. This has also led them to choose relatively easy approaches to development, such as focusing on practical courses in applied arts and social sciences in order to accumulate capital. This approach has had the benefit of making start-up fairly easy, but at the same time, it has been difficult to develop accumulated experience in systematic curriculum development.

The adoption of a flexible personnel system has also had some negative results, making it difficult to build a stable teaching contingent, since part-time teachers tend to play the dominant role. Most of the part-time teachers come from public higher institutions nearby, and among them are graduate students, part-time teachers, and retired teachers. It is very interesting to see how places where public higher education is highly developed are also where private higher education has sprung up most quickly, a phenomenon that might be explained in terms of a kind of synergy. We can understand some of the weaknesses of private higher institutions arising from this situation. Although the availability of experienced part-time and adjunct faculty have decreased their costs greatly, this has led to a kind of parasitism, which has limited their ability to develop and shape their own academic style and characteristics.

Another serious problem of private higher institutions is the tendency toward a family style of management, a phenomenon also seen in China's burgeoning private industry (Guo 2005). Only too often the founder or leader of a private higher institution appoints his or her relatives to posts such as director of financial affairs or other key positions rather than appointing the most-qualified professionals. This kind of practice has exposed the short-sighted decision making of many leader–founders. Although they retain some professionals to take charge of teaching affairs, they maintain a tight hold on decision making. Their financial policies and practices are thus not transparent, and the income they gain from tuition fees is often mixed with income from other business activities, something that has negatively influenced their prestige (Cheng 2006).

Since private universities are market dependent, tuition fees play a very important role, and the recruitment of students is their first task. If they want to recruit students successfully, they must have popular programs that will attract students, and the tuition fees cannot be too high (L. Li 2007). For this reason, they always adopt an expansive approach, with rapid increases in enrollment as their main policy of development (Guo 2005). For the most part, they lack any long-term vision for their institutions, and they do not see their future as depending on quality enhancement, the gaining of prestige, improvement in their service to students, and soliciting other sources of income. Because private higher institutions have made expansion their highest priority, the government has continued to control student quotas. It is hard to imagine what would happen if the government stopped imposing quotas. So the key to success for private higher institutions is getting the desired quota of students from government, and all private higher institutions give greatest importance to getting their staff to take on the duty of recruiting students.

Currently, private universities are mainly oriented to higher vocational education, since their history is very short. For practical reasons, this arrangement fits their profiles and allows them to establish their programs based on the needs of the market and to cooperate with relevant industries in order to nurture qualified talent that is adaptive to market needs. Overall, it can be seen as an effective way of using the market to figure out which institutions are successful or otherwise.

The new phenomenon of independent colleges might be seen as a kind of monster because they are neither public nor private, and enjoy the double advantages that come from affiliation with major public universities and their legal status as private institutions (H. Li 2006). For example, they can establish their programs entirely on the basis of market needs, while charging much higher tuition fees than either public or private universities. They can recruit students in the name of the public university, and their core leaders come from the sponsoring public university. In reality, they have thus become a new hybrid class of higher institution. They can in some cases recruit more highly qualified students than ordinary private universities and many ordinary public universities, especially those at the provincial or local level.

Today, many people think that the private universities have reached a critical stage in their development, since the expansion of enrollment has come close to a saturation point (Jia 2002). Thus, if they want to develop further, they must compete on the basis of quality, not on price. While the potential for price enhancement is minimal, the potential for quality enhancement is unlimited. If they want to follow this path, they must establish transparent standards for the management of their institutions.

Otherwise, it will be difficult to make real progress. They need to turn away from the profit-making motive and devote much more effort to developing a strong contingent of full-time teaching faculty who are dedicated to their work. It will not do to continue relying on retired teachers or graduate students who serve on a part-time basis. The experience of private higher education internationally has a clear message: World-class universities are nonprofit ones. Frankly, the profit motive is the crucial factor that is preventing the development of excellence in higher education in China.

Case Three: What Can We Learn from Traditional *Shuyuan* or Academies?

The *shuyuan* played a very important role in Chinese academic development. Song neo-Confucianism or the School of Principle, which developed in the Song and Ming dynasties, represents the peak of Chinese academic development. It owes its birth and development to the scholarly conditions provided by the *shuyuan* (Jiang 2003; C. Li 2005). The *shuyuan* system has contributed many important elements to China's cultural heritage. Its system of free discourse on academic topics was the true starting point for Classical teaching to set aside dogmatic forms of recitation as the main learning style and pursue a rational understanding of the social and natural worlds alongside self-reflection. The *shuyuan* discussions and debates between famous scholars were promoted as a way of probing important academic topics, and these dialogues became front-page news. The most famous case was the electrifying debate between Zhu Xi and Lu Jiuyuan known as the Ehu Conference.

It was common for scholars to move around and study at different places, learning from encounters with a variety of scholars. This promoted communication among different schools of thought, and encouraged the integration of ideas and the advancement of knowledge. If we analyze this situation, we see that objectively the feudal officials of the time were simply incapable of fostering scholarship, while subjectively, they were relatively open politically to various forms of schooling. Maybe there is a rule in academic development: the less government control, the better it will be for academic progress. In other words, the relation between government and university is always of crucial importance in academic development.

If we develop the analysis further, the reason that *shuyuan* were able to develop freely lay in the fact that they were relatively independent economically. First of all, their geographical locations were often rather remote, which made it very difficult for the government to control them. Secondly, they owned their own property, which guaranteed a kind of economic independence and ability to provide for their own needs. Thirdly, they attracted a number of famous scholars, who made scholarship the focus of their careers, which is an essential condition for sound academic development. Finally, *shuyuan* were generally at some geographic distance from urban centers, which meant that their scholars could be totally bound up in their academic work (Deng 2007). This suggests that academic development is best when scholars keep some distance from both politics and the market, when they earnestly practice what they advocate, and when they are able to be independent. In later times, when the *shuyuan* became too intimately involved in politics, it resulted in interference from the government and the *shuyuan* declined. The historical record suggests that the main reason for decline was too much involvement in politics (F. Wang 2000).

Objectively, it is impossible to separate the academic world entirely from politics, but academic institutions can be independent to some extent. If academic institutions are too dependent on politics or interfere too much in politics, it is likely to bring calamity. Based on Chinese traditional culture and practice, we think there are two main reasons that have led to Chinese academia not functioning as an independent profession. One is the outcome of the long-standing pattern of "studying to become an official" and the other is the lack of an institutional mechanism for the protection of free academic expression, which would ensure that academics keep a suitable distance from politics. The early *shuyuan* were able to maintain this distance by virtue of geographic remoteness and economic independence, but once these factors were lost, it became very difficult to keep this suitable distance from politics.

Today, it is impossible to imagine keeping a genuine geographic distance or having full economic independence, since we are part of an information era. However, geographic distance can still have some meaning in enabling us to escape from immediate pressures of the market. At the same time, we also can use geographic distance and asymmetry in information flow to enjoy a degree of academic freedom. In other words, geographic distance can still play a role today. However, it is currently very difficult to maintain independence, and difficult to imagine how a university can be maintained and run well without government support. Therefore, the most crucial issue is how to build up a rational mechanism for the relations between government and university, which will be protected by law and guarantee that the university can be freely involved in academic creation.

Case Four: The Future of Confucius Institutes

The fact that Confucius Institutes have been set up has wide-ranging significance. This can be seen not only as a remarkable initiative in cultural communication between China and foreign countries, but also as an important development in Chinese higher education (Han and Shi 2010). It is, in fact, epoch-making for Chinese universities, since it has brought about a transformation in relations with the wider world, from the past one-sided "importation" of external ideas and models to a two-way "interaction" between China and the outside world. Since the Opium Wars, China has introduced foreign university models, whether German, American, or Soviet, which suggests that China had no model of its own. When Confucius Institutes were set up, as a Chinese native brand, if not a Chinese university model, they at least shed some light on features of a possible Chinese model. The purpose of Confucius Institutes is, of course, to disseminate Chinese Culture. Confucius is a highly symbolic figure in Chinese Culture, and Confucius Institutes represent Chinese universities to some extent. In reality, Confucius Institutes are at arm's length from Chinese universities, and might be seen more as a window to the universities. At the present time, they give priority to the teaching of Chinese language and culture, and do not pay much attention to other disciplines. This is useful in terms of advancing an understanding of China in the world, but it cannot begin to reflect the academic level of Chinese universities or the real situation of Chinese universities.

What is most significant about Confucius Institutes is not the teaching content or the curriculum, but the approach to management. It is well known that Confucius Institutes are not run by the Chinese government, but by some famous Chinese universities, which are, in turn, cooperating with foreign universities. Obviously, it is an innovative approach to university management, which has been commented on positively by a number of comparative educational scholars (H. Wang 2010a).

China has a long history of cooperation with foreign countries in running universities, but the cooperation has been interrupted by the changing international situation. Only in this new century has China published its first ordinance or law on cooperation in running universities between China and foreign countries. This was done in order to respond to the conditions of entry to the World Trade Organization. Since then, the procedures for cooperation in running universities have been speeded up, and multiple forms of cooperation have developed. In addition to the cooperation on Master's programs that began in the 1990s, cooperation subsequently expanded to the undergraduate level and to doctoral programs, and most recently, campuses of foreign universities have been set up in China. No matter what kind of cooperation, in all cases, the foreign university tends to play the dominant role, with the Chinese university serving as an assistant in providing classrooms, recruiting students, coordinating the curriculum, and providing teachers for a small part of each program. Certainly, the goal of cooperation in running a university is a complicated one, including an interest in international partnership and learning from the management practices of foreign universities, as well as the all-important consideration of potential profit making. The cooperation between Nanjing University and Johns Hopkins University in running Master's programs is one of the earliest examples of cooperation. Later, there were many cooperative efforts in running MBA programs and in preparatory education programs for those wishing to study abroad. [4]

Now a new kind of cooperation has developed, exemplified in the collaboration between Wanli College and Nottingham University, which resulted in the building of a whole campus for Nottingham University in Ningbo, a coastal city in Zhejiang province. Another case is the partnership between Xi'an Jiaotong University and Liverpool University, which built a campus in Suzhou, Jiangsu province. All these partnerships essentially take the form of an extension of the foreign university to China; in other words, introducing a foreign university model directly, including the curriculum, the teaching faculty, the examinations, and the diplomas from the foreign university. Moreover, this kind of education is a kind of high-consumption type, only available to very few people; so its influence is likely to be small. Nevertheless, it is an important modality for more extensive experience of cultural communication with foreign universities and for learning from them.

By contrast, Confucius Institutes require those who run them to be very adaptable and fit in with local educational conditions where they are located, which involves the gradual adoption of new mindsets. They have to be open-minded and engage in a process of active learning, or otherwise, it will be difficult to find acceptance and take root. Therefore, in the process of running Confucius Institutes, the Chinese side must have a world of openness to accept new things and adapt to new ways of doing things. This could be seen as a dialogue between Chinese culture and foreign culture. Perhaps, it is this process that stimulated the imagination of Ruth Hayhoe as she developed her hypothesis about a Chinese university model.

It is quite conceivable that Confucius Institutes will be successful in introducing aspects of Chinese Culture to foreign countries, and especially in making known certain fields or disciplines that are unique to China. If so, they will be increasingly capable of reflecting the academic level of Chinese universities and making indigenous Chinese ideas known internationally, which will in turn promote the influence of Chinese scholarship in the wider world. This situation will lead to some effective communication and dialogue, and advance the level of cooperation. Of course, the most important partners of dialogue are Western universities and most particularly American universities. Only now are we in a position to understand the American model in a new way.

Conclusion: Is the Aim to Build a New System?

In my mind, no matter whether the Confucius Institutes or the 985 universities, whether private universities or China's traditional *shuyuan*, they all embody elements of Chinese traditional culture though none of them can independently give birth to a new university model that has genuine Chinese characteristics. This is because none of them have yet fully imbibed the spirit of the Western university model, and because the soul of the Western university model is infused with a notion of value-neutral academic knowledge. Therefore, in the future, the construction of a Chinese university model must take place through a fusion of the soul of the Western university system and the spirit of Chinese culture into one body. In the very first place, the model must establish the idea of an independent academic standard, which is the foundation of a university; without its own academic standard, no real university can exist. I think the issue of an academic standard is the core value of the Western university model, which is the source of academic freedom, university autonomy, and the principle of value neutrality in knowledge.

Although the 985 universities demonstrate the dominant role of government, which is one characteristic of Chinese traditional culture, strong government leadership will be futile if the universities do not establish their own firmly rooted academic standard. Chinese private universities have succeeded in bringing a market mechanism into their university management, and recognizing the capacity of students to assert and express their interests, but they still have not established an academic standard of their own, and this will jeopardize their future. Traditional Chinese *shuyuan*, which had a strong sense of academic freedom, met with calamity in the process of dealing with politics, due to the absence of any form of value neutrality. Confucius Institutes are open to learning from Western university models, but the impact of this learning is limited, due to their main function as institutions for language learning, lacking a high academic status.

All these points make it clear that the construction of a genuinely Chinese university model requires an appropriate relationship between university and government, and a way of establishing its own independent academic standard. This task is the core problem for the establishment of a modern university system in China and it is attracting extensive attention from Chinese academics. To put it another way, the establishment of a modern university system calls on us to face the question of how we can develop a Chinese model of the university.

If we focus all questions around the Chinese model of the university on a single point, it is the question of how the principal leader of the university is selected. If we imagine a situation in which the leader is chosen by election from among the professors, he or she would also be accountable to the professors and not just to his or her superiors in government. Such a mechanism for selecting the president could achieve the double aim of establishing an academic standard, and reducing government dominance over the university. If the leader does not care about what the professors think, the will of administrators will be viewed as the will of the university. Today, the phenomenon of "over-administration" of universities is the result of the traditional appointment system for leaders. Furthermore, only when the selection mechanism is changed can the system of management be changed from within. Only then can the academic foundation become a genuine one and the professors have an independent voice in academic decision making. An academic standard means that the right of professors' freedom in academic creation must be respected, and interference from the administration should be minimized. Every effort should be made to guarantee that professors have freedom for independent action and are able to make their own decisions on the basis of their academic conscience. Therefore, the university's administrators must respect the professors' choices and provide suitable conditions for them. Surely, we can assume that professors will be self-disciplined, will adhere to the principle of value neutrality, and thus be successful in resisting both the lure of the market and that of official position. Without academic self-discipline, academic freedom will not be protected, and there will be no academic foundation.

I conclude that Professor Ruth Hayhoe has made a correct judgment in suggesting that a Chinese university model must be based on a dialogue between Chinese and Western cultures. The Chinese university model certainly has to take the current model of the university in Western circles as a reference in the globalization process, but Chinese universities must have their own interpretation of what constitutes Chinese cultural characteristics. In addition, they should reform their institutions according to their own practical needs, while recognizing that reform is, in fact, a process of creation. It is not appropriate to try to build a pure Chinese model of the university and there is no future in copying Western models. The right way to go is creating a suitable model according to the needs defined by ourselves. Certainly, it is pivotal to recognize what we need. We know that the traditional system results in universities becoming more and more hamstrung by administration, and in academic creativity being suppressed more and more. So universities must be emancipated from the cage of administration, and academics must balance the power of administration with a firm academic standard. Obviously, there is no point in denying the function of administration at the present time, which, maybe, can enable universities to make temporary progress as did the traditional Chinese *shuyuan*, but it cannot sustain their development forever. The history of the traditional *shuyuan* tells us that we have enough imagination for academic freedom in Chinese culture, but we lack the mechanism of self-discipline, and it is on this point that we should respond in a creative way when we learn from the Western university system.

As long as we persist on the pathway of change and reform, deepen our understanding of the soul of the Western university system, set up a mechanism for self-discipline in university development, and ensure that the government gives more money to universities and puts fewer constraints on academic freedom, Chinese universities will release their huge power of creativity and a Chinese model of the university will emerge. Unavoidably, this will take a very long time to implement and we cannot expect results in a few days and nights. We must be more tolerant and wiser, in order to allow more time for the exploration of the Chinese university model. Once we overcome our eagerness for quick success and instant improvement, a preeminent group of Chinese universities will come forth. We believe that Chinese people have a huge potential for creativity, but this creativity has to come from a conscious effort, it is impossible for it to appear in a random way. So getting rid of eagerness for quick success and instant benefits is the first step in establishing a Chinese model of the university.

NOTES

1. Deng Xiaoping had given an epigraph for Jingshan Middle school, Beijing, China in 1983, which said, Education Should Face Modernization, Face the World, Face the Future. This is the famous "Three orientations," and this slogan is applicable to the whole of education. "Face the world" has the implication of world-class standards. So this slogan appeared in the formal education reform document "Central Committee of CPC Decision on Education System Reform" in 1985.
2. Before mid-1990s, in mainland China, if a scholar wanted to discuss anything openly, he had to prove that he had a highly socialist consciousness, and based on the Marxism principle. This phenomenon is always called the result of traditional left-wing politics by today's Chinese academia.
3. In 2011, five private universities (including Beijing City College) got the right to begin the Master's program, which is a big news to Chinese private universities.
4. This refers to many international institutions under Chinese universities, for example, The International College at Beijing (ICB) is an integral part of China Agricultural University (CAU). ICB was founded on April 20, 1995, as the result of a joint venture educational program between itself and the University of Colorado at Denver (UCD). 中国农业大学国际学院, http://baike.baidu.com/view/2099347.htm.

REFERENCES

Chen, Xuefei [陈学飞]. 2006. "理想导向型的政策制定" ["Idea Orientation Policy-Making: Analysis of '985 Project' Policy Process"]. 北京大学教育评论 [*Peking University Education Review*] 1: 145–157.

Cheng, Zhixiang [程志翔]. 2006. "民办高校的产权、合理回报和法人治理结构" ["Property Rights, Rational Return and Corporation Governance Frame of Private Colleges"]. 无锡南洋学院学院学报 [*Journal of Wuxi South Ocean College*] 2: 1–5.

Deng, Hongbo [邓洪波]. 2007. "八十三年来的中国书院研究综述" ["Review on the Research on Chinese Shuyuan over 83 Years"]. 湖南大学学报(社科版) [*Journal of Hunan University (Social Science edition)*] 3: 68–74.

Guo, Jianru [郭建如]. 2003. "民办高等教育的市场化与民办高校的组织管理特征—以陕西民办高等教育为例" ["The Marketization of Private Higher Education and Characteristics of Organization and Management of Private Universities and Colleges—By Taking the Private Higher Education of Shanxi Province as Example"]. 高等教育研究 [*Journal of Higher Education*] 4: 68–74.

Guo, Jianru [郭建如]. 2004. "民办高等教育地域性发展的多维分析" ["Dimensions of Analysis of the Regional Development of Chinese Private Higher Education"]. 高等教育研究 [*Journal of Higher Education*] 6: 44–52.

Han, Yingxiong [韩映雄], and Shi Mei [石梅]. 2010. "论高等教育强国建设中的海外办学—以孔子学院为例" ["A Discussion of Higher Education Great Powers' Activity in Running Schools Overseas—The Case of the Confucius Institutes"]. 比较教育研究 [*Comparative Education Review*] 10: 40–44.

Jia, Shaohua [贾少华]. 2002. "民办高校可持续发展的思考" ["Pondering over the Sustainable Development of the Non-State-Run Colleges"]. 浙江师范大学学报(社会科学版) [*Journal of Zhejiang Normal University (Social Science)*] 3: 111–113.

Jiang, Di [江堤]. 2003. 书院中国 [*Shuyuan in China*]. Changsha: Hunan People Press.

Li, Caidong [李才栋]. 2005. 中国书院研究 [*Research on Chinese Shuyuan*]. Nanchang: Jiangxi College Publishing House.

Li, Donghu [李东湖]. 1990. "论鸦片战争打断了中国社会正常发展的进程" ["Opium Wars Broken in the Ordinary Process of China's Social Development"]. 武汉教育学院学报(哲学社会科学版) [*Journal of Wuhan Educational College (Philosophy and Social Science)*] 2: 35–43.

Li, Hongmei [李红梅]. 2006. "独立学院独立性问题研究综述" ["Summary of the Research on the Independency of the Independent College]. 浙江树人大学学报 [*Journal of Zhejiang Shuren University*] 6: 32–36.

Li, Liyun [黎利云]. 2007. "民办院校面临的困难及其自强路径探析" ["A Brief Analysis of Difficulties Private-Owned College are Confronted with and

Ways to Develop]. 湖南涉外经济学院学报 [*Journal of Hunan International Economics University*] 3: 31–34.

Li, Liyun [黎利云]. 2010. "民办高校办学风险调查与分析" [Risk Investigation and Analysis of Running Private Colleges and Universities]. 湖南涉外经济学院学报 [*Journal of Hunan International Economics University*] 1: 5–9.

Li, Meng [李猛]. 2003. "如何改革大学——北京大学人事改革草案逻辑的几点研究" ["How to Reform Higher Education? A Study on the Logic of Beijing University's Personnel Reform Draft"]. 书城 [*Book City*] 8: 39–51.

Li, Xiaobo [李晓波], and Chen Bin [陈斌]. 2002. "论我国民办高等教育发展的前景及对策" ["Trial Remark on the Development Prospect of Civilian-Run Higher Education and the Way to Handle It"]. 黄河科技大学学报 [*Journal of Huanghe S&T University*] 2: 35–38.

Liu, Niancai [刘念才] , Cheng Ying [程莹], Liu Li [刘莉], Zhao Wenhua [赵文华]. 2002. "我国名牌大学离世界一流有多远" ["Comparison of Top Chinese Universities with World-Class Universities"]. 高等教育研究 [*Journal of Higher Education—China*] 2: 19–24.

Min, Wenfang [闵文方], and Wen Dongmao [文东茅]. 2010. 学术的力量——教育研究与政策制定 [*The Power of Scholarship: Educational Research and Policy Making*]. Peking: Peking University Press.

Mo, Dai [牟岱]. 1997. "论中国多元文化" ["On the Multi-Cultures of China"]. 社会科学辑刊 [*Compile of Social Sciences*] 6: 28–33

Wang, Fengyu [王凤玉]. 2000. "中国书院与欧洲中世纪大学的不同历史命运及文化潜因" ["Potential Culture Cause of the Different Historical Fate of China's Ancient Academies and Western Universities in Middle Ages"]. 河北师范大学学报(教育科学版) [*Journal of Hebei Normal University (Educational Science)*] 4: 18–23.

Wang, Hongcai [王洪才]. 2010a. "对露丝•海霍 '中国大学模式'命题的猜想与反驳" ["Speculation and Argumentation regarding Ruth Hayhoe's Idea about a Chinese Model of the University"]. 高等教育研究 [*Journal of Higher Education—China*] 5: 6–13.

Wang, Hongcai [王洪才]. 2010b. 大学校长: 角色·使命·选拔 [*University President: Role, Mission and Selection*]. Shanghai: Shanghai Jiaotong University Press.

Wang, Yingjie [王英杰]. 2001. "规律与启示——关于建设一流大学的若干思考" ["Rule and Revelation: Some Thoughts on the Building of World-Class University]. 比较教育研究 [*Comparative Education Review—China*] 7: 1–8.

Yan, Fengqiao, and Wu Peijuan [阎凤桥, 吴沛娟]. 2005. "中国民办高等教育研究: 回顾、比较与展望" ["Private Higher Education Research in China: Retrospection, Comparison and Prospect"]. 高等教育研究 [*Journal of Higher Education Research*] 5: 45–50.

Zhang, Weiying [张维迎]. 2005. 大学的逻辑 [*The Logic of University*]. Peking: Peking University Press.

Chapter 9

Achieving Balance among Competing Challenges in Chinese Higher Education

Robert F. Arnove

All countries face a number of daunting balancing acts with regard to their education systems. These challenges are intensified by the convergent forces of globalization and are remarkably dramatic in the case of China. Among the principal challenges are these:

- Balancing the competing demands of equity, quality, and efficiency;
- Coordinating the contributions of the private sector with public resources and oversight;
- Balancing institutional autonomy and academic freedom with public accountability;
- Achieving a harmony between the instrumental and intrinsic goals and purposes of an education system;
- Drawing upon the best practices of other countries while building on the historic strengths of indigenous educational institutions and traditions.

In examining these fundamental policy issues, it is necessary to keep in mind these questions (Arnove 2005). To what ends are reforms in education undertaken? Who initiates change efforts and who benefits from them? Finally, what role can comparative educators play in contributing to more informed policy and enlightened practice?

Balancing Equity, Quality, and Efficiency

Since 1949, China has undergone dramatic swings in state priorities in the economy, society, and education. Political scientists, such as David Apter (1965), have viewed China as a "mobilization regime" as compared with the "representational regime" of India. As such, China, since liberation, has mobilized society and schooling around the compelling challenges of overcoming past decades of neocolonialism and underdevelopment and placing the country on the path to national sovereignty, economic growth, and a more equitable society for all. Depending on the period, priority has been given to education as a means of (a) equalizing the society and forming the new socialist citizen with a collectivist orientation or (b) modernizing the society and becoming a global power with more emphasis placed on an individual entrepreneurial spirit.[1]

A prominent example of state mobilization of societal resources has been the dramatic expansion of Chinese higher education since the late 1990s, to reach previously excluded populations, principally rural, working-class, and national minority populations. In 1990, only 3 percent of 18–22 year olds were undergoing tertiary-level education. By 2006, 15 percent of the age cohort was enrolled, what is considered to be the threshold for the "massification" of this level of education. According to Postiglione (2011, 25): "By 2010, about 30% of 18–22 year olds—roughly 30m students—were enrolled in 2,263 colleges and universities, including 1,079 universities and 1,184 higher vocational and junior colleagues." China now has the largest higher-education system in the world. At the same time, China has pursued a policy with its 211 and 985 initiatives to modernize previous structures and create an elite set of world-class universities.[2]

These two state drives—expansion and modernization—have diversified China's higher-education system along several dimensions: whether institutions are organized and funded at the national, provincial, and municipal/local level or whether they are public, private, and semiprivate entities (Lin 2004; Ma 2007). Increased differentiation of higher education, in China as elsewhere, poses the potential problem of stratification with different quality education being offered to those teaching and studying in an elite system (national public and especially designated universities, for example) and those in the nonelite system (private, provincial, and what have been called "second-tier institutions"). As described by Liu and Wang (2010, 8):

> Over the last decade…Chinese education has evolved into a hierarchical and diversified system: national universities remain at the top ambitiously

focused on attaining "world-class" status and promoting national competitiveness and prestige; local public universities remaining in the middle, acting as the major providers for higher education and contributing to local
development; and private institutions are largely at the bottom, focusing on
vocational programs.

One indication of differences in the two systems is the per-student funding gap between national and local higher-education systems. According
to Liu and Wang (2010, 7), "the gap increased from 3,708 RMB in 1998
to 8,396 RMB in 2006."

Another factor affecting the quality of education in the different sectors of the higher-education system is that most enrollment growth took
place in local colleges and universities. Between 1998 and 2008, enrollment in the nonnational sector grew from 2.58 to 14.578 million, while the
national sector grew minimally from 1.541 to 1.705 million (Liu and Wang
2010, 7). The following results are not surprising: overcrowded classrooms,
lack of adequate resources, and inferior teaching and research conditions
that characterize many of the newly created institutions, both public and
private. Students in the nonelite institutions not only experience, in many
cases, an inferior education, but less promising career opportunities and
life chances.

The discrepancy in public resources allocated to different sectors of
higher education is further reflected in the gap in access to resources
and a quality education between urban and rural areas and between the
coastal and interior regions of the country at primary and secondary levels
of schooling. As a case in point, Sargent and Hannum (2005) document
significant differences in teacher quality between rural and urban areas of
mainland China.

Inequities in Chinese education reflect the growing inequities in society as a whole since the country embarked upon the path of integrating
the country into the global economy and introducing a different economic model based on notions of "market socialism." Although mainland
China has reduced poverty more than any other country in the world
(the astounding figure of 200 million people no longer count as poor),
the People's Republic of China (PRC) also ranked among the bottom
one-third of countries in equality of income distribution according to the
United Nations Development Programme (UNDP 2002; Ross and Lou
2005, 242). The country's GINI coefficient, a frequently used measure of
income inequality (with 0 representing perfect equality and 1 representing
absolutely inequality), increased between 1978 and 2007 from 0.18 percent
to 0.42 percent, and may have been as great as 0.47 in 2010—with zero
representing perfect equality (for further discussion, see Chen et al. 2010).

The growing inequality is most noticeable between leading coastal urban and inland rural areas, with differences in educational attainments contributing significantly to inequitable income distribution (Luo and Zhu 2008). In 2009, China ranked 101[1] out of 187 countries overall on various measures of human development (UNDP 2011). With the closure of many state enterprises and the disintegration of rural collectives, millions have become destitute and are without the social safety net that once protected them. Such are the consequences of the neoliberal economic agenda that has been implemented all around the world with its ideological underpinnings promoting the privatization and decentralization of economic enterprises and social services, respectively, owned and provided by the state.

The neoliberal agenda also views the achievement of efficiencies in education in problematic ways. Supposedly, the "invisible hand" of the market efficiently determines the distribution of resources based on the law of supply and demand. According to this logic, parents and students will elect to go to the best-run schools and they will prosper, while inferior schools will lose students and eventually close. Furthermore, with regard to educational expenditures, leading international financial and technical assistance agencies, such as the World Bank (the main source of external funding of education systems), view efficiency not in terms of optimizing the output of given resources, but in cutting resources allocated to education (see, for example, Klees et al. 2012). Schools and universities then scramble to compensate for the loss of public revenues with funds garnered from charging fees for services once provided free, soliciting private donations, and in the case of universities, increasing tuition, setting up second-tier institutions, seeking competitive research grants, starting businesses, and establishing joint enterprises with private industries.

Coordinating the Private, Civil, and Public Contributions to Education

One way to respond to the increased demand for higher education is to permit, if not encourage, the establishment of private universities (Cao and Levy 2005). Since the mid-1990s, the number of private institutions has increased rapidly from virtually none to well over 1,500. While public institutions enroll the vast majority of students, the number of private institutions has proliferated in recent years to approximately the same number as public ones. Most private institutions, however, lack official accreditation and the authority to offer undergraduate degrees. Among the more than 1,500 private institutions offering various types of post-secondary education in 2004, only 228 were state accredited (Lou 2006). As of 2009, fewer than 20 private institutions were granted authority to offer undergraduate academic degrees.

Quality varies enormously across these institutions as do fees charged. Generally, however, tuition fees tend to be substantially higher than in public universities.[3] One attraction of private institutions is that they provide a second chance for students who fail university entrance examinations. Public universities also have established "second-tier" affiliated institutions that serve many of the same populations catered to by private institutions.

Yellow River University, which in 1999 became the first private institution authorized to grant undergraduate degrees, represents many of the positive features of this sector of higher education. Its motto, "Dare to be the first under Heaven," is committed, in the words of its President, to "sharing the nation's sorrow, and relieving the people's suffering." This institutional vision translates into providing "an environment where they [students] could gain self confidence, identify their own interests and abilities and prepare for professional work in areas of need at the local level" (Hayhoe et al. 2011b, 397).

Blue Sky University, another private institution included in the Hayhoe et al.'s (2011c) study of 12 Chinese universities, offers an example of efforts to provide services to an historically neglected population—students with disabilities. Its visionary founder, Yu Guo, crippled by polio at a relatively early age, played a key role in designing a campus accessible to students with a disability. Since it was established in 1994 (it was accorded degree-granting authority in 2005), Blue Sky has graduated approximately 2,000 students with a disability. Moreover, Blue Sky, in 1995, created "Yu Guo's Fund for Helping the Outstanding Poor and the Disabled Students," which disbursed by 2007 a total of 14.93 million *yuan* to help more than 10,000 students (Lin and Zha 2011, 443).

Private universities, furthermore, are seen as bolstering an emergent civil society and the contributions it can make to the provision of important social services, including education for nontraditional populations. Hayhoe et al. (2011b, 397) in their case study of Yellow University "saw evidence of many types of student-initiated organizations, and of study programs that incorporated internships, opportunity for community service and a deep-level integration of theory and practice, knowledge and action."

These exemplary cases, however, do not characterize the quality of education provided in most private institutions. Moreover, despite the promotional materials provided by many private institutions that paint a glowing picture of the attractive jobs that await their students, reality is something else. In a highly competitive context of limited high-paying and prestigious jobs in the modern sectors of the Chinese economy and a massive number of graduates from a substantially expanded higher-education system, students from nonelite institutions are at a decided disadvantage. (They tend to be seen as inferior students due to their low scores on the national university examinations and coming from less academically rigorous institutions.) Also disappointing is that some second-tier colleges appear to have fraudulently duped high-tuition-fee-paying poor students with the promise of their degrees bearing the seal of the sponsoring more prestigious university. Sadly, they discovered that the promise was supposedly "a printing mistake" in promotional materials (see, for example, Hayhoe et al. 2011a, 331, fn 36).[4]

China, as is true of any highly differentiated education system, faces the challenge of establishing an effective legal framework and regulatory system that facilitates and strengthens constructive aspects of the private system of higher education while limiting abuses. The same observation pertains to coordinating effectively different levels and types of public education.

To be sure, both the state and the market can play positive roles in contributing to greater access, individual choice, and more robust pluralism in the society as nongovernmental forces are strengthened. As Jamil Salmi (2002, 8), coordinator of the World Bank's Tertiary Education Thematic Group, reports: With the state's direct involvement in the funding and provision of tertiary education diminishing internationally, it, nonetheless, can protect the public interest by "guiding tertiary education institutions with a coherent policy framework, an enabling regulatory environment, and appropriate financial incentives." What is required is "a clear vision for the long-term development of a comprehensive, diversified, and well-articulated tertiary education" (ibid.). Along the same lines, Schugurensky (2007, 371) agrees that "the government regulations can help monitor standards, avoid duplication, and improve efficiency and social responsibility." At the same time, he concedes that "market practices and values can promote the adoption of better managerial procedures and a close relationship with business in which both partners benefit equally" (ibid.).

The key concern here is that of equal-status interactions among higher-education institutions, the market, and the government. Not without good reason, Schugurensky (2007), like Altbach (2002, 11) and numerous others, are concerned that accountability measures established in recent years by governments to establish rewards and punishments will substantially reduce the autonomy and academic freedom of higher-education institutions while pushing them toward a narrow range of goals unrelated to the formation of participatory citizens, democratization of their polities, the revitalization of national cultural heritages, and the achievement of more just societies.

Balancing Institutional Autonomy and Academic Freedom with Public Accountability

The issues of institutional autonomy and academic freedom are critically related to China's development agenda of creating a significant number of "world-class" universities. There are differing notions of what this means. In any listing of defining attributes, the internationally recognized excellence of faculty and the quality of the research they produce and the services they provide would be primary considerations. Moreover, according to Altbach (2006a, 7):

> Academic freedom and an atmosphere of intellectual excitement are central to a world-class university. This means that professors and students must be free to pursue knowledge wherever it leads and to publish their work freely without fear of sanction by either academic or external authority. (also see Altbach 2006b)

For Ruth Simmons (2003), president of Brown University in the United States, world-class universities

> promote the capacity of scholars to develop original work that is not immediately applicable or useful. Great universities are not only useful in their own time but in preparing for future times. What allows a great university to do that is as little interference from the state as possible. The role of the state is to provide resources, but to give wide latitude to universities' leaders to decide how scholarship is to advance. (cited in Mohrman 2004)

In the case of China, achieving a desirable balance between external oversight and institutional internal management has been problematic since 1949, with the worst excesses of external disruption of university functioning occurring during the Great Proletarian Cultural Revolution (1966–1976). Since 1978, state initiatives to modernize the society in all spheres have placed an emphasis on developing expertise and creating world-class universities. In accordance with initiatives to decentralize the provision of educational and other social services, the relationship between state control over the mission and functioning of the university has given way gradually to a more balanced relationship, although not one without tensions. As described by Zha (2011, 462): "The State promotes decentralization of steering and management in exchange for institutional performance and accountability on the one hand, and tightens control over normative criteria for knowledge production on the other."

He continues:

> State control, which used to reside mainly in the organizational process, has penetrated into the knowledge production process, which is now often driven by a kind of State willpower or managerialism, according to a technical rationale. Put explicitly, knowledge production no longer arises from scholars' individual interest, but has become an integral part of national efforts to fulfill the century-long dream of China's resurgence. In return, the government looks at higher education as a driver of the country's future, and is compelled to give priority to supporting its development. (2011, 462)

Rui Yang's (2010, 10–11) case study of personnel reforms at Peking University illustrates the tensions inherent in balancing forces internal and external to the university in improving the quality of higher-education institutions. He describes how initially top-down initiatives from the state and institutional leaders encountered internal resistance from faculty, particularly in the humanities and social sciences who saw the market-inspired restructuring efforts to change teacher appointment and promotion policies as not a meaningful reform but as an effort to "castrate the university, an issue of life and death concerning China's traditional culture. They raised the matter to the level of principles and accused the reformists of breaking the law."

Arguing in favor of major changes in personnel policies were presidents of a number of leading higher-education institutions, including the University of Science and Technology of China, Xiamen University, Beijing University of Science and Technology, and Renmin University, who saw efforts to encourage competitive faculty recruitment and "promote the flow of personnel when its high-ranking positions were filled, by and large, and not a single high-paid teacher was willing to leave," as central to improving the quality of their institutions (Yang 2010, 10).

How this clash of interests plays out is yet to be determined. For Yang (2010, 10–11), "the most meaningful part of the debate was...the idea of the [Chinese] university." The Peking University case "illustrated China's long standing struggle to strike a balance between dominant Western models and carrying forward its own rich cultural and educational traditions. The experience reiterated the complexity of the internationalization of Chinese universities" as they strive to become internationally ranked institutions.

Hayhoe and Liu's (2010, 82) conceptualization of autonomy and academic freedom is particularly pertinent to this discussion as they illustrate how differing notions of autonomy and academic freedom are influenced by traditional Chinese thought. As they note:

> After many years of reflection on why the core values of the Western university—autonomy and academic freedom—did not fit well in the Chinese context, Chinese educational commentators and others realized that Chinese knowledge traditions are more suited to a notion of autonomy as self-mastery, rather than autonomy as freedom from government intervention. Chinese scholars have always had a strong sense of their responsibility to serve the nation…However, this has not meant the university was wholly subordinate to the state, rather, its scholars felt responsibility for developing a vision of their own, which they can convey to national leaders in the form of criticism, advice, and/or direct service.

Hayhoe and Zhong (2001) contrast "two widely used Chinese terms for autonomy, one meaning self-government (*zizhi*), which is used for the autonomous regions within China, and the other meaning self-mastery (*zizhu*), which is usually used to express the concept of university autonomy. The university supports the state, yet its scholars are responsible as 'masters' of their own domain to develop their own independent visions, insights and ideas" (cited in Hayhoe and Liu 2010, 88).

Hayhoe and Liu (2010, 88) also find it difficult to apply Western notions of academic freedom to the Chinese context, not only because of what they call "the restrictions of a socialist regime," but also what they consider to be "Chinese traditions of epistemology, which privilege applied knowledge, holistic knowledge, and knowledge that is socially useful, over theoretical and specialist cannons of knowledge."

One danger of drawing such sharp contrasts involves essentializing cultures and seeing them in dichotomous terms. Certainly from my own knowledge of United States universities and the American professoriate, many of the features defined by Hayhoe and Liu as characteristic of Chinese notions of autonomy (self-mastery by scholars who are committed to contributing to the common good) and academic freedom (scholars engaged in applied research that is socially useful) pertain as well to Western scholarly traditions. In fact, these competing notions of institutional autonomy and academic freedom are hotly contested in the Americas and Europe, as substantial numbers of both faculty and students oppose the current ascendant neoliberal agenda with its emphasis on applying a commercial discourse and market logic to the functioning and outcomes of their education systems.

Research on the Chinese professoriate indicates that faculty experience conflict over their roles in effecting meaningful change in their institutions and society at large as they are buffeted by the forces of globalization. As universities endeavor to upgrade the quality of their research and teaching to improve their national and international rankings, increased demands are placed on faculty by their institutional leaders as well as by the state (Postiglione 2011). On a positive note, David Zweig (1992, 162), for example, views the opportunities provided by the state's opening to international currents and market forces, as being like "water to a man dying of thirst, [because] global resources offered China's universities and intellectual resuscitation, rejuvenation, and even a source of life for new organizations" (cited in Ross and Lou 2005, 249). By contrast, Wang Yuechuan raises the prospect that Chinese intellectuals have experienced a "legitimation crisis" as "their role in Chinese society has shifted from sometimes vital, sometimes social conscience to entrepreneurs in a world of corporate managerialism" (Ross and Lou 2005, 250).[5]

All these state initiatives to change the role of universities in society raise the fundamental question—education for what ends?

Intrinsic versus Extrinsic Goals of Education

What kind of education makes sense for China or any other country that seeks to improve the life chances of its young and the overall well-being of its population? Here we return to the critical question of the purposes and means of education? Unquestionably, there is a convergence of educational emphases globally. Education is increasingly defined almost exclusively in narrow instrumental terms of preparing individuals for the workforce, for the new "knowledge or informational economy," which will improve the competitive position of a country in the worldwide capitalist system— notwithstanding adding the descriptor noun "socialism" to the key word "market." If education is a human right (Tomasevski 2005)—integral to what it means to be human and live a life of dignity—then, it certainly does not need to be justified in such extrinsic terms. However, if we are to think of how it can contribute to individual and societal flourishing (Brighouse 2010), then other goals need to be considered. They include such traditional goals as preparing individuals for participatory citizenship, social solidarity, cultural continuity as well as developing in all individuals, young and old alike, higher-order reasoning skills, ethical commitments, aesthetic sensibilities, tolerance and respect for differences among people, and, importantly, the abilities of individuals, according to Noble Laureate Amartya Sen (1999, 285), to lead lives they "have reason to value."

At the same time that the instrumental, extrinsic value of education has been emphasized, there also has been, according to certain scholars, a growing concern with the need to emphasize the cultural and spiritual dimensions of education. For example, Nina V. Borevskaya (a researcher in the Institute of the Far East, Russian Academy of Sciences) has pointed to a possible shift in the educational modernization strategy and paradigm in China. She claims that:

> During the last 25 years of reforms, Chinese scholars learned from the negative experience of many countries, where the educational model, based purely on the need for economic development, failed…It has to be substituted by another one, where a human-being and the "all-round development of the quality of his [sic] life" became a more important manifestation of modernization than its economic achievements. (Borevskaya 2003, 26–27, citing Gun Xiaoping 1998, 15–19)

Borevakaya's observations were confirmed by a number of Chinese scholars who attended the World Congress of Comparative Education held at Beijing Normal University in 2005.

Balancing the contributions of an education system to economic prosperity with other worthy goals (such as enhancing individual fulfillment and strengthening social solidarity) will continue to be a challenge to China, as it is to countries all around the world. Tensions faced by students themselves have been identified by Wang (2010, 9) in examining postcompulsory education and training in China designed to tighten the relationship between schooling and workforce participation. While many older students enter the postgraduate system with the hope of being guaranteed a good job, the programs were "set up to provide opportunities to improve themselves to 'be a better person,' which implies a strong sense of learning as moral duty—a trait deeply ingrained in Confucian culture." However, according to Wang: "It is ironic that programs established with such moral goals have turned into an economic market exchange of credentials and not even real knowledge and skills." Not only Confucian culture, but socialism itself, especially as manifested in various state education policies since Liberation in 1949, stresses the ethical dimensions of education, of improving oneself so as to contribute to the collective well-being. Yet, this is true of Western traditions as well.

Balancing External and Internal Cultural and Knowledge Traditions in Higher Education

As discussed by Yang earlier in this chapter, China confronts the challenge of drawing upon the best of Western traditions while building on the strengths of its own educational traditions. For Simmons (2003), truly excellent universities are rooted in the culture of their societies. Based on this notion, Mohrman (2004) makes the point that "[i]t would be quite interesting to learn of a new definition of a world-class university that is not simply an imitation of Harvard but a creative blend of the East and West."

What the outlines of an emerging Chinese university of the twenty-first century might be are explored in the Hayhoe (2011) case studies of 12 institutions representing public comprehensive, education-related, science and technology, and private universities. In undertaking the study, they set out to determine whether the emerging model "might be found and whether it could be interpreted in relation to persisting elements of China's cultural and scholarly traditions" (ibid. 13). Among those traditions were the *shuyuan* or classical academies. Established during the Tang and Song dynasties, the *shuyuan* were independent centers of learning that functioned for over a millennium as a kind of counterforce to the civil service examination system (Hayhoe and Liu 2010, 87–88). Over the centuries, China also has borrowed what it considered best practices from other countries, including Japan, Germany, France, the United States, and the Soviet Union. At the beginning of the twenty-first century, however, China is poised to achieve a more balanced, if not harmonious, relationship between external influences and its own rich cultural traditions.[6] As recalled by Hayhoe and Liu (2010, 94), "the president of a leading institution recently selected a telling phrase from the Confucian classics, *he er butong*," which can be translated as "harmonious co-existence within diversity," or "harmony but not conformity." The university president "suggested that traditional Chinese culture might become a spiritual force in the third millennium … [as] he reflected on the mission of contemporary Chinese universities."

Hayhoe and Zha (2010, 91–92) envision that universities with their "own unique ethos, rooted in its own civilization" would

> stress international exchange and cooperating in teaching and research, integrating into its curriculum knowledge in areas such as world history, geography, and international finance. It would try to be a visible channel for attracting the talented and absorbing the very best elements of diverse cultures from around the world. (cited in Hayhoe and Liu 2010, 94)

Achieving such a well-rounded curriculum is not without its problems as China's universities have to overcome the previous specialization that characterized them. It is not surprising that several of China's universities—specifically those with a history of specialization in the sciences and technology—score well in the Academic Ranking of World Universities (of Shanghai's Jiao Tong University), which gives greatest weight to research and publication in these fields but neglects such important traits as institutional ethos (Hayhoe and Zha 2010, 13). These universities, however, rank lower in the system developed by the Times Higher Education Supplement, which employs, according to Hayhoe and Zha (2010, 13), "a broader array of indicators" that might capture, for example, teaching quality and educational reputation.

Change from Within

Within the context of state initiatives to expand and modernize higher-education systems, the most likely source of progressive institutional reform is expected to come from the vision of extraordinary educators. Although I would like to believe that teachers and students constitute the principal agents of institutional change, historically, this has not been the case. From the May Fourth Movement of 1919 onward, certainly professors and students have been major advocates for significant educational and social change, and they certainly will need to be key players in any major reforms in higher education. Their support is essential to state and institutional initiatives. But, in examining specific cases of institutions that have risen to national, if not international, prominence, there invariably is a pioneering educator who provided the inspiration, vision, and leadership. This is true of the 12 universities in the Hayhoe et al. (2011) study; and in her 2006 study of 11 influential Chinese scholars of the twentieth century, all of them played a central role in developing major universities and defining disciplinary fields, such as comparative education.

The Contributions of Professor Ruth Hayhoe to the Field of Comparative Education

Indeed, Ruth Hayhoe is one of those extraordinary individuals who have made significant contributions to defining the field of comparative and international education, and especially the subfield of comparative higher education. It should be obvious from my extensive references to the work of Ruth that she is not only an authoritative source, but, in my judgment, the foremost scholar of Chinese higher education. As an educator and scholar, she has built bridges between China and Canada and the rest of the world. She has been an exemplary teacher and mentor of generations of students from around the globe who have gone on to achieve distinguished careers. Equally exemplary are her relations with colleagues on research projects in China, and elsewhere; relations that are democratic and characterized by mutual respect and dignity.

Her scholarship illustrates the possibilities of a dialogue among civilizations that enriches scholarly perspectives and ways of understanding differences as well as common interests across cultures and societies—the elements of continuity and change that need to be taken into account in formulating education policies reflective of local realities, even as they are buffeted by global forces (Hayhoe and Pan 2001). Her research brings the lenses of history, the social sciences, and philosophy to the study of education systems as they evolve over time in interaction with international political, economic, and cultural currents. The multidisciplinary perspectives she employs illuminate the paths to more equitable education systems, more just societies, and, hopefully, to international understanding and peace. These, after all, are the very worthy goals of comparative education, to which she has contributed so much over a glorious career.

Notes

1. The swing between what more generally has been called "red" and "expert" is noticeable in the Great Leap Forward (1958–1960), followed by a return to an emphasis on expertise, followed by the Great Proletarian Cultural Revolution (1966–1976), and then the "Four Modernizations" (1977 to the present in various manifestations). For further discussion, see Arnove (1984) and Rao et al. (2003).
2. The 211 (beginning in 1993) and the 985 projects (beginning in 1998, in conjunction with the hundredth anniversary of the founding of Peking University) respectively provide priority investment to the top 100 and an even smaller number of elite universities (43 in 2010).
3. Even where tuition is not higher in private and public second-tier institutions, the costs pose serious obstacles for a significant percentage of students (see, for example, Li 2011, 77). Even in relatively rich provinces like Guangdong, students at Zhongshan University pay tuition fees (depending on courses taken) that are 1.5 to 2.5 times greater than average per capita monthly salary in the urban area of Guangzhou (Mok 2000, 116).
4. By contrast, an example of a successful second-tier college is Zhejiang University City College (ZUCC) co-operated by the Hangzhou Municipal Government, Zhejiang University, and the Zhejiang Post and Telecommunications Bureau. Created in 1999, ZUCC is able to draw upon the excellent resources of Zhejiang University and the employment opportunities provided by the cosponsoring government and public utility company.

5. In this process, university teachers and staff often tend to feel powerless. In a recent international study of the Changing Academic Profession in 18 countries, the researchers (Cummings et al. 2010) found that faculty in China ranked among the lowest three countries in perceptions of their ability to influence the governance and management of their institutions. Although this chapter has focused on faculty roles and perceptions, Chinese university students, historically, also have been important agents of progressive institutional and societal change. Among the reforms students have championed is the right to due process being accorded to them in disputes with institutional authorities with regard to disciplinary actions and civil liberties—for example, the right to marry (Zhang 2005).

6. The harmonious melding of external forces with traditional Chinese values, as well as the historical role of the academies as a counterforce to the state bureaucracy, however, are not considered unproblematic. Some scholars view these assertions as an idealized version of the past and wishful thinking about East–West relations.

REFERENCES

Altbach, Philip G. 2002. "Asia: Trends and Development in Higher Education." *International Higher Education* 29 (Fall): 10–11.

Altbach, Philip G. 2006a. *International Higher Education: Reflections on Policy and Practice*. Chestnut Hill, MA: Boston College Center on International Higher Education, esp. pp. 71–76. (This chapter on "The Costs and Benefits of World-Class Universities" may be found elsewhere, including *Academe*, January–February 2004).

Altbach, Philip G. 2006b. "Chinese Higher Education in an Open-Door Era." *International Higher Education* 45 (Fall): 15–17.

Apter, David. 1965. *The Politics of Modernization*. Chicago: University of Chicago Press.

Arnove, Robert F. 1984. "China and India: A Comparative Perspective." *Comparative Education Review* 28: 378–401.

Arnove, Robert F. 2005. "To What Ends: Educational Reform around the World." *Indiana Journal of Global Legal Studies* 12 (1): 79–96.

Borevskaya, Nina. 2003. "The PRC Educational Modernization Strategy: The Shift of a Paradigm?" *Berliner China-Heft* 25 (October): 13–29.

Brighouse, Harry. 2010. "Flourishing and Justice: Reimagining a More Humane Education." CIES 2010 Kneller Lecture. Comparative and International Education Society (CIES), Annual Meeting, Chicago, March 3.

Cao, Yingxia, and Daniel C. Levy. 2005. "China's Private Higher Education: The Impact of Public-Sector Privatization." *International Higher Education* 41 (Fall): 14–16.

Chen, Jiadong, Dai Dai, Ming Pu, Wenxuan Hou, and Qiaobin Feng. 2010. "The Trend of the Gini Coefficient of China," *BWPI Working Paper* 109,

January. Manchester, UK: Brooks World Poverty Institute, University of Manchester.

Cummings, William K., William Locke, and Donald Fisher. 2010. "Faculty Perceptions of Governance and Management." *International Higher Education* 60 (Summer): 3–5.

Hayhoe, Ruth. 2006. *Portraits of Influential Chinese Educators*. Hong Kong and Dordrecht, The Netherlands: Comparative Education Research Centre, University of Hong Kong and Springer.

Hayhoe, Ruth. 2011. "Introduction and Acknowledgements." In *Portraits of 21st Century Chinese Universities in the Move to Mass Higher Education*, ed. Ruth Hayhoe, Jing Lin, Jun Li, and Qiang Zha (pp. 1–18). Hong Kong and Dordrecht, The Netherlands: Comparative Education Research Centre, University of Hong Kong and Springer.

Hayhoe, Ruth, and Julia Pan. 2001. "A Contribution to Dialogue among Civilizations." In *Knowledge across Cultures: A Contribution to Dialogue among Civilizations*, ed. Ruth Hayhoe and Julia Pan (pp. 1–21). Hong Kong and Dordrecht, The Netherlands: Comparative Education Research Centre, University of Hong Kong and Springer.

Hayhoe, Ruth, and Jian Liu. 2010. "China's Universities, Cross-Border Education and the Dialogue among Civilizations." In *Border Crossings in East Asian Higher Education*, ed. David W. Chapman, William K. Cummings, and Gerard Postiglione (pp. 77–102). Hong Kong and Dordrecht, The Netherlands: Comparative Education Research Centre, University of Hong Kong and Springer.

Hayhoe, Ruth, and Qiang Zha. 2010. "The Polytechnic Universities in China's Transformation." *International Higher Education* 60: 11–13.

Hayhoe, Ruth and Ningsha Zhong, 2001. "University Autonomy in Twentieth Century China." In *Education, Culture and Identity in 20th Century China*, ed. Glen Peterson, Ruth Hayhoe, and Yongling Lu. Ann Arbor: University of Michigan Press.(p.265–296).

Hayhoe, Ruth, and Jun Li, with Min Chen and Guangli Zhou. 2011a. "Huazhong University of Science and Technology—A Microcosm of New China's Higher Education." In *Portraits of 21st Century Chinese Universities in the Move to Mass Higher Education*, ed. Ruth Hayhoe, Jing Lin, Jun Li, and Qiang Zha (pp. 307–344). Hong Kong and Dordrecht, The Netherlands: Comparative Education Research Centre, University of Hong Kong and Springer.

Hayhoe, Ruth, and Jing Lin, with Baomei Tang. 2011b. "Yellow River University of Science and Technology—Pioneer of Private Higher Education." In *Portraits of 21st Century Chinese Universities in the Move to Mass Higher Education*, ed. Ruth Hayhoe, Jing Lin, Jun Li, and Qiang Zha (pp. 374–399). Hong Kong and Dordrecht, The Netherlands: Comparative Education Research Centre, University of Hong Kong and Springer.

Hayhoe, Ruth, Jing Lin, Jun Li, and Qiang Zha, eds. 2011c. *Portraits of 21st Century Chinese Universities in the Move to Mass Higher Education*. Hong Kong and Dordrecht, The Netherlands: Comparative Education Research Centre, University of Hong Kong and Springer.

Klees, Steven, Joel Samoff, and Nelly P. Stromquist. 2012. *The World Bank and Education: Critiques and Alternatives*. Rotterdam: Sense Publishers.

Li, Jun. 2011. "Equity. Institutional Change and Civil Society. The Student Experience in China's Move to Mass Higher Education." In *Portraits of 21st Century Chinese Universities in the Move to Mass Higher Education*, ed. Ruth Hayhoe, Jing Lin, Jun Li, and Qiang Zha (pp. 58–93). Hong Kong and Dordrecht, The Netherlands: Comparative Education Research Centre, University of Hong Kong and Springer.

Liu, Jian, and Xiaoyan Wang. 2010. "Expansion and Differentiation in China." *International Higher Education* 60: 7–8.

Lin, Jing. 2004. "Private Higher Education in China: A Contested Terrain." *International Higher Education* 36: 17–18.

Lin, Jing, and Qiang Zha. 2011. "Blue Sky: A University for the Socially Marginalized." In *Portraits of 21st Century Chinese Universities in the Move to Mass Higher Education*, ed. Ruth Hayhoe, Jing Lin, Jun Li, and Qiang Zha (pp. 422–449). Hong Kong and Dordrecht, The Netherlands: Comparative Education Research Centre, University of Hong Kong and Springer.

Lou, Jingjing. 2006. "Diversifying Chinese Higher Education: A California Model or a Chinese Model? Perspectives about Private Universities and Vocational Education." Paper presented at the March 14 meeting of the Comparative and International Education Society in Honolulu, Hawaii. Available from the author at [jlou@indiana.edu].

Luo, Xubei, and Zhu Nong. 2008. "Rising Income Inequality in Education: A Race to the Top." Policy Research Working Paper #WPC 4700. Washington, DC: World Bank.

Ma, Wanhua. 2007. "Globalization and Paradigm Change in Higher Education: The Experience of China." In *Changing Education: Leadership, Innovation and Development in a Globalizing Asia Pacific*, ed. Peter D. Hershock, Mark Mason, and John N. Hawkins (pp. 163–182). Hong Kong and Dordrecht, The Netherlands: Comparative Education Research Center, the University of Hong Kong and Springer.

Mohrman, Kathryn. 2004. "World-Class Universities and Chinese Higher Education Reform." *International Higher Education* 39: 1–3.

Mok, Ka Ho. 2000. "Marketizing Higher Education in Post-Mao China." *International Journal of Educational Development* 20: 109–126.

Postiglione, Gerard. 2011. "University Challenge." *China Economic Quarterly* (July): 22–25.

Rao, Nirmala et al. 2003. "Primary Schooling in China and India: Understanding How Socio-Contextual Factors Moderate the Role of the State." In *Comparative Education: Continuing Traditions, New Challenges, and New Paradigm*, ed. Mark Bray (pp. 153–176). Dordrecht, The Netherlands: Kluwer Academic Publishers.

Ross, Heidi, and Jingjing Lou. 2005. " 'Glocalizing' Chinese Higher Education: Groping for Stones to Cross the River." *Indiana Journal of Global Legal Studies* 12 (1): 227–250.

Salmi, Jamil. 2002. "New Challenges for Tertiary Education: The World Bank Report." *International Higher Education* 28: 7–9.

Sargent, Tanji, and Emily Hannum. 2005. "Keeping Teachers Happy: Job Satisfaction among Primary School Teachers in Rural Northwest China." *Comparative Education Review* 49 (2): 173–204.

Schugurensky, Daniel. 2007. "Higher Education Restructuring in the Era of Globalization: Toward a Heteronomous Model?" In *Comparative Education: The Dialectic of the Global and the Local*, ed. Robert F. Arnove and Carlos Alberto Torres (pp. 257–276). Boulder, CO: Paradigm Publishers.

Sen, Amartya. 1999. *Development as Freedom*. New York: Knopf.

Simmons, Ruth. 2003. "How to Make a World-Class University." *South China Morning Post*, January 18.

Tomasevski, Katarina. 2005. "Globalizing What: Education as a Human Right or as a Traded Service." *Indiana Journal of Global Legal Studies* 12 (1): 1–78.

United Nations Development Programme (UNDP). 2002, 2004. *Human Development Reports, China*. New York: UNDP.

UNDP 2011. *Sustainability and Equity: A Better Future for All. Table 1.* New York: UNDP

Wang, Qi. 2010. "Postcompulsory Education and Training in China." *International Higher Education* 60 (Summer): 8–9.

Yang, Rui. 2010. "Peking University's Personnel Reforms." *International Higher Education* 60 (Summer): 10–11.

Zha, Qiang. 2011. "Is There an Emerging Chinese Model of the University?" In *Portraits of 21st Century Chinese Universities in the Move to Mass Higher Education*, ed. Ruth Hayhoe, Jing Lin, Jun Li, and Qiang Zha (pp. 451–470). Hong Kong and Dordrecht, The Netherlands: Comparative Education Research Centre, University of Hong Kong and Springer.

Zhang, Ran. 2005. "The Responsive Roles of Chinese Universities: The Redefinition of University-Student Relationships." Paper delivered at the annual meeting of the Comparative and International Education Society, March 23. For further information, Ms. Zhang may be contacted by e-mail at [razhang@indiana.edu].

Zweig, David. 1992. *Internationalizing China, Domestic Interests and Global Linkages*. Ithaca, NY: Cornell Studies in Political Economy.

Chapter 10

One Hundred Years in Pursuit: The Idea of University Autonomy in China

Ningsha Zhong

The idea of university autonomy, as understood in the West, appeared in China with the emergence of modern universities in the late nineteenth century. However, only in 1985 did socialist China begin a dramatic reform of higher education to serve the needs of modernization. Since then, the theme of university autonomy has dominated the discourse of higher education. One focus has been on the delegation of power from the government to universities, leading to the enactment of the Higher Education Law of the People's Republic of China in 1998. Another has been on the universities' self-initiated activities related to institutional development and expansion. The campus revolutions that took place much earlier in the West have now swept over China—the transition from elite to mass higher education, equality in women's enrollment, and technological innovations leading to the modernization of programs and resources (Wildavsky 2010). Today, China has built the largest higher-education system in the world. Its next goal is to achieve academic excellence throughout the system.

The connection between the idea of university autonomy and the expansion in higher-education capacity reflects the traditional Chinese value of the relationship between knowledge and action. Ruth Hayhoe (2006, 15) once commented: "One of the features of Chinese educational philosophy that I have found most striking is the connection between knowledge and action, the belief that experience is the fundamental basis of knowledge. Another side of this is the view that knowledge can only finally be demonstrated as true or valid through its expression in action, not merely through logical argument or critical testing." It is the focus on the unity of knowledge and action in Chinese universities that has characterized the Chinese practice of university autonomy, making it unique (Hayhoe and Zhong 1997).

Within this framework of the understanding of knowledge as including action, the discussion of university autonomy in China only makes sense if we examine university activities and outcomes in connection with the concept. In the following sections, I will reflect on Chinese experience related to the development of university autonomy from 1911 to the present. The concept will be analyzed through university activities at the international, national, and institutional levels. Discussions on "professorial governance" will be considered at the different historical stages. My position is that the Chinese commitment to the unity of knowledge and action has positively influenced university actions that have led to a redefinition of autonomy throughout China's modern history.

The discussion begins from two preliminary assumptions: First, university autonomy is a matter of degree rather than an all-or-nothing affair. It refers to "the degree of independence which university members as a corporate body are able to exercise over all internal decision-making, and in relation to authorities such as those of Church and State in the society" (Hayhoe 1984, 6). Second, university autonomy in China is exercised within the framework of the government's policies, with differences from the practice of universities in Western European countries such as France and Germany or public universities in North America, where universities have the freedom to function as a corporation within the framework of government policies (Mahoney 1994).

Historical Roots—Knowledge and the Institutions

The unity of knowledge and action has always been highly valued in Chinese tradition (Chiang 1963; Zhang 1982; Li 1994). The word "knowledge" traditionally had two main meanings in Chinese: to know, to investigate, or find out or the capacity to know; and acquaintance. It has encapsulated new meanings from "experience" over the modern era (Zhang 1982, 495). Understanding of knowledge covers several key questions: Is knowledge possible? How is knowledge obtained? What is the relationship between knowledge and action? What is the relationship between the method of seeking knowledge and morality? Both Confucian and Taoist schools emphasized the integration of theory and practice from different angles.

Knowledge is both innate or inborn, and empirical, as received by the mind from outside through the senses. Wang Yangming (1472–1529), a Neo-Confucian philosopher, held that knowledge became possible when a unity between the inner and outer was recognized. Knowledge could be obtained through a combination of the inner and outer, a process which includes study, inquiry, thinking, discrimination, and action (Chiang 1963). While Wang approached knowledge by being focused on the mind for the development of "virtue," another prominent neo-Confucian master Zhu Xi (1130–1200) focused on "the search for truth in the world of affairs and things" (ibid., 58). Both were united in their views with regard to the relation between knowing and doing. Zhu regarded knowing and doing as "the two wheels of a carriage," "the two wings of a bird," and stated that it was impossible for one to function without the other. Wang went further and firmly claimed: "To do with clear sight and conscious effort is knowing and to know with true insight and definite idea is doing." He also said: "Knowing is the beginning of doing, doing is the accomplishment of knowing... knowing is for the purpose of doing, and doing is to put into effect what you know" (ibid., 64). Wang's theory has been significant in modern Chinese education. This is evident in the following definition of knowledge by Chiang Monlin, who served as President of Peking University from 1931 to 1945: "enlightened consciousness which implies a knowledge of the whole act—rational conviction with clear insight and definite purpose, absolute obedience to the dictation of the inner voice, and the will power to carry the rational conviction into action" (ibid., 146–147).

To Chinese thinkers, the purpose of seeking knowledge is not for its own sake, but must be expressed in conduct. Confucius took conduct as the standard to judge the value of knowledge. He said: "They who know the truth are not equal to those who love it, and those who love it are not equal to those who delight in it" (Huang 1997, 83). Mencius (c. 372–289 BCE) believed that the purpose for the superior man to make advances in learning was to get hold of the essence of learning in himself so that he could have the greatest freedom in life (Zhang 1982, 5). Liang Shuming (1893–1988), a self-educated scholar and a professor at Peking University who was hired by Cai Yuanpei (1868–1940) in 1917, claimed that "I did not pursue knowledge merely for knowledge's sake. I had feelings for, and was excited by, the problem of China. I was anxious to find a solution to it and accordingly traced the problem back to China's history and culture" (Fung 2010, 12).

Zhang Dainian (1909–2004), a famed Chinese philosopher and professor in Peking University, pointed out that Chinese philosophers always attached great importance to cultivation of the self in the method to seek knowledge. According to Zhuangzi (369–286 BCE), an influential Taoist philosopher, one must become a true person before one can obtain true knowledge. Xunzi (c. 310–220 BCE), a great early Confucian philosopher, insisted that great learning should have an impact on changing one's behavior so that talking and action become one unity and that a good experience of learning should culminate in the leveraging of one's good deeds (Zhang 1982, 10).

Institutions such as the state and the school are main actors in human activities related to knowledge creation, transmission, interpretation, and application. Confucianism and Taoism hold different views on the functions of the state and the school, but are complementary to each other in real life. On the one hand, the ideal state in Confucianism is benevolent, with the ideal function of securing peace, order, and prosperity for the people. A well-governed state is established on well-ordered families which themselves depend on cultivated persons. Furthermore, the school of Confucianism has a state function that is to teach people proper human relations. These are clearly expressed by Mencius in terms of the mutual devotion of parents and children, of the sovereign and ministers, of the husband and wife, of youth and elders, and of friends (Chiang 1963). A formal education system is built on the belief in educating students to acquire knowledge and skills to serve in the government. On the other hand, Taoism is skeptical of the state's role in the life of individuals, where the ideal world would be a "natural state" where people live together free from the social ties imposed through moral codes and institutions (ibid., 11). The school is not beneficial to people unless it leads to a natural fulfillment in harmony with the rest of the world. The school should be informal, aimed at developing human capacity to follow the Tao and avoiding all unnatural behaviour through self-directed ways of learning.

Accordingly, China's traditional system of higher education was established with both formal and informal schools of higher learning, along with a civil service examination system managed by the state. While formal schools, such as the *taixue* and *guozijian*, taught students specialized knowledge of the classics, which was to be applied in government office, private schools, such as the *shuyuan*, allowed students to pursue knowledge for their personal interest in a relaxed and informal manner. It was possible for individuals to achieve social mobility through any of these schools or even without schooling through the civil service examination system. Academic values were linked to the ultimate purpose of knowledge, which was a matter of self-accomplishment, either in seeking an official position in order to build up a harmonious social order or in moving away from society to search for universal laws that would be fundamentally beneficial to humanity.

The idea of autonomy was associated with administrative power shared between intellectuals and rulers. It was reflected in intellectuals' collective authority over the state and the integration of higher education into the state administration. There was no collectivity in the Western sense of a corporation that could identify itself with a particular institution within the higher-education system. A group of intellectuals who shared power with the emperor organized the government and formed schools, constituting government officials and school members. Within the bureaucratic system of the state, intellectuals enjoyed the right to regulate knowledge for the emperor. The close relationship between higher education and the government shaped the form of autonomy.

University Autonomy 1911–1949

University autonomy in the Western liberal tradition is well accepted for its legal features in connection with the concepts of the charter, corporations of faculty and students, and freedoms to decide on what, how, and who to teach and who is to be admitted (Thomson 1961; Cowart 1962; Monahan 2004). These ideas did not exist in Chinese traditional institutions of higher education, however, and only gradually did they develop along with the growth of modern universities.

The first university act, the Imperial University Act (1902), brought in the Western concept of university autonomy and reflected from a legal point of view what a university was and how it should approach its goal. The Act defined a university as an institution of learning committed to graduating individuals with specialized knowledge whose faculty was composed of a group of scholars separate from state officials and dedicated to education and research. Science education was highly emphasized (Xin 1992). These legal provisions marked the beginning of a separation between the state and the school and identified the faculty by their role as educators within academic settings.

After the founding of the Republic of China in January 1912, the new government continued to enhance the state's role in developing legal provisions for higher education. It strengthened public education while allowing private and religious institutions to grow on their own and supplement the public sector. Universities went through what has been described as a Chinese renaissance after the May Fourth Movement of 1919, that is, the fundamental idea of what a university should be was well accepted and academic communities grew on campus. Peking University under the presidency of Cai Yuanpei (1868–1940) set up a new model for Chinese universities (Hayhoe 1996).

By 1927, when the Nationalist Party (Kuomintang) established its government in Nanjing, the national educational system had been changed twice, once in 1912, and the second time in 1922. Modeled after American patterns, the 1922 system emphasized decentralization in governance, the development of science education, the adoption of the credit system in curriculum, and an orientation toward serving the local economy and society. In the subsequent years up to 1949, the state increased its role in higher-education governance through financial investment in the expansion of public universities and efforts to strengthen ideological education by introducing courses on the Three Principles of the People—nationalism, democracy, and people's well-being. A stronger national system of higher education was established, composed of three types of institutions by structure—universities, independent colleges, and specialized schools, with public institutions having a dominant role.

During the Republican period, Chinese intellectuals made every attempt to search for a right road to modernization, from "seeing the West through Japanese eyes" (Chiang 1963) to fiercely debating how to be modernized without colonization (Hayhoe 1989). These efforts resulted in action for change in higher education and led to an increasing role for the state and the incorporation of science and democracy into the university setting. Edmund Fung (2010) studied three ideological schools of thought over this period and suggested that active debates in the intellectual community contributed to scholarship in the university and the development of higher education, especially during the period after the May Fourth Movement. First was Westernized Radicalism that advocated political changes toward modernization through the wholesale importation of Western patterns. Proponents of this approach believed that any new institutions should be built upon a foundation from which the old ones were completely removed. Second was Cultural Conservatism whose proponents were concerned about how Chinese modernity should be constructed and sought a fusion of Western and Chinese sensitivities. They defended the Chinese cultural heritage and wanted to revitalize it so that it could claim a global space and make a contribution to world civilization. The third was a Liberalism that sought constitutional government, sociopolitical changes, the rule of law, and belief in the dynamics of free intelligence. It encouraged individual freedom and gender equality, and identified with science and democracy, liberty, and progress. However, all three had some overlap, both in the concepts embraced and in the orientation of the advocators themselves. Some liberal intellectuals identified themselves with cultural radicalism, for example, while some cultural conservatives came to embrace liberal ideas.

As most of the leading thinkers in these schools were faculty members at the time, the universities gained the greatest benefits through these debates and created their own patterns through an integration of the Western ideas of university autonomy and Chinese values. This came about through their experience with various models of higher education including the Japanese, English, French, German, and American. The most influential universities in China began during this period and their practices of university governance demonstrated how university autonomy was incorporated into the Chinese intellectual world.

University autonomy in Peking University (founded in 1898) was developed from the time when Cai Yuanpei became president in 1917. The university encouraged academic freedom and the integration of knowledge and social practice. The internal governance followed the practice in the German university with the dominant decision-making power residing with professors and a combination of teaching and research under one roof. A faculty association was formed and there was an academic council as the highest decision-making body to determine academic issues. The university adopted a principle of inclusiveness to form an intellectual community that promoted scholarship, inquiry into knowledge, and excellence in education. Many famous scholars gained appointments at this university, despite very different political views (e.g., the Communist Chen Duxiu, 1879–1942, and the liberal Hu Shi, 1891–1962), also different educational backgrounds (e.g., the Confucian Liang Shuming). The academic council had a regulation that the university president was not allowed to hold a government position while in office for fear of the university losing its autonomy (Ma 1997). Nevertheless, the university did not give up its duty of social responsibility inherited from the Chinese tradition. Culturally, Peking University also revived the Chinese traditional value of knowledge always holding a moral purpose. Patriotism and social progress were also core values of the university, which led to strong expressions of individualism, patriotism, and gender equity in the May Fourth Movement in 1919 and later in the Anti-Japanese War (Peking University 2011).

Nankai University, established in 1919, had a unique profile as a locally founded private institution with great flexibility in governance and a focus on excellence in education and in business. Created by educator and entrepreneur Zhang Boling (1876–1951), Nankai integrated Chinese values of moral education with Western knowledge of science and democracy. By 1937, the university was well established with three faculties—arts, sciences, and commerce. As a graduate from the Beiyang Navy School and St. John's University, Zhang believed that modern education that followed Western principles of science and democracy could make the nation strong. From 1904 onward, he co-founded a series of Nankai educational enterprises—Nankai school, Nankai University, Nankai women's middle school, Nankai primary school, and Chongqing Nankai middle school. Moral education was a core value in the university, reflected in the motto, set by Zhang, as dedication to the public interest, acquisition of all-round capability, and aspiration for daily progress (Zheng 1989; Nankai 2011).

When the Anti-Japanese War broke out in 1937, Peking University, Tsinghua University, and Nankai University moved inland to Kunming in Yunnan province, merging into the National Southwestern Associated University (Lianda, 1938–1946). Lianda was in fact an academic alliance comprised of two national universities and one private university, which chose to stand by the Chinese government in the national crisis. A collegiate governance model was established and the president of each institution took turns to provide leadership to the university. The university had a considerable degree of autonomy that ensured teaching and research to continue under the most difficult circumstances. There were five faculties—arts, science, law, engineering, and teacher education— with over 30 departments and specialties. Scholarly activities continued and many new courses were developed under those difficult physical conditions. For example, Wang Li (1890–1986), a professor in Chinese language, offered new courses in linguistics based on his comparative research on the Chinese and Vietnamese languages (LaPolla 2006). Jin Yueling (1895–1984), a professor in philosophy, wrote a comprehensive philosophical work "On Epistemology," which combined Western theories and neo-Confucianism to clarify the role of the individual in relation to others in the process of knowing (Bunnin 2003). Lianda's faculty and students spent the war years striving to uphold a model of higher education that sought to preserve liberal education, political autonomy, and academic freedom. It was successful in the face of wartime privations, enemy air raids, and Kuomintang pressure. During its eight-year history, Lianda graduated more than 2,000 individuals, many of whom became backbone scholars in professional fields and also state leaders (Israel 1998).

In this period, the Western value of autonomy was introduced to China in a way in which the modern university was defined through law, and the university was separated from the state. A modern higher-education system was established under the influence of various foreign models, with the American and French models probably having the greatest influence on Chinese higher education (Hayhoe 1989). On campus, university members formed professional groups and began to identify with their institutions. The collective leadership of professors was strengthened through institutional development and the growth of academic communities. Nevertheless, Chinese universities were seen to have a strong political mission. Higher education aimed at national development in order to get rid of poverty and backwardness in China, and also to resist imperialism. In practice, the universities demonstrated a strong sense of social responsibility that included the support of economic and military modernization and the adoption of a watchdog role over governmental inaction and corruption (Hayhoe 1996, 117). Political parties became involved in higher education and a national ideology was inserted into the curriculum. Consequently, due to the national crises caused by China's political situation as a country without full sovereignty, university autonomy remained limited in this period.

University Autonomy, 1949–1978

Ruth Hayhoe (1996) observed that in the socialist period from 1949 to 1978, universities joined the state to support economic development and nation building while sacrificing the freedom of inquiry that had been developed since the 1911 revolution, and eventually becoming a victim of the Cultural Revolution (1966–1976).

When the People's Republic of China was founded in 1949, the debates inspired by various schools of thought in the prior period came to an end, with one perspective predominating: that only socialism could save the country. This claim had good grounds, which might not have been well understood by the West at the time (Fairbank 1949). Politically, China was worn out by a prolonged period of internal wars and by the Japanese occupation. A new isolation imposed by the West and the breakout of the Korean War in 1950 pushed China into a corner. Economically, there was extreme poverty among Chinese people and an over 80 percent illiteracy rate in the overall population.

To tackle the problems, China prioritized economic development and decided to create a new educational system which was to be national, scientific, and mass oriented, with an emphasis on science and technology, the integration of knowledge and practice, and serving the needs of socialism. Strategically, China adopted a policy of leaning on the Soviet Union to transform higher education. It was regarded, in a recent study, as a strategy to obtain scientific and technological supports for the purpose of becoming eventually self-sufficient and independent (Bernstein and Li 2010). From a practical perspective, the Soviet Union, which had a shared belief in Marxism, was the only country that was capable and willing to help China out.

The restructuring of the higher-education system began in 1952, and by 1957, a more balanced system than that of the previous regime was established, reflecting political and economic needs at the national and provincial levels. It was modeled after Soviet higher education and the state assumed all responsibilities for the provision of higher education; yet, it also revived some elements of tradition. For the purpose of efficiency, the new system was highly centralized and completely integrated into the state planning process, with a well-balanced mapping of institutions over six administrative regions of China. In each region, there were 11 types of institutions: comprehensive (arts and sciences), engineering, teacher training, agriculture, forestry, medicine, finance, law and political science, music, fine arts, and sports. A system of specialties was introduced, laying the foundation for the curriculum. Research was no longer seen as a necessary task for the university. To better use the resources and achieve higher efficiency, the government established separate institutions to conduct research following the practice of the Soviet Union and also France (Hayhoe 1989).

The development of People's University (1950) embodied the idea of a new type of university for socialism. The university was founded in 1950 on the basis of three vocational universities for political leaders run by the Communist Party of China. Hayhoe (1989) noted that People's University was modeled after the Moscow Planning Institute and aimed at integrating knowledge drawn from the Soviet experience into the new Chinese socialist system and providing high-quality training for leaders in law, economics, and planning. A majority of faculty members came from the Soviet Union in the beginning stage. The delivery of programs was based upon a fixed schedule of courses with little flexibility for students to choose according to their interests. University governance reflected the leadership of the Party in collaboration with professional governance with the authority residing in the president. One of the university's objectives was to cultivate students with socialist beliefs and loyalty to the communist cause. The first president, Wu Yuzhang (1878–1966), was himself a Marxist, who had received a Western education and participated in the 1911 revolution. He strongly believed that the tasks of the new type of university included integration of theory and practice, mastery of advanced knowledge in science and technology, and the education of students (Chen 2007). People's University became a national model for Chinese universities in the socialist period.

With regard to the concept of university autonomy, the first layer of meaning might be seen to lie in the international context. With the establishment of a socialist regime, institutional history was assimilated into the national narrative. Considering university autonomy as a political notion linked to educational sovereignty, Chinese universities and colleges finally got away from any form of foreign control and became public institutions. Private and religious universities had been integrated into the public system by 1953. The end of religious higher education that had been introduced from abroad was regarded as an increase in autonomy for China in the larger international context and in relation to imperialism.

The second layer of meaning was regarding the relationship between the state and the university at the national level. As the higher-education system was integrated into the state planning, universities functioned according to the role that was defined for them by the state in relation to the social, economic, and political needs of the country. However, their role was limited to providing training services, with little opportunity for exercising leadership in terms of intellectual development or of continuing the role of watching over potential government wrongdoing. Universities were administered respectively by the Ministry of Higher Education or central ministries and agencies at the central level, and by provincial governments at the local level. These two kinds of leadership put universities in such a position that they had to operate within government policies at both levels. Their freedom and power were derived from their relationship with the government, especially with the central government. As Hayhoe (1989) pointed out, the closer a university was to the central government, the more power and authority it had. The idea of "professorial governance" was still alive; however, it was transformed into an understanding of conformity to the state's needs.

The meaning of autonomy at the third layer was related to operational settings at the individual institutional level. Within the university, the governance system was characterized by the political leadership of the Communist Party of China (CPC). Compared with the Nationalist Party before 1949, which was never able to penetrate effectively into internal academic governance, the CPC firmly claimed the leadership of the university and gradually established its cells on campus. In September 1958, a directive regarding educational aims and principles issued by the Central Committee of the CPC and State Council stated that "All schools should receive the leadership of the Party" (Li 1989, 162). Hence, the Party committee system or a university council system was to be put in place. Under such systems, the Party committee played a leading role in the decision making in that all important matters were to be discussed and passed within the committee first and then given to the president for implementation. The Party's leadership in the universities was further strengthened by the directive "Temporary Working Regulations on the National

Higher Institutions" issued by the Ministry of Higher Education in 1961. As the university was integrated into the state administration, both the Party committee and the president were accountable to the government or superior party organization, respectively. In fact, it became a common practice that the university president or secretary of the Party committee had a cross-appointment in the government or seat on the decision-making board at a higher level, something that had been resisted with difficulty by the national universities in the previous regime. Therefore, autonomy at the institutional level became very limited.

Furthermore, both faculty and students were integrated into the state personnel system as civil servants or future civil servants. Their nationally defined status weakened their identity as a professional group. As a result, it was hard for them to find a clear identity. Politically, faculty and students were classified as petty bourgeois, but they could become a part of the working class if they continued thought reform and identified with the working class. Some scholarly activities did continue in this period, but they were conducted selectively based on the country's needs. Opportunities were particularly good in the areas in which knowledge was applied to social practice and economic development. For instance, in this period, Professor Wang Li in Beijing University, whom I mentioned in the previous section on the National Southwestern Associated University, continued to produce original research and apply his knowledge to the reform of the Chinese language to improve literacy in China. Moreover, national universities were able to participate in state key projects in scientific research and innovation.

University Autonomy since 1978

It is recognized that the national system of higher education modeled after the Soviet pattern had laid a solid foundation for the state to play a key role in higher education for economic development (Bernstein and Li 2010), but at the same time, it limited the freedom of each institution to define its role in society. In the end of 1978, the Chinese leaders launched a national reform, aimed at speeding up economic development for modernizations. The reform was initiated in agriculture and industry first but soon spread to higher education.

Deng Xiaoping (1904–1997), the great leader and reformer who led China to a market economy in the 1980s, strongly believed in the application of Marxist materialism to socialist practice. His theory about emancipating the minds and seeking truth from practice set up a theoretical foundation for universities to take self-initiated actions for change (Deng 1978). Under his leadership, higher-education reform began in 1985 and was aimed at expansion and development to suit the needs of a market economy. The new direction in higher education reflected a revival of liberal ideas of modernization that emphasized legal and constitutional development. Gradually, the government relaxed its control over universities in terms of their operational settings. In 1998, a Higher Education Law was issued, providing legal protection for the rights of universities in a wide range of areas. As long as the Law is followed, universities may run on their own, responding to the needs of society. The areas for self-initiated action encompass student admissions, curriculum planning and development, pedagogy, research and innovation, internal governance regarding academic issues, resources, and personnel arrangements, also the management and use of the funds allocated by the state, the property provided by sponsors, and the contributions and donations received.

Furthermore, the state policies increased the national profile of universities in a move to boost enrollments and to create academic excellence through the strategic development of a set of national key projects, such as the 211 and 985 Projects, and other key national programs. The 211 Project was put forward in 1993 to develop 100 key universities and some key programs to a level of excellence comparable to the best in the world during the twenty-first century. Universities were expected to improve significantly the quality of their education, research, management, and institutional efficiency, and become the bases for training high-level professional manpower and solving major problems for the country's economic construction and social development. The 985 Project was announced in 1998 and aimed at creating a number of "first-rate universities of international advanced level." By 2009, 39 out of the 115 universities included in the 211 Project were selected for the more elite 985 Project. It included China's most prestigious universities, such as Peking University, Tsinghua University, Fudan University, and Zhejiang University. These universities have been entitled to a large amount of funding to develop research centers, host international conferences, and attract top researchers and academic leaders from overseas (Gu et al. 2009).

Along with the expansion in capacity, new state projects have also been put in place to improve the overall quality of higher education and to build a critical mass of scientists and innovators. One of these is The National Basic Research Program (also called the 973 Program), which was initiated in 1997 to launch innovation studies on major scientific issues relating to sustainable development, such as agriculture, energy, information, resources and environment, population and health, and materials. A second is the New Century Talent Project, which plans to identify 100 world-class scientists and specialists, 1,000 nationally recognized academic and innovative leaders, and 10,000 young scholars and scientists who have achieved success in their field of learning and play a leading role in their institutions. In company with this special recognition, the state also allocates a large sum of funding to each individual for development. These individuals are expected not only to provide leadership in education and research in their areas of expertise, but also to be upheld as role models for the whole nation (Du 2001).

The dynamics of these projects have changed the map of Chinese higher education. The universities administered by the Ministry of Education (MOE) have been strengthened by the state's substantial investment and become comprehensive and research oriented. Most specialist ministry universities have been given to provinces to administer or merged with universities under the MOE. Local universities also went through a similar exercise to participate in national and provincial programs. City universities rose as a result of new efforts made by local governments to contribute to higher-education development. Some of these have gradually merged into provincial or even national universities.

In this period, the government formally recognized university autonomy as an important factor in higher-education development. Autonomy as a way of thinking and a principle of action has served to liberate the minds of university members, as they have embraced the goal of ensuring higher education's contribution to the various modernization agendas. At the international level, the state has protected educational sovereignty through keeping universities as public institutions and aided some national universities to strive for world-class status. The fundamental principles regarding educational sovereignty have been consolidated in the Higher Education Law, which rules that Chinese universities must be controlled by the state and that a university president must be a Chinese citizen.

Global education, as a new initiative in higher education since 2000, has been developed according to state policies (Zheng 2009). Chinese universities have been proactively involved in global activities that include, but are not limited to:

- Satellite campuses and partnerships with foreign universities for student exchange, joint research, knowledge transfer, and even for-profit activities;
- Memberships in international university networks, such as the Worldwide Universities Network (WUN 2011);

- Connection with world-renowned scientists, scholars, and experts through academic appointments or awarding of honorary doctorates to foreign professors;
- Confucian Institutes in foreign countries established through partnerships with universities or other nongovernment organizations abroad, under the general guidance of the Chinese government;
- Enrollment of international students at all levels—doctoral, master's, undergraduate, visiting, and language studies. In 2010, there were 265,090 international students from 194 countries and regions. About 40 percent of the total student population were studying for academic degrees (Wang 2011).

At the national level, the meaning of autonomy is modified by the relationship between higher education and the government. While being protected by law, higher education has been continuously incorporated within the state under principles of macro planning and functions under the general direction of state policies. For instance, the newly published Outline of China's National Plan for Medium and Long-term Education Reform and Development (2010–2020) by the CPC has put universities on the path to achieve the development of a larger mass of critical scientists and the improvement of quality education over the next ten years (Yue et al. 2010). Universities have taken these policies as new opportunities to develop their capacities to respond to the needs of society. During this period, the expansion in capacity has been without precedent. In 1980, there were 675 higher-education institutions, with 1,144,000 full-time students. By 2010, there were 2,358 institutions, with student numbers increased to 22,317,929. Thus, within 30 years, students increased by 1,851 percent, with much of that growth coming in the first decade of the new century. Adult education and Internet-based courses have also increased greatly. The data available show that in 1995, there were 2,570,100 students in these forms of education, while by 2010, the number had reached 9,891,831, an increase of 285 percent within 16 years. Now China has the largest student population in the world, with an enrollment of 32.8 million students in all forms of higher education (Educational Statistics 2010).

The development and integration of adult education into the higher-education system has been an important factor in the transition from elite to mass higher education. Historically, there were conflicts between formal and informal or adult education, which reflected different ideological orientations. The support for informal education was aimed at maximizing opportunities for the majority of people, as against the formal education rooted in the scholar-official tradition and consolidated throughout the republican and socialist periods, which benefited a small percentage of the population. Hayhoe observed that during this period, "a renewed adult higher-education system was built upon the heritage of the non-formal sector" (1996, 118). Now the system has expanded to include independent institutions with programs offered through television, evening, adult, correspondence, and in-service types of adult education universities; schools of adult education within universities; the state national examination for self-studies, which was initiated in 1981 and gradually became institutionalized at the national, provincial, and local levels. Academic degrees are applied to adult education programs and their graduates enjoy the same treatment in employment, promotion, and admission to higher degree programs as graduates from a formal institution of higher education.

At the institutional level, the meaning of university autonomy is reflected in the activities that are identified under the category of "acting on one's own" and outlined in the Higher Education Law. This has resulted in both diversity and expansion in each institution individually. The university's tasks have been expanded beyond teaching and research to encompass social services, community development, and global education. Each institution has been able to set up its own development goals and undertake self-directed activities to achieve them. A case in point is the process of applying for admission to national key projects such as the 211 Project.

The leadership of the CPC on campus is continued through a governance model defined as a presidential responsibility system under the leadership of the Party committee. The president undertakes overall responsibility for the institution's teaching, research, and administrative affairs, while important decisions, such as the appointment of academic administrators at the department level and above, are made by the Party committee. Thus, a dual system of governance by the Party and the academic leadership exists across all organizational structures at university, college/school, and department levels. However, as the Party's role has been reshaped by the agenda of reform, the dual system has created a new mechanism to check internal operations and to keep a balance among various groups on campus.

Faculty's identity has been defined by law and consolidated through institutionalization of academic appointments and professional titles. Faculty as a professional group has grown enormously along with the changes in higher education. Their number increased from 247,000 in 1980 to 1,343,127 (of which 46 percent were females) in 2010 (Educational Statistics 2010). There are faculty councils, teaching and research centers, and many types of self-regulated committees. Teaching is no longer separated from research. Faculty are expected to be specialists in specific subject areas and become a role model for students. Ongoing faculty evaluation has been introduced and is connected with one's appointment, promotion, and pay.

Universities' expansion and diversification have enabled students to have more freedom and opportunities to pursue learning. While the enrollment is still largely determined by the national entrance examination, there are alternative admission methods that accept the assessments made by individual institutions including high schools and universities. In addition, a variety of adult-education programs and courses open a new path for students to pursue learning. Higher education is no longer free, as it was under the planned economy, as tuition fees have been introduced for almost all programs. At the same time, financial aid and loans are available to help students. Upon graduation, students must look for jobs by themselves as employment is no longer a governmental responsibility. Accordingly, student services on campus have expanded enormously to meet these needs.

These initiatives demonstrate a great degree of university autonomy, which can be observed in practical and even quantitative forms, such as enrollment expansion, new programs and specialties, student aid and services, personnel reform and appointment systems, institutional management, social development in terms of the emergence of all sorts of groups on campus, short- and long-term planning. In the center of these activities, it is evident that Chinese universities are always linking their own goals with national development.

Conclusion

The concept of university autonomy has been redefined in China along with the development of Chinese modern universities and one of the important factors is the application of knowledge to social practice. In the past century, Chinese universities have gone through a dramatic transformation from a closed system that served the state solely through preparing government officials to an open one that has embraced and critically adapted Western ideas of science and democracy for modernization. The transition has been quite dynamic. Before the Revolution of 1911, there was intellectual authority, which reflected the unity of the state and higher-education institutions. In the Republican period (1911–1949), university autonomy in the Western sense grew and took shape in the form of professorial governance on campus in particular and encouragement of innovative thinking among different schools of thought in general. In the Socialist period (1949–1978), university autonomy was replaced by a new form of bureaucracy—the unity of specialized knowledge and political authority, through which the state successfully incorporated the higher-education system into its macro planning. On campus, there was a loss of the professorial governance that had been established in the previous stage. In the Reform period (since 1978), the concept of university autonomy has taken a new form, as universities moved away from bureaucratic control toward a new status as legal persons, protected by law, and a scope of practice that has enabled them to initiate action for change in society. It is evident that in this process, the government's role in higher education has been transformed, too.

After all these years of learning from the West and from their own tradition, Chinese universities have ultimately stood up and identified themselves as a unique model. They have been shaped by a variety of models from the West, but no longer identify themselves with any Western model (Hayhoe 1996). Their focus on the unity of knowledge and action in the exercise of autonomy within government policies has demonstrated innovativeness and zeal for change, and Chinese universities' pursuit of knowledge in line with social progress has provided invaluable experience to the development of higher education in the world. This chapter has tried to summarize their experience of seeking knowledge in practice, as they have developed over the twentieth century.

REFERENCES

Bernstein, Thomas P., and Hua-yu Li, eds. 2010. *China Learns from the Soviet Union, 1949-Present.* Lanham, MD: Lexington Books.

Bunnin, Nicholas. 2003. "Contemporary Chinese Philosophy and Philosophical Analysis." *Journal of Chinese Philosophy* 30 (3–4): 341–356.

Chen, Sihui, ed. 2007. 新中国著名大学校长 1949–1983 [*Presidents of the Famous Universities in New China*]. Wuhan: Hubei Renmin Press.

Chiang, Monlin. 1963. *Chinese Culture and Education: A Historical and Comparative Survey.* Taipei: The World Book.

Cowart, Billy F. 1962. "The Development of the Idea of University Autonomy." *History of Education Quarterly* 2 (4): 259–264.

Deng, Xiaoping. 1978. "Emancipate the Mind, Seek Truth from Facts and Unite as One in Looking for the Future." *People's Daily,* Dec. 13. Beijing: Communist Party of China. Available online at: http://english.peopledaily.com.cn/dengxp /vol2/text/b1260.html.

Du, Minghua. 2001. "China to Launch New Century Talents Project." *People's Daily*, March 16. Beijing: Communist Party of China. Available online at: http://english.peopledaily.com.cn/english/200103/16/eng20010316_65224.html.

Ministry of Education, China. 2010. *Educational Statistics in 2010*. Beijing: Ministry of Education. Available online at: www.moe.edu.cn.

Fairbank, John K. 1949. "Communism in China and the New American Approach to Asia." In *Next Step in Asia* (pp. 1–24). London: Oxford University Press.

Fung, Edmund S. K. 2010. *The Intellectual Foundation of Chinese Modernity: Cultural and Political Thought in the Republican Era*. New York: Cambridge University Press.

Gu, Jianmin, Xueping Li, and Lihua Wang, eds. 2009. *Higher Education in China*. Paramus, NJ: Homa and Sekey Books.

Hayhoe, Ruth. 1984. "German, French, Soviet and American University Models and the Evolution of Chinese Higher Education Policy since 1911." PhD diss., University of London, London, UK.

Hayhoe, Ruth. 1989. *China's Universities and the Open Door*. Armonk, NY: M. E. Sharpe.

Hayhoe, Ruth. 1996. *China's Universities 1895–1995: A Century of Cultural Conflict*. New York and London: Garland Publishing Inc.

Hayhoe, Ruth. 2006. *Portraits of Influential Chinese Educators*. Hong Kong: Comparative Education Research Centre.

Hayhoe, Ruth, and Ningsha Zhong. 1997. "University of Autonomy and Civil Society." In *Civil Society in China*, ed. Timothy Brook and B. Michael Frolic (pp. 99–123). Armonk, NY: M. E. Shape.

Higher Education Law of the People's Republic of China. 1998. Beijing: Ministry of Education of the People's Republic of China Available online at: www.moe.edu.cn.

Huang, Chichung. 1997. *The Analects of Confucius*. Trans. by Chichung Huang. New York: Oxford University Press.

Israel, John. 1998. *Lianda: A Chinese University in War and Revolution*. Palo Alto, CA: Stanford University Press.

LaPolla, Randy. 2006. "Wang Li." In *Encyclopaedia of Language and Linguistics* (pp. 514–515). 2nd ed. Oxford: Elsevier. Available online at: www.sciencedirect.com.

Li, Lihua. 1989. "校长负责制" ["President Responsibility"]. In 教育管理词典 [*Encyclopedia of Education Administration*]. ed. in chief Ji Li (p. 162). Haikou: Hainan Renmin Chubanshe.

Li, Zhehou. 1994. 中国现代思想史论 [*On History of the Chinese Modern Thought*]. Hefei: Anhui Wenyi Press.

Ma, Yong. 1997. 蒋梦麟教育思想研究 [*On Jiang Menglin's Educational Thought*]. Shenyang: Liaoning Education Press.

Mahoney, David. 1994. "Government and the Universities: The 'New Mutuality' in Australian Higher Education—A National Case Study." *Journal of Higher Education* (Mar–Apr): 123–146.

Monahan, Edward J. 2004. *Collective Autonomy: A History of the Council of Ontario Universities 1962–2000*. Waterloo, ON: Wilfred University Press.

Nankai University. 2011, "About Nankai University." Tianjin: Nankai University. Available online at: www.nankai.edu.cn/english/.

National Basic Research Program of China. 2011. *The National Basic Research Program*. Beijing: National Basic Research Program of China. Available online at: http://www.973.gov.cn/English/Index.aspx.

Peking University. 2011. "Message from the Chair of the University Council." Peking: Peking University. Available online at: http://english.pku.edu.cn.

Thomson, James S. 1961. "The Responsibility of the University." *Canadian Universities Today*, ed. George Stanley and Guy Sylvestre. Toronto: University of Toronto Press.

Wang, Peng, ed. 2011. "Over 260,000 International Students Studying in China in 2010." *Ministry of Education of China News Update*, March 14.

Wildavsky, Ben. 2010. *The Great Brain Race: How Global Universities are Reshaping the World*. Princeton, NJ: Princeton University Press.

Worldwide Universities Network Homepage (WUN). 2011. Aukland: Worldwide University Network. Available online at: www.wun.ac.uk/.

Xin, Fuliang. 1992. 各国高等教育立法 [*Higher Education Law in Selected Countries*]. Shanghai: Shanghai Jiaotong University Press.

Yue, Xuying, Zongtang Zhang, Jing Wu, and Chao Zhao. 2010. "A Blueprint for Educational Modernization." July 31. Beijing: Ministry of Education. Available online at: www.moe.edu.cn.

Zhang, Dainian. 1982. 中国哲学大纲 [*The Outlines of Chinese Philosophy*]. New edition. Beijing: Zhongguo Shehui Kexue Press.

Zheng, Lin. 2009. "Chinese Universities' Motivations in Transnational Higher Education and Their Implementations for Higher Education Marketisation." In *Internationalising the University: The Chinese Context*, ed. Tricia Coverdale-Jones and Paul Rastall (pp. 33–56). New York: Palgrave Macmillan.

Zheng, Zhiguang, ed. 1989. 张伯苓传 [*Biography of Zhang Boling*].Tianjin: Tianjin Renmin Press.

Part III

Inquiries into Chinese Education Inspired by Ruth Hayhoe

Chapter 11

Childhood, Youth, and Globalization: Some Theoretical Perspectives with Reflections on China

Irving Epstein

It is a great privilege to participate in this book honoring the work of Ruth Hayhoe. Ruth has been a wonderful mentor and friend for over 25 years, and it is not an exaggeration to say that her support is largely responsible for the professional success I have achieved in my own career. Having said this, I do need to additionally note that it has occasionally been difficult being one of Ruth's colleagues. We, as academicians, are socialized into comparing our work and productivity with those of our colleagues and friends, not necessarily in the spirit of competition, but really, in order to measure our own impact upon our fields of engagement. And this is where it can be downright depressing to acknowledge that one is a colleague of Ruth's. As the foremost international scholar of Chinese higher education in the world, having also served as an academic administrator at the highest level in Hong Kong after successfully serving as an important Canadian diplomat, one cannot help but become depressed when Ruth has raised the bar for success to such an impossibly high degree. Such feelings are fleeting however, when one recognizes Ruth's exceptional achievements as a scholar, colleague, and above all, friend. That exceptionalism, which is not transferable to others, is evident in the ways in which her scholarship reflects her personal values, a connection that I find to be seamless.

What Ruth has taught me most is that ideas really do matter, and that they have an influence that extends beyond their origination. The notion that ideas travel across continents and cultures, and do impact different social groups in important and significant ways is not new. However, when applied to the Chinese case, where notions of Chinese cultural uniqueness have been traditionally promulgated by sinologists of all persuasion, be they from Asian, North American, or European backgrounds, the view that ideas have cross-cultural resonance regardless of their state of origin has not always met with strong support. Of course, Ruth not only documented the ways in which Chinese syncretism manifested itself in historical and contemporary contexts within the realm of higher education, but she encouraged others to look for similar patterns.

To be sure, Ruth has not only written about Chinese higher education but has made important contributions to the study of higher education globally where again, the power of ideas, particularly through her application of the ideas of Peace Studies theorist Johan Galtung, has proven persuasive and engaging (Hayhoe 1989). However, in doing so, the Chinese case is not simply held up to be an exemplar for other national/cultural cases, but it is used to further understand and appreciate the power and limits of global trends. In this chapter, my aim is to follow a similar structure, offering some comments regarding the sociology of the body literature and its impact upon our theoretical understanding of globalization forces, particularly as they are affecting children and youth, while examining the ways in which the contemporary Chinese case offers evidence for support for and/or resistance to the concepts and assumptions that have categorized these literatures.

Globalization and the Sociology of the Body

Globalization has become a buzz word over the past three decades for a number of phenomena, some of which are related to one another and some of which are discrete. For the purposes of our analysis though, we focus upon the ways in which it has fueled consumerist desire and the ways in which global consumption has influenced our understanding of children and youth. A basic premise of this chapter is that consumerism and consumption are not only artifacts of globalization, but are intrinsic to the ways in which global capitalism functions, as the insatiable demands for the fulfillment of consumerist desire have reached global dimensions, with very negative effects upon the lives of children and youth. To be sure, modes of global consumption also speak to other aspects of globalization, many of which are interrelated. Globalization can be associated with forces that challenge and contest conventional notions of fixed authority, as defined by the state and its political or geographical borders, as structured by conventional political and social institutions, and as formed by traditional ethnic, cultural, and social identities. Conventional categorizations of children and youth are being similarly contested. In the midst of such decenteredness, Zygmunt Bauman (2004) has argued that a focus upon "body" as a social site becomes critical to the expression of authority because it is the one space where individuals believe they have the ability to exercise control over the fundamental aspects of their own lives. Even if such control is ephemeral or contingent, it still is indicative of an intimacy with one's person that makes the prospect of control of one's life a rational possibility while surrounded by the prevailing uncertainty that globalization trends perpetuate. In any event, the importance of the "body" as a contributing mechanism to the understanding of globalization is clear because the increasing importance of consumerist desire, manufactured within the framework of those neoliberal principles that emphasize unregulated competition as a means of fueling such desire, speaks to many of the ways in which the "body" is being reconceptualized, creating dramatic effects upon the lives of children and youth. Although notions of childhood and youth have always been subject to construction and reinvention in response to larger social, economic, and political contexts, the contention here is that globalization trends have fundamentally altered long-standing views of children and youth.

Childhood and Globalization

It can be argued that this is a particular affectation of contemporary postindustrial societies where the blurring of childhood, youth, and adulthood has become even more prominent than may have previously been the case. What, for example, do conventional understandings of the distinct developmental stages of childhood and youth mean when 30-year-olds now regularly live at home with their parents, where teenagers are given some say in protecting their reproductive freedom, or when youth under the age of 16 years can be tried as adults for the commission of violent crimes (Mintz 2006)? And what does such blurring portend for children of all social classes, living in radically different circumstances within the developing, emerging, and postindustrial societies of the twenty-first century? However, aside from boundary issues involving the definitions of childhood, youth, and adulthood, an even more significant issue to be addressed involves the quality of children's lives, and whether it has changed significantly in a globalized era. One could assert that in actuality, the quality of children's lives has not changed greatly as a result of globalization. Few would disagree with the assertion that children have always been the victims of domestic violence and abuse, that they have perpetually lacked access to a decent education, and that they have traditionally been the first casualties of poverty. When one examines the practices affecting children that do not respect nation-state boundaries, be they early conscription and child soldiering, sex trafficking and exploitative child labor, or the spread of illness and disease that effect children specifically even when cures and treatments are available, it is difficult to argue with the conclusion that the state of the world's children reflects conditions that have always been present. According to this line of reasoning, it is the enhanced access to information and the increased speed with which information is transmitted that is different in the twenty-first century, making us more aware of the pervasive nature of those practices that continue to harm children, not any fundamental difference in the nature of those practices. Others can point to declining rates of infant mortality and increasing rates of years of school completion as indices of an actual improvement in the lives of children in the broadest of terms (United Nations Development Program 2011; United Nations Population Division 2011).

The alternative argument holds that something *is* qualitatively different because of the increasing tendency to reject the values of modernism, with its assumptions that discreet categories of past, present, and future exist and are viable. The worth of the child in the twenty-first century, it can be argued, is no longer defined by or tied to the future, either the child's own future, the family's future, or society's future. A corollary of this position is that without a future, the child is not worth preserving, protecting, or developing; her or his inherent or potential value is thus fundamentally compromised. Instead, the child holds ephemeral value only, intertwined with her or his perishability. Under such conditions, the lives of children are significant only insofar as their supply is never-ending and the opportunities for their exploitation boundless. Children thus exist in the twenty-first century in order to be consumed and then thrown away, as the draconian conditions governing their lives are continually reproduced with impunity. Indeed, the prevalence of sex trafficking, other exploitative forms of child labor, and child soldiering, is tied to their profitability, generated because of the small investment one has to make in order to perpetually exploit their services (Bales 2004).

Of course, we are used to notions of planned obsolescence as an affectation of the consumer culture that pervades contemporary life. However, it is only in the late twentieth and twenty-first centuries that the dehumanization that characterizes consumerism has become associated with the way in which we view children and youth. The association of a child with a perishable object, worthy only as an object of consumption, leads to a corollary view, forcefully articulated by Henry Giroux (2012): that children are contaminants that need to be expelled from the social body, disposed of, or eliminated completely. Their extinction thus becomes a necessary social good. How else can the following admittedly extreme examples be explained?

1. Politicians in the United States argue that the provision of the 14th amendment to the Constitution guaranteeing citizenship to anyone born within U.S. borders should be repealed, because children who fall into that category are undeserving of U.S. citizenship and should be deported (Benen 2010).
2. Roma children are systematically denied access to earliest forms of education (UNESCO 2007).
3. Juveniles are repeatedly imprisoned as adults in Iran, Saudi Arabia and Sudan, and continue to be executed for committing criminal offenses (Tomasevski 1986; Human Rights Watch 2010).
4. Street children face violence and death as paramilitary police in South America seek to drive them from visible urban spaces (Shinealight 2002).

In all of these cases, children and youth are viewed as contaminants with their presence generating inherent social harm. The ambiguity of their status and identity as children and youth vis-à-vis that of adults not only creates the license that legitimizes their exploitation, but it further leads to widespread social fear that, if acted upon, would logically lead to their extermination. To be sure, societies of all types experience differing forms of moral panic, whereby traditional values and conventional assumptions are questioned. The implementation of the one-child-family policy provoked such an occurrence in China, during the late 1970s and early 1980s, for example, as thoughtful individuals questioned the impact of the excessive spoiling of the single child upon her or his growth and character development, even without convincing evidence in support of such concern (Davin 1991). However, previous examples of moral panic, as the Chinese case illustrates, are qualitatively different from the vehemence with which contemporary children and youth are sometimes depicted. In the past, the handwringing that accompanied the discourse was voiced as part of conventional support for existing social institutions that simply needed to be reformed, be they the family, schools, or other social service providers. The subjects of their care were not directly attacked in the ways that contemporary children and youth experience.

Of course, there is an inherent contradiction in viewing the child (or more precisely her or his body) as being consumable, where one is in control of the object of exchange (buying, selling, producing), and the fear of the child (body) as a contaminant, where one needs to take extraordinary measures to prevent the child/body/other from taking over and inflicting harm upon the owner. How do we reconcile this contradiction? It seems to me that here, the notion of money as filthy lucre (or shameful profit) is instructive. The self-empowerment one feels through controlling the body by ridding oneself of the undesirable (feces) is no different in my view from efforts to depict children and youth as moral contaminants that can and should be physically and culturally eliminated. The process of objectifying children and youth and transforming them into commodities allows the owner to both accumulate the object and rid himself or herself of it; such actions are not mutually exclusive. Hence, what we have done in the twenty-first century, in the worst instances, is to treat children and youth as being no more or less than excrement, deserving of a treatment commensurate with that status. This is not to imply that children and youth necessarily and willfully accept such a status, but the concerted assault upon their basic dignity is structural and widespread.

This process of course plays out within a context of neoliberalism and globalization. The competitive pressures to secure short-term profit at any cost, enhanced with the understanding that the state will not intervene to protect its citizens from the negative consequences of the race to the bottom, define the neoliberal/globalized world. In such situations, there can be no permanent trust in institutions of the state, and the conditions under which collective social action occurs are tenuous, particularly because there is no consensus as to whether social goods exist or what they might entail. With such rabid individualism in play, every person becomes a threat to everyone else's survival.

However, the assumption that one can single handedly exert control over one's own body is not sustainable either, if one understands the body as a social site. The body as the sole source of authority becomes as ephemeral as the more traditional institutional structures that have been attacked in the neoliberal era. It is the unforgiving nature of neoliberalism that guarantees profit as forever being short term, and that artificially manufactures consumerist desire by creating the possibilities of exercising more and more individual choice, the results of which offer, at best, temporary satisfaction. Under such circumstances, competition not only rules but dehumanizes. The victims of neoliberal consumption and consumerism thus are not only the children and youth who are forced to lead lives where their dignity and personal worth are continuously compromised. From a broader perspective, the victims include the affluent as well, who equate their self-worth with the objects available for their consumption. The consequences of neoliberal dehumanization thus affect the affluent teen who equates her or his self-worth with the smart phone she or he wishes to possess, as well as the young girls and boys working in the factory sweatshops under slave-like conditions, who manufacture the very smart phones that are the objects of consumerist desire. Thus, in making the argument that our conceptions of childhood and youth have fundamentally changed in a globalized era, one necessarily views childhood and youth as being compromised regardless of social class, country of origin, or the extremely coercive circumstances one may confront in one's efforts to survive. The universalism of the values that equate human dignity with consumption has thus served to redefine childhood and youth generically and categorically. The fact that such values are exchanged and transferred among cross-cultural contexts reiterates Ruth Hayhoe's generic faith that the power of ideas and the practices they encourage is not constrained by geopolitical, national, or cultural boundaries.

Responses: Children, Youth, and the Children's Rights Field

What can one say about children's rights as a field, and how does such discourse influence policies that directly affect children's lives? Historically, the human rights movement arose in Europe when the expansion of print and other media touched the sensibilities of a nascent bourgeoisie, communicating the importance of the values of empathy and universality, preconditions for the acceptance of human rights as a viable concept (Hunt 2007). Early notions of human rights as entities to which autonomous individuals were entitled were revised with the growth of the nation state and nineteenth-century European nationalism. Not only did the state assume the role of chief protector of individual rights, but also the communitarian notion of nationhood asserted dominant-group control over the state, in defining what human rights could and should be protected. The international structures and instruments that were created in the twentieth century in order to promote and preserve human rights were constructed in ways that affirmed the primacy of the nation-state system among the various nation-state players became a key strategy within the human rights movement, as the right of the consensus-building state to determine how best to serve its citizens would remain unchallenged, except perhaps to avoid mass atrocity or similar human catastrophe (Hunt 2007).

With regard to children, it was therefore assumed that the family as a whole, rather than its individual members, was a viable independent economic unit, deserving of protection and support from the state but subject to minimal state interference. Even when the economic viability of the family unit was challenged by industrialism and the growth of the factory system, the state was reluctant to interfere: either through enforcing compulsory education laws or restricting child labor within factories. Again, these were concerns best left to the heads of households to resolve. As a result, the protection of children was never viewed as a fundamental obligation of the state; instead, the state would serve as a default when the family unit proved to be dysfunctional. The primacy of the family unit in traditional Chinese society, with its emphasis upon filial piety and reciprocity of obligation on the part of children and parents, also created contexts whereby the state was either reluctant to interfere in family matters so as to protect the rights of children, or it faced resistance when it did so (Wolf 1984).

The Convention on the Rights of the Child (CRC) was written with these assumptions in mind. Not only, as is true of all contemporary international instruments, was the Convention written to depend upon United Nations (UN) members to enforce its provisions, but its authors expressed conventional assumptions that viewed the family in traditional terms, and argued that parents were in the best position to address the needs of their children. It is noteworthy, though, that the authors of the Convention understood that children could not be solely dependent upon adults to protect their rights, hence the provision in the Convention that it be promoted in schools, and that youth be encouraged to have a formal say in policies determining their welfare (Articles 9, 13, and 15) (Office of UN High Commissioner for Human Rights 1990). Indeed, there has been a notable global expansion of human rights education as a part of school curricula, due in part to the worldwide growth of nongovernmental organizations (NGOs) working in this area (Ramirez et al. 2007). However, schools in actuality have had at best a mixed record in encouraging students to express themselves with a collective voice: their uncontested control of the formal and hidden curriculum proves to be a significant barrier in this regard (Cox et al. 2010).

The CRC has received near-unanimous ratification by the member states of the UN (the United States and Somalia being the two notable exceptions). And a rigorous reporting system to the Commission on the Rights of the Child, allowing NGO evidence to supplement formal state reports, has helped to promote international consensus-building with regard to what universal principles determining the best interests of the child really mean. However, as a late-twentieth-century document, it is clear that the CRC also has significant limitations that influence its effectiveness in the global climate we currently experience. The contradiction that we have noted, between relying upon the traditional family unit as protector of the child, while encouraging child self-advocacy because of the ineffectiveness of the former, is not its only limitation. Because of its reliance upon the nation state as the ultimate guarantor of the child's interests, the original Convention's effectiveness in addressing cross-national and cross-cultural problems, whether they involve migration, sex trafficking, or child soldiering, was limited. Thus, optional protocols on child soldiering and trafficking, designed to explicitly address these issues, were constructed after the adoption of the original document. A final criticism involves the modernist assumptions of the Convention with regard to the efficacy of state institutions acting in good faith to protect children's interests. In short, the very institutions that failed children in the past—schools, welfare agencies, juvenile justice systems—were promoted as having the potential to protect children for the present and in the future. The Convention thus has little to say to the children living in failed states, whose families have been destroyed by AIDS or civil unrest, and have no prospect of obtaining an adequate support system that would allow them to survive, let alone thrive. As will be discussed later, the China case both conforms to and offers contradictory evidence for these trends.

What then can be said about the "field" of children's rights? The rules of the children's rights field are fairly explicit. First, the use of the term "best interests of the child," as opposed to the more explicit use of rights language as a part of the discourse involving the state of children globally, demonstrates the limits to which adults recognize children's individual autonomy as thinking and feeling individuals, and their identity as a cohesive social group. Normally, the use of the term "right" involves a recognition of the need to protect an individual or group that because of its status, class position, and others (O'Neil 1996). Yet, as has been noted, the ambiguity that accompanies the definition of what constitutes a child is translated into institutional ambivalence with regard to her or his protection, let alone the roles of the state in offering such protection. The CRC framework thus creates a set of vertical hierarchical relationships between the child (individual) and her or his family, and relevant state institutions, whereby one's cultural and social capital is spent on negotiating space within this hierarchy: as family member, student, worker, and the like. The contradictions that arise when the rules within the field break down become clear: Family membership is sacrificed as children are forced to leave the unit in order to work full time, away from home; the imperative placed upon schools to foster citizenship is compromised as students realize the disconnect between what their education promises and what it delivers, with regard to employment opportunity and participatory civic engagement. It is therefore not surprising that children and youth no longer play conventional roles and instead are forced into accepting ones that are characterized by their ambiguity rather than ones that clearly mark distinctions between childhood, youth, and adulthood. As a result, they look to different forms of social and political capital that resonate more clearly with their habituses (learned dispositions acquired through daily interactions with one's external environment). The emotional capital that African girls employ in pursuing university education in spite of profound cultural and structural obstacles that are placed in their pathways (Manion 2007), the practical survival strategies that street children effectively employ that allow them to survive with their dignity and self-worth in place, and the reliance that former child soldiers display in reconnecting to families and reintegrating with their home communities upon their release from captive situations (Boyden and de Berry 2004) are examples of the ways in which children and youth bend and transform the negative and at times hurtful roles to which they have been traditionally ascribed, without depending upon conventional modernist state institutions to do so.

It would be overly simplistic to argue that twenty-first-century children and youth have shown an ability to express an independent, collective voice, in opposition to the structural violence that has so often threatened their physical existence. And, it would be naïve to suggest that the effects of state institutions upon children and youth—through their policies and practices that practice inclusion through decontextualization, or exclusion through categorization—are easily resisted. This is particularly true with regard to schooling. However, the very forces that state institutions have such difficulty confronting—transnationalism, capital and cultural flows, technological innovation, and consumption—have affected some children and youth in ways that occasionally ameliorate the worst excesses of global neoliberalism and have allowed them to exert a degree of agency that is quite surprising. The growth of social networking and the ease with which youth have embraced newer technologies to promote engagement with the global dimensions of music, art, fashion, and politics give rise to some hope that information and cultural flows can be structured to support actions that are inherently liberating.

From a structural perspective, the information age has encouraged the growth of horizontal rather than vertical social relationships (Castells 2001), and such relationships, marked by the speed and flexibility of their communicative character, further encourage twenty-first-century youth to engage in hybrid identities and a multiplicity of social roles. Youth who live in the Middle East, and are devoutly religious, text their global friends or listen to hip hop while wearing traditional clothing, without seeing any contradictions in their behavior, negotiating between the multiplicity of identities those different roles imply, expressing comfort in each of them.

Young South Asian women participate in local beauty pageants, but seek to balance indigenous and exogenous notions of commercialized beauty in the process (Lukose 2008). Youth-oriented NGOs have had beneficial effects upon reforming educational and social policies, including the limiting of corporal punishment in Nepalese schools, or the promotion of children's radio programming in Ghana (Manful 2010). Furthermore, as recent events in the Middle East suggest, highly educated Egyptian youth, with all of the reasons in the world to feel politically alienated if not embittered, given the disconnect between their educational attainment and their work opportunities, engage in the highest levels of participatory democracy through using the tools of the Internet and social networking to help bring down an authoritarian government through nonviolent means.

Two concepts that have particular relevance to our discussion include "glocalization" or the ability of groups to think globally while acting locally, balancing their awareness of global tendencies with an understanding of local context (Robertson 1995), and "cosmopolitanism," or the view that all human beings belong to a single community that should be cultivated (Appiah 2006). Both views are salient to an understanding of the ways in which twenty-first-century youth balance the practical and ethical demands of living in societies where fixed identities as expressed through conventional political and social roles no longer make sense to them. Certainly, the notion of cosmopolitanism assumes that global awareness invites an ethical imperative, while the concept of glocalization (along with softer forms of cosmopolitanism) asserts that an understanding of universalist policies need not compromise an affinity for local practices, although it might create some pressure for redefining and reinventing those practices. As alternatives to the fetishizing of individualism present within classical notions of Western liberalism, or the rigidity with which groups are defined and bounded within traditional conceptions of communitarianism, these concepts can be viewed as progressive. To the extent that they argue against the determinism implicit in conventional understandings of globalization, they are informative, and they speak to the aspirations a significant number of children and youth express.

To sum up, there are contesting claims as to whether or not the state of children and the ways in which children and youth are perceived are fundamentally different in a globalized era from those of previous centuries. Competing views are also offered as to whether the consumerism that characterizes twenty-first-century globalization is inherently degrading and destructive of children's dignity, let alone their ability to materially survive, or whether the contingent nature of social relationships and organizations as an artifact of the information age offers children and youth new possibilities for pursuing self-expression, even if those possibilities are subject to movement and flux. Although it can plausibly be argued that both sets of arguments contain degrees of truth, to me, it is the view that children and youth are being perceived and treated in fundamentally different ways from those of previous centuries that is more compelling.

The China Case

One can also examine the China case as it refers to the lives of contemporary children and youth from varying perspectives. However, underlying such analyses are perceptions of China itself and its relationship with globalization trends. To be sure, both the strengths and weaknesses of Edward Said's *Orientalism* framework (1979) can be applied to the China case. As a tabular rasa for Western scholars who constructed images of China conversant with their own values, it is easy to see how scholars have situated Chinese history, politics, and culture within a frame of reference with which they felt comfortable. Indeed, Jesuit efforts to reconceptualize Confucius according to Christian terms represent one historical example of this effort (Jensen 1997). More recent scholarly writing that promotes Chinese economic development as the embodiment of global capitalism gives further evidence for this contention. To be sure, the association of Confucian values with economic success was noted by both Western and Chinese intellectuals, particularly with the rise of the Four Tigers (Hong Kong, Singapore, Taiwan, and South Korea) as NICS (newly industrialized countries) after 1970 (Tu 1996). And, the essentialism that characterizes the depiction of neo-Confucianism through the promotion of its global dissemination is problematic regardless of the source of authorship be they Western or Chinese intellectuals. However, one can also view the construction of Pacific Rim Studies in the 1980s as a hegemonic attempt on the part of the West to mark and control scholarly discourse about Asia (Dirlik 1997). Thus, the admonition that fitting the study of China within a globalization framework is simply another attempt to reify a Western perspective, and place discourse about China within that perspective, should be taken seriously.

Nonetheless, while cognizant of the fact that China was a distinct political entity prior to the emergence of the nation-state concept, issues regarding the appropriate ways of defining national identity continue to be salient to the Chinese people in an era where the globalization processes that have been previously noted are so prominent. Hence, whether the economic and political changes that have occurred within China over the past four decades—including rapid economic development accompanied by economic liberalization, political decentralization, privatization and the corporatization of local politics, foreign investment, and growing structural economic and social inequality, or the country's use of soft power to expand its presence as a world power—are characteristics that affirm the traditional cultural values of the Chinese people or reiterate the basic characteristics of neoliberalism and global capitalism, it seems fair to note that Chinese citizens and policy makers are at the very least more aware of their global standing and are more apt to measure the worth of these policies in comparative terms.

Addressing questions of globalization and national identity with specific reference to the lives of children and youth offer ambiguous answers. One can argue, for example, that Chinese children and youth have borne the harsh effects of global capitalism enforced according to Chinese norms. In doing so, one would point to the negative effects political decentralization and global investment policies have had generally, upon large sections of the Chinese population, with children and youth suffering directly from their implementation. The sweatshop conditions young girls confront when migrating from rural areas to urban locations have been documented for three decades, yet their presence remains undeterred as the suicide attempts at the Foxconn Longhua factory plant in March 2010 (Ricker 2010; Duhigg and Barbarosa 2012) or the horrific conditions at the KYE factory in Dongguan in June 2010 attest. Such events speak to larger concerns regarding environmental justice as well, given the preponderance of e-waste recycling that has created adverse health conditions in rural areas, the ultimate product of the sweat equity the young girl and women migrants produce for an electronics industry that benefits from lax governmental regulation (Worldwatch Institute), nor are the educational opportunities for migrant children, who make up 19.82 million of the over 120 million members of China's floating population, particularly robust (Wei and Jou 2010). The creation of special schools for these children by migrant families themselves, supported by philanthropic external funding, speaks to the few incentives regular school administrators have in opening their doors to these children. Given the second-class citizenship that is structured by a registration system that makes it nearly impossible for rural migrants to obtain the appropriate residence permit, there are minimal incentives for schools to abandon exclusive policies that restrict the enrollment of these children, particularly at the middle and upper secondary levels (Wei and Jou 2010). The private or nonprofit alternatives that have been created are generally acknowledged to have inferior resources (Kwong 2004). In short, educational policies serve to ossify class distinctions between migrants and the permanent urban working populations within Chinese cities (Solinger 1995, 1999).

Similarly, non-Han ethnic minority children confront the effects of unequal educational opportunity even when one controls for geographical region and family (Hannum 2002), while gender discrimination remains pervasive particularly in rural areas (Hannum et al. 2009). To be sure, in spite of China's laudable and largely successful efforts to implement basic universal and compulsory education, the discrepancy of resources, the disparate poverty their families confront, and lack of an effective social service safety net strongly work against rural children staying in school and reaping the benefits of significant educational attainment (Hannum and Adams 2009).

Looking at the state of Chinese children from a larger perspective, in spite of China's overall impressive economic development over the past 30 years, over 100 million are still living on less than two dollars a day, their health conditions are similar to those living in poor countries, and China remains one of the top five countries in the world for infant mortality below the age of five years (UNICEF-China 2011). Interestingly, even in urban China, children remain uncovered by the State Council "Decision on Establishing Basic Medical Insurance System," established in late 1998, while services provided for maternal and infant care are not always free (Law Library of Congress). With regard to the sale and trafficking of children, China remains in the Tier 2 category as assessed by the United States State Department, as enforcement of the Criminal Law remains inconsistent (Law Library of Congress). Six hundred and fifty thousand Chinese children are estimated to be HIV/AIDS infected and half of all new HIV infections occur among young people (UNICEF-China), with the stigma attached to the illness affecting treatment and prevention.

However, even children and youth who reap the advantages of China's market economy face pressures that reflect neoliberal and consumerist priorities. In spite of efforts to reform school curricula, one's educational experience remains examination driven, with the competition for placement in higher-status institutions made even more severe through efforts to concentrate resources in secondary schools with high-performing students, the pressures for creating "world-class" higher-education universities driving many of these competitive pressures. The match between educational attainment and employment opportunity lacks congruence, and the fears of being unemployed or underemployed are very real for Chinese youth regardless of their educational level, fears exacerbated by neoliberal policies (Zhang 2006). Not surprisingly, discussions of children's rights within schools, as required by the CRC, do not occur on a regular basis, and as we are aware, efforts on the part of the government to control Internet usage, blogging, and the social networking that results from technology usage are pervasive. Thus, one could argue that the results of globalization are affecting Chinese children and youth in much the same way as their counterparts throughout the world: Consumerist desire that legitimizes global capitalist principles is in fact commodifying the lives of Chinese children and youth in ways that threaten their safety, survival, and basic humanity.

In making the alternative argument, however, one would stress the existence of other factors that allow us to come to a differing conclusion. One could note, for example, the fact that the expansion of basic educational provision to most of the country's children is an accomplishment that should not be underestimated. One could argue that with regard to the basic protection of children on a formal basis, the Chinese state has not done badly given its population size, with implementation efforts rather than central governmental policy per se hindering initiatives in this area (the field of juvenile justice would be a notable exception to this rule). While acknowledging the lack of formal curricular space for children and youth to understand children's rights issues within schools, one can point to growing efforts to introduce environmental awareness to children and youth in educational settings (Lin and Ross 2004; Li and Dong 2010). And, one can view the growth of Internet usage in spite of censorship pressures, as allowing Chinese youth to critique political corruption and unfairness through the power of social networking that such usage invites in powerful and compelling if not always positive ways (Zheng 2008; Liebold 2010).

To be sure, survey research has indicated that Chinese youth express strong familiarity with and appreciation for Western consumer and cultural artifacts. Their values include an anti-authoritarian individualism and a reluctance to engage in formal political participation, coupled with a strong nationalist belief in China's future ascendancy as the premier world power. However, they also express faith in a better future, future employment worries notwithstanding (Rosen 2009). One also notes evidence of glocalization in the Chinese context, as documented by James Watson in his study of Asian fast-food restaurants and the traditional cultural artifacts they assimilate into their operations, or aspects of transnationalism, as migration flows between China and the West are no longer solely unidirectional, nor geographically bounded (Watson 2005, 2010). Certainly, the recognition of Western discourses involving early childhood education signify the ability of China's growing middle class to syncretize competing value claims (Hoffman and Zhao 2008), an ability one can argue China's youth also express. In short, the alternative argument emphasizes both the persistence of cultural values and norms that have allowed at least a significant number of Chinese people to negotiate the neoliberal principles of global capitalism according to their own terms, and Chinese youth represent one sector of this group.

Conclusion

In this chapter, I have rejected the contentions that the struggles children confront in the twenty-first century are similar to those of their predecessors. Globalization truly involves a set of conditions that are not only unique, but reframe traditional notions of childhood in compelling ways. I also reject the view that there are multiple childhoods, so distinct from one another that the use of the term can be questioned. To be sure, the conditions to which the world's children and youth are subjected vary tremendously, but it is my view that the ethos of consumerism, buttressed by neoliberal and global capitalist principles, categorically and uniformly marks the lives of children and the way in which they are viewed in spite of the immediate circumstances to which they are exposed. If one agrees with this contention, then the sociology of the body literature becomes particularly informative when one considers the body as a contested social site and a source of legitimacy for policies and practices to which children and youth are exposed, a site that also becomes authoritative and self-referential for youth themselves.

The Chinese case supports this view but is also illustrative of its limitations. Chinese children and youth are certainly affected by the consumerism that global capitalism promotes, often in ways that are no less harsh than those that threaten the lives of the poorest children in the world. With the exception of child soldiering, every major issue that negatively affects children's lives on a global basis is present in China. And, even those youth privileged enough to enter China's nascent middle class confront the competitive pressures for educational and employment advancement that are more frequently being defined in global terms. At the same time, the ethos of choice that consumerist culture legitimizes, and the tentative agency that it has the potential to sponsor, is also present in the behavior and attitudes of contemporary Chinese youth. The impact of new media, while fostering the same types of digital divides that are common between privileged and less-privileged social groups in the global context, is also apparent in China. Hence, the opportunities for engaging in social networking and building social capital are as evident there as in other international settings, if not more so.

Yet, there are significant differences that are apparent as well. First, the Chinese version of global capitalism, while encouraging a decentralized corporatism at local levels, concomitant with creeping privatization of education at the higher levels, has yet to abandon, at least rhetorically, the view that education is a basic social good that is deserving of political and social protection. The contention that educational opportunity provides the best means of guaranteeing a better future regardless of one's social position remains ideologically potent, and even fuels the growing materialism among those youth entering China's nascent middle class (Rosen 2010; Wang and Ross 2010). Second, although Chinese youth do use electronic technology and the media as a means of expressing their voices in ways that are autonomous, independent and at times critical of the formal policies of government agencies, they demonstrate conflicting levels of civic engagement and political participation. On the one hand, even state-sanctioned youth-oriented NGOs stake out autonomous positions for themselves that are surprising for their independence (Lu 2010). In addition, their use of social networking has assisted in efforts to combat corruption and cronyism, providing a powerful voice in the absence of more permanent organizations one would conventionally see as promoting civil society. However, one can also view the attitudes of Chinese youth as less liberal and more individualistic when compared to their global counterparts (Rosen 2010). Their willingness to disavow formal political engagement while expressing strong nationalist views is not a characteristic that is clearly in evidence globally.

Suffice it to conclude that in this area, as in so many others, Ruth Hayhoe's belief in the power of ideas to shape policies and practices, be they progressive or regressive, is reaffirmed. The challenges globalization forces create for those who care deeply about the lives of children and youth are daunting; the possibilities they invite with regard to advancing new forms of expression, new types of social relationships, and new avenues for exercising personal agency are intriguing. The Chinese case further reiterates that context matters: that traditional beliefs that speak to the importance of moral cultivation, the unity of thought and action, and the importance of education for purposes of individual and collective transformation maintain some influence in a society that is part of a world marked by its increasingly transitory nature. At the same time, the authoritarian tendencies that continue to shape Chinese politics and society remind us that there are large parts of the world resistant to the positive transformative possibilities globalization forces invite. Those of us concerned about the lives of children and youth in the twenty-first century would do well to take into account the Chinese case as a necessary corrective against analysis that is overreaching. At the same time, those of us concerned about our understanding of Chinese children and youth specifically would do well to move beyond holistic cultural narratives

222 IRVING EPSTEIN

that do a disservice to the complex ways in which they and their parents resist, address, negotiate, and embrace practices influenced by globalization forces.

REFERENCES

Appiah, Kwame. 2006. *Cosmopolitanism: Ethics in a World of Strangers.* New York, NY: Norton.

Bales, Kevin. 2004. *Disposable People: New Slavery in the Global Economy.* Berkeley, CA: University of California.

Bauman, Zygmunt. 2004. "A Sociological Theory of Postmodernity." In *Contemporary Sociological Theory,* ed. Craig Calhoun, Joseph Gerteis, James Moody, Steven Pfaff, and Indermohan Verk. Oxford, UK: Blackwell.

Benen, Steve. 2010. "House Republicans Call for Deportation of U.S. Citizens." *Washington Monthly,* April 28. Available online at: www.washingtonmonthly.com.

Boyden, Jo, and Joanne de Berry. 2004. "Introduction." In *Children and Youth on the Front Line,* ed. Jo Boyden and Joanne de Berry. New York, NY: Berghan Books.

Castells, Manuel, 2001. *The Internet Galaxy.* New York, NY: Oxford.

Cox, Sue, Robinson-Pant, Anna, Dyer, Caroline, and Schweisfurth, Michele. 2010. "Introduction." In *Children as Decision-Makers in Education: Sharing Experiences across Cultures,* ed. Sue Cox, Anna Robinson-Pant, Caroline Dyer, and Michele Schweisfurth (pp. 1–5). London: Continuum.

Davin, Delia. 1991. "The Early Childhood Education of the Only Child Generation in Urban China." In *Chinese Education: Problems, Policies and Prospects,* ed. Irving Epstein. New York, NY: Garland.

Dirlik, Arif. 1997. *The Postcolonial Aura: Third World Criticism in the Age of Global Capitalism.* Boulder, CO: Westview Press.

Duhigg, Charles, and David Barbarosa. 2012. "In China, the Human Costs that Are Built into an iPad." *New York Times,* January 25. Available online at: www.nytimes.com.

Giroux, Henry. 2012. *Disposable Youth: Racialized Memories and the Culture of Cruelty.* New York: Routledge.

Hayhoe, Ruth. 1989. *China's Universities and the Open Door.* Armonk, NY: M.E. Sharpe.

Hannum, Emily. 2002. "Educational Stratification by Ethnicity in China: Enrollment and Attainment in the Early Reform Years." *Demography* 39 (1): 95–117.

Hannum, Emily, and Jennifer Adams. 2009. "Beyond Cost: Rural Perspectives on Barriers to Education." In *Creating Wealth and Poverty in Postsocialist China,* ed. Deborah Davis and Fang Wang. Palo Alto, CA: Stanford University.

Hannum, Emily, Peggy Kong, and Yuping Zhang. 2009. "Family Sources of Educational Gender Inequality in Rural China: A Critical Assessment." *International Journal of Educational Development* 29 (5): 474–486.

Hoffman, Diane, and Guoping Zhao. 2008. "Global Convergence and Divergence in Childhood Ideologies and the Marginalization of Children." In *Education and Social Inequality in the Global Culture*, ed. Joseph Zadja, Karen Biraimah, and William Guadelli. New York, NY: Springer.

Hunt, Lynn. 2007. *Inventing Human Rights*. New York, NY: Norton.

Human Rights Watch. 2010. *Iran, Saudi Arabia, Sudan: End Juvenile Death Penalty*. New York: Human Rights Watch. Available online at: www.hrw.org.

Jensen, Lionel. 1997. *Manufacturing Confucianism: Chinese Traditions and Universal Civilization*. Durham, NC: Duke University Press.

Kwong, Julia. 2004. "Educating Migrant Children: Negotiations between the State and Civil Society." *China Quarterly* (180): 1073–1088.

Law Library of Congress. *Children's Rights: China*. (n.d.). Retrieved April 5, 2011. Washington, DC: Library of Congress. Available online at: www.loc.gov.

Li, Xiaoyun, and Qiang Dong. 2010. "China's Environmental Education." *Chinese Education and Society* 43 (2): 6–15.

Liebold, James. 2010. "More Than a Category: Han Supremacy on the Internet."*China Quarterly* (203): 539–559.

Lin, Jing, and Heidi Ross. 2004. "Environmental Crises, Governmental Policies, and 'Green Schools' in China." *Chinese Education and Society* 37 (3): 5–102.

Lu, Yiyi. 2010. "The Autonomy of Chinese NGOs." In *Politics of Modern China: Volume IV: Democratization*, ed. Yongnian Zheng, Yiyi Lu, and Lynn T. White. New York: Routledge (reprinted from *China: An International Journal* 2007, 5 (2): 173–203).

Lukose, Ritty. 2008. "The Children of Liberalization: Youth Agency and Globalization in India." In *Youth Moves: Identities and Education in Global Perspective*, ed. Nadine Dolby and Fazal Rizvi. New York, NY: Routledge.

Manful, Esmerana. 2010. "Children's Participation: Radio as a Medium in Ghana." In *Children as Decision-Makers in Education: Sharing Experiences across Cultures*, ed. Sue Cox, Anna Robinson-Pant, Carolyn Dyer, and Michele Schweisfurth. London: Continuum.

Manion, Carolyn. 2007. "Feeling, Thinking, Doing: Emotional Capital, Empowerment and Women's Education." In *Recapturing the Personal: Essays on Education and Embodied Knowledge in Comparative Perspective*, ed. Irving Epstein. Charlotte, NC: Information Age Publishing.

Mintz, Steven. 2006. *Huck's Raft: A History of American Childhood*. Cambridge, MA: Harvard University.

O'Neill, Onora. 1996. "Children's Rights and Children's Lives." In *Children's Rights Revisioned: Philosophical Readings*, ed. Rosalind. E. Ladd. Belmont, CA: Wadsworth.

Ramirez, Francisco O., David Suarez, and John W. Meyer. 2007. "The Worldwide Rise of Human Rights Education." In *School Knowledge in Comparative and Historical Perspective*, ed. Aaron Benavot and Cecilia Braslavsky. Hong Kong and Dordrecht, The Netherlands: Comparative Education Research Center: University of Hong Kong and Springer.

Ricker, T. 2010. "Five Foxconn Workers Attempt Suicide in Last Month, Are We the Cause?" New York: *Engadget/AOL*. Available online at: www.engadget .com.

Robertson, Roland. 1995. "Glocalization: Time-Space and Homogeneity-Heterogeneity." In *Global Modernities*, ed. Mike Featherstone, Scott Lash, and Roland Robertson. London, UK: Sage.

Rosen, Stanley. 2009. "Contemporary Chinese Youth and the State." *Journal of Asian Studies* 68 (2): 359–369.

Rosen, Stanley. 2010. "The Victory of Materialism: Aspirations to Join China's Urban Moneyed Classes and the Commercialization of Education." In *Politics of Modern China: Volume III: Political Sociology*, ed. Yongnian Zheng, Yili Lu, and Lynn T. White (pp. 27–51). New York: Routledge (reprinted from *The China Journal* 2004, 51).

Said, Edward. 1979. *Orientalism*. New York: Vintage Books.

Shinealight. 2002. *The Current Conditions of Street Life in Colombia*. Sao Paolo, Bogota and Mexico City: Shinealight. Available online at: www.shinealight .org.

Solinger, Dorothy. 1995. "The Floating Population in the Cities. Chances for Assimilation?" In *Urban Spaces in Contemporary China*, ed. Deborah Davis, Richard Kraus, Barry Naughton, and Elizabeth. Washington, DC: Woodrow Wilson Press.

Solinger, Dorothy. 1999. *Contested Citizenship in Urban China: Peasant Migrants, the State and the Logic of the Market*. Berkeley, CA: University of California Press.

Tomasevski, Katerina. 1986. *Children in Adult Prisons*. New York, NY: St. Martins Press.

UNESCO. 2007. *Towards Quality Education for Roma Children: Transition from Early Childhood to Primary Education*. Final Report. Paris: UNESCO. Available online at: http://unesdoc.unesco.org.

Tu, Wei-ming. 1996. *Confucian Traditions in East Asian Modernity: Moral Education and Economic Culture in Japan and the Four Mini-Dragons*. Cambridge, MA: Harvard University Press.

UNICEF-China. n.d. *HIV/AIDS*. New York: UNICEF. Available online at: Unicef.org/china/hiv_aids.html.

United Nations. 1990. *Convention on the Rights of the Child*. New York: Office of Untied Nations High Commissioner on Human Rights. Available online at: www2.ohchr.org/english/law/crc.htm.

United Nations Development Programme (UNDP). 2011. "Human Development Report: Table 2, Human Development Index Trends 1980–2011." New York: UNDP. Available online at: http://hdr.undp.org.

United Nations Population Division (UNDP). 2011. "World Population Prospects: The 2010 Revision." New York: United Nations Population Division. Available online at: http://esa.un.org/unpd/wpp/index.htm.

Wang, Yimin, and Heidi Ross. 2010. "Experiencing the Change and the Continuity of the College Entrance Examination." *Chinese Education and Society* 43 (4): 75–93.

Watson, James L. 2005. "China's Big Mac Attack." In *The Cultural Politics of Food and Eating: A Reader*, ed. James L. Watson and Melissa L. Caldwell (pp. 70–79). New York, NY: Wiley-Blackwell.

Watson, James L. 2010. "Forty Years on the Border: Hong Kong/China." *ASIANetwork Exchange* 18 (1): 10–23.

Wei, Jianwei, and Jiawei Hou. 2010. "The Household Registration System, Education System, and Inequalities in Education for Migrant Children." *Chinese Education and Society* 43 (5): 77–89.

Wolf, Margery. 1984. "Marriage, Family, and the State in Contemporary China." *Pacific Affairs* 57 (2): 213–236.

Worldwatch Institute. n.d. *China's E-waste Problem: Facing Up to the Challenge.* Washington, DC: Worldwatch Institute. Available online at: www.worldwatch .org.

Zhang, Libin. 2006, February 28. *Globalization and Its Effects on Youth Employment in China* Beijing: Ministry of Labor and Social Security. Available online at: www.slideshare.net.

Zheng, Yongnian. 2008. *Technological Empowerment: The Internet, State, and Society in China.* Palo Alto, CA: Stanford University Press.

Chapter 12

Sustainable International Cross-cultural Collaboration: Transcending "Brain Drain" and "Borrowing" Models

Vilma Seeberg and Haiyan Qiang

Introduction

This is the story of an expanding net of international collaborations that grew out of an innovative Canada–China higher education development aid project. The main actors are Chinese and North American scholars.[1] The story traces three expanding circles of scholars and their ripple effects as China opened to the world and before an elite had accumulated enough wealth to send its children to North American universities.

The story is noteworthy because it shows how a government-sponsored development assistance project resulted in the formation of an international network of educator–activists rather than the all-too-common unidirectional *brain drain* from China to the West. This story is characterized by a *reverse flow*[2] of knowledge and scholars that characterizes instead a "global cultural dialogue" (Yang 2011).

In this chapter, we focus on collaborations initiated by scholars at a Chinese national-level university and Professor Ruth Hayhoe in the field of education. We make no claims of scientific representativeness; rather, we will describe the perceptions of three main actors regarding second-generation projects and other diverse offshoots, and offer an analysis of the scholars' interpretation regarding the essential elements that lead to expansion, diversification, and sustainability.

The story is far from over. The collaborations continue to evolve transcontinental projects. We suggest that the knowledge and resource transfers of these kinds of collaborations are so fruitful, though unquantifiable, that they may go a long way toward counterbalancing the losses of the unilateral, easily quantifiable, *brain drain*. These are vital educational programs, originating and operating in civic space that support equality of access to quality public education. The affiliated projects have been knit together by the actions of individuals. We can observe that individual, private efforts can lead to public nongovernmental organizations, and can implement locally controlled, appropriate educational projects that have far-reaching and beneficial effects both locally and internationally.

Methodology

To fulfill the purpose of the study, we chose a descriptive and interpretive methodology, starting with a narrative description of interview findings, and identifying emerging themes and patterns along the way. The participants member-checked the descriptions and interpretations for authenticity and accuracy. Three open-ended questions served as the interview protocol. The three key participants were asked to reflect on the how and why of the many educational collaborations and exchange activities:

1. Describe the international collaborations, their origin and history (first generation).
2. Describe the sideline or offshoot projects or subsequent funded and unfunded projects that grew out of them (second generation).
3. What are the reasons that the original government-sponsored one-way development aid projects were succeeded by multiple, diverse, collaborative projects?

We found that themes that emerged in the interviews fell within theories of multiculturalism and cross-cultural relations, and therefore we used a multicultural analytical lens for organizing the subjective interpretations of the participants.

Reconceptualizing International Scholarly Relations in Education

Worldwide, the larger context of international scholarly exchange has been development education. In the postcolonial reconstruction era, projects were funded to transfer advanced countries' educational systems or parts thereof to countries that were lagging economically. This practice simulated economic and power relations between countries that divided the international community into borrowers and lenders (see Arnove 1980 for a longer review of world systems theory) to the extent that Boli and Ramirez (1992, 15) maintain that "the European model of a national society (and its public educational system) has become so deeply institutionalized as a world model. . . .that in late-developing countries. . . . it is. . . . [simply] imposed." By the 1970s, voices in "developing" nations and among "Western" educators were raising strong critiques of education development aid programs as designed to profit the donor or lending economies rather than benefiting the recipients or borrower nations. By the 1990s, the *brain drain* was widely lamented and was of particular concern in higher education development projects (Cao 1996).[3]

After China joined the United Nations, higher-education assistance projects by individual country governments or the World Bank often included funding for scholarly exchanges. The directional flow was largely toward Europe and North America (Hayhoe 1989; World Bank Educational Lending Projects I-III).

As participants in the projects examined for this study, we experienced a counter-hegemonic discourse on international mobility of knowledge. In these projects, we experienced mutually beneficial processes and outcomes that multiplied in number, impact, and sustainability, rather than borrowing or draining of talent. Whereas governmental development aid projects often assume expertise on one side and need for it on the other, civic space offered flexibility for stakeholders to define their interest collaboratively and negotiate mutually beneficial projects without limitations.

Very little systematic information and analytical literature exist on international collaborations in education. In the 1990s, collaboration initiated by returned scholars was still minimal, and where it existed, it was "facilitated by Chinese scientists and engineers who have kept in touch with their U.S. advisor" (Johnson 2001). In this context, Hayhoe was invited to lead the Canadian–Chinese governmental scholarly exchange.

The Story of Three Circles of International Scholars

The story is told from the perspective of three scholars, Ruth Hayhoe, Haiyan Qiang, and Vilma Seeberg, professors at three different universities, who brought their respective circles of colleagues into contact with each other. For reasons of space, we hold the focus rather tightly on these three circles and the second-generation projects that grew out of the original development aid program. Many other scholars have created offshoots and large third-generation projects with wide impact on scholarly relations and have contributed substantially to cross-cultural literature on education.

From 1990 to 1995, the first Canada–China University Linkage Project (CCULP-1) went into effect. CCULP-1 was a "joint" doctoral program for Chinese education academics conducted under Hayhoe's leadership at the University of Toronto with six major Chinese *key*[4] teacher education institutions. A second linkage program (Canada–China Special University Linkage Consolidation Program [CCSULCP-2]) followed a number of years later and focused on training young Chinese women and national minority scholars in multicultural higher education. Significantly, these were called the Canada–China university "linkage" projects.

The First Circle

Haiyan Qiang, who at the time of this writing was a faculty member in a key pedagogical university in South China, is at the center of the first circle of relationships. She told her story as follows. She and visiting scholars from her university had participated in a few shorter-term university-level academic exchanges with North American universities. When her colleague F. Zhun returned, he was appointed Dean of the Faculty of Education at Shaanxi Normal University (SU). In 1987, under his initiative, SU established a *Center for the Study of North American Education*. Hayhoe was sent to visit the Center shortly after she was appointed cultural attaché at the Canadian embassy in Beijing. A few years later, SU and six other key pedagogical universities were designated partners in CCULP-1 under Hayhoe's direction, and Qiang and several doctoral students came as visiting scholars to the University of Toronto.

The following year, as part of this first linkage project, several professors from the University of Toronto and other North American educational institutions visited SU to conduct training and participate in joint conferences in areas of educational specialization, such as special education, psycholinguistics, and administration out of which evolved ideas for new projects, which led to several third-generation collaborations that are still impacting many (see several of the participants in the May 2011 conference *Education and Global Cultural Dialogue: A Tribute to Ruth Hayhoe*; for details of project outcomes and affiliated scholars, see Boyd and Pan 2001). For example, Hayhoe, when conducting an in-depth investigation into higher education, collaborated with Qiang on her fieldwork travels throughout northwest China, which resulted in a book chapter published by Hayhoe in North America (1996) and another authored by Qiang in China. By 1994, the SU *Center for the Study of North American Education* had held its seventh annual conference. Only a year later, Qiang and eight other Chinese scholars returned to University of Toronto for a conference on a future cooperation focused on education for women and minorities in China. Out of this conference came the application for the follow-up CCSULCP-2, submitted to the Canadian International Development Agency (CIDA) by Hayhoe, but under the direction of seven China-returned CCULP-1 scholars. From 1996 through 2001, CCSULCP-2 extended into many different and overlapping areas at the institutions in the network (see Boyd and Pan 2001, for detailed descriptions).

Most of the CCULP-1 scholars were promoted into important positions upon their return to China, evidencing the expansion and hierarchical layering of social networks. For example, G. Tin was appointed dean of the faculty of education at a premier university in East China. G. Wen became a Director in the National Research Center in the Ministry of Education. Qiang was appointed Associate Dean of the Faculty of Education at SU and later Associate Director of the Center for Women's Studies. F. Zhun moved to a premier key normal university in East China as full professor and head of the School of Education (for Early Childhood and Special Education). More of the outcomes of CCULP-1 will be discussed in the context of the second circle centered on Hayhoe.

Qiang directed one project called *Women and Minorities as Education Change Agents* under CCSULCP-2, which involved many young Chinese scholars in international and intercultural education, resulting in the publication of a four-volume textbook edited by Qiang on women in education that was adopted for instruction in all the teacher education institutions originally involved in CCULP-1. Second-generation projects included (1) a comparative empirical study of school management models in China and the United Kingdom, headed by Qiang and supported by both the British Council and the Ministry of Education of China, from which five young Chinese scholars returned after significant academic experience abroad and (2) a research project funded by an ecumenical international educational assistance foundation, called the *University Curriculum Development for Gender Equity Education*, under which Qiang organized an international conference by the same name at SU in 2000. At the conference, Qiang brought together three circles of relations between China and North America.

The research in minority ethnic knowledge and bilingualism under CCSULCP-2 led to a large ancillary creation, bilingual immersion schools in China. Qiang of SU along with M. Huang of NU of CCULP-1 cofounded along with North American scholars what Qiang calls the most successful example of educational *adaptation*. We make a clear distinction here between *transposition* and *adaptation*. *Transposition* is part of the borrower–lender model, whereas *adaptation* is a process of learning and transformation. The Early English Immersion Program (EEIP) operated, and still does at the time of this writing, in more than 50 kindergarten, primary, and secondary schools in several big cities including Beijing. It has become an enduring China–North American collaboration that enrolls students in kindergartens through eighth grade. This is the first activist or clinical project that grew out of the scholarly work ensuing from the development aid. In 2011, in its fourteenth year, it thrives on its own momentum without any outside funding. Qiang expects the research to make important contributions to educational modernization in China by preparing a new Chinese generation for participation in a global information society (for publications, see Boyd and Pan 2001).

In sum, under the auspices of the two Canada–China University Linkage Projects, about 30 North American scholars and doctoral students paid academic visits and collaborated with Chinese scholars at SU and other normal universities in the network. More than 20 Chinese scholars visited North American universities, all but two of whom returned to China, five more scholars returned from extended study in England, and several senior scholars returned from many study tours in North America. The network of seven Chinese key normal universities continued strong and spun off many projects by the time of this writing. Returned scholars in China have produced the following independent second-generation output in China: eight smaller joint projects, two books on Canadian education, four textbooks on gender and women's education (Qiang et al. 1999–2002), four new courses, and five international conferences all held in China and relevant to the Chinese context.

Qiang reflected on why such a wealth of educational exchange activities and local projects developed in such a short period of time: First, the key participants shared a commitment to a mutually beneficial academic network. Second, the key participants shared a commitment to explore multicultural issues in the societies and education of their partners. Third, the key participants were senior educational scholars and had a deep understanding of the other culture. Key participants had had previous experience in the universities of the other country and spoke each other's languages. Whereas the former three points were essential, she wrote, the previous experience and language familiarity facilitated the work logistically, but played less of a role as time went by.

The Second Circle

In 1986, Ruth Hayhoe, then a newly appointed professor of comparative international higher education at University of Toronto, received a call from her director that a Chinese education official at the ministerial rank had requested the university to help Chinese normal universities establish doctoral programs in education. The director called Hayhoe not only because of her position but also because she was known to be fluent in Chinese, having spent decades in Hong Kong. The call led to Hayhoe becoming involved with grant-writing to fund such projects, which, she said, she mastered after several years with the approval by CCULP-1 (Hayhoe's email to Seeberg in March 2001).

Hayhoe directed the North American component of CCULP-1 and -2, and was personally responsible for introducing her circle of scholars to the Chinese scholars and their circles of relationships. Due to her extraordinary effort in initially and continuously seeding, nurturing, and growing networks, the three circles of relationships mentioned above have intersected at several points.

Hayhoe (2001) said that she was able to really express her "intention and passion" about the nature of these Chinese–North American interactions in the conceptualizing and organizing of the *Knowledge across Cultures* conference of 1992 at the University of Toronto. It was so successful that the Chinese partners organized a follow-up conference in China in 1994. These conferences brought together multicultural scholars from throughout North America with Chinese educators, among them, Seeberg. The first conference produced a book (Hayhoe and Pan 2001), and the second produced *East-West Dialogue in Knowledge and Higher Education* (Hayhoe and Pan 1996), both published in the United States, and another published both in Chinese and English in China (Hayhoe et al. 1993). The impact of these works has gone well beyond the intention of the original government development project.

During the second development project, when Qiang and Hayhoe conducted their investigation into education in northwest China, Hayhoe visited a number of poor rural schools. With the help of returned scholar

J. Huang and his wife, both professors at NU, Hayhoe arranged to donate starter libraries to four of the poorest schools in remote ethnic Muslim prefectures of southern Gansu. Then, in the summer of 1998, when she and her husband visited these schools, they were taken aback by the sharp decline in the number of girl students in each higher grade. Again with the help of J. Huang, they established a scholarship for 10-12 girls yearly to finish primary school, which has continued for over a decade. It is the second activist or clinical project that grew out of, but went beyond the intent of the original governmental development aid project through the active participation of intentional and attentive scholars.

By 1998, Hayhoe had taken a position as president at a teachers' college in Hong Kong and joined the board of a worldwide organization providing relief to children in poverty, Save the Children Hong Kong (SCHK). The latter had funded school-building projects in remote areas of China and wanted Hayhoe to link these schools with the teachers' colleges in the university linkage network. SCHK for half a decade funded university graduate students and young scholars from the CCULP-1 and 2 normal university network to supervise on-site teacher training and develop libraries and professional training in its rural schools and Hayhoe's scholarship schools. Over time, rural schools in Hubei, Qinghai, Xinjiang, Guangxi, and Gansu, were included—all remote border provinces with large minority nationality populations. Qiang and a colleague at SU managed one of the projects. Seeberg later conducted a project review of the SCHK schools in northwest China with the help of one of Qiang's graduate students connecting the three circles (Seeberg 2008).

As an offshoot of a research project conducted by Hayhoe, a modest scholarship had grown into unique support system for rural education in China by linking the CCULP-1 network with SCHK and is continuing to sponsor 10 or more village girls, one of whom has reached the tertiary level. This second-generation impact again surpassed the original government development project's intent.

Hayhoe accounted for the first- and second-generation successes and diversifications of the international cooperation by the participants' genuine commitment to mutuality from the beginning, and added that the North American government officials administering the CCULP-1 office may not have understood or cared about this. Young and older participating Chinese scholars were eager to learn from their North American colleagues and genuinely respected their own culture and heritage. They were committed to making their experience available to their Chinese colleagues by taking up leadership in their own institutions. On the North American side, all those involved were equally committed and got enticed into various "sideline" activities as they worked with Chinese colleagues.

This, for example, is how the bilingual immersion project and the girls' scholarships came about. In 2000, one of the North American scholars who worked with the second-generation English immersion schools project led a group of local Canadian teachers, all paying their own way, to the final CCSULCP-2 conference in China. Hayhoe emphasized that participants did not see themselves as experts or teachers and students, but as colleagues across borders. The North American scholars, Hayhoe commented, were the "best scholars in North America and they got excited about what they could learn from Chinese colleagues" (Hayhoe's email to Seeberg in May 2001).

A ripple effect from China to North America is illustrated by one of the CCSULCP-2 advisory scholars, a Chinese Canadian from Taiwan who taught in a university in Toronto. In 2002, she held "a wonderful workshop on feminist pedagogy in Toronto, supported by Ford Foundation, and involving many of the same Chinese women scholars—it lasted two weeks, and I met with the group three times. Xing was proud to see it also as part of our expanding circles of collaboration" (Hayhoe's email to Seeberg in March 2003).

Hayhoe's emphasis on the participants' interest in the scholarly and clinical work per se rather than their personal career advancement is echoed by Stead and Harrington (2000) as an essential ingredient for egalitarian collaboration. Hayhoe did not comment in her reflections on her work promoting education for poor rural girls, as if it was understood that this was a necessary consequence of doing research in the region. This activist orientation is common to the field of multiculturalism and originates in a personal commitment and willingness to act on social justice principles.

The Third Circle

The two circles around Qiang and Hayhoe intersected with Vilma Seeberg at the *Knowledge across Cultures* conference in Toronto in 1992. Seeberg, a professor studying Chinese education, had been doing research in sociology of higher education in China collaborating with among others J. Xue of Beijing Normal University.[5] During field research in China in 1990, Seeberg introduced Xue to Hayhoe at the Canadian embassy in Beijing, which resulted in her involvement with Qiang's second-generation women-in-education textbook and college course development project. Xue later was active in the Chinese organizing committee for the Fourth World Conference on Women in Beijing in 1995, demonstrating the combination of scholarship and activism common to the participants in this network. When Seeberg returned to conduct follow-up research in China in 1995, Hayhoe connected her with the Canada–China university linkage network and particularly two "promising returned scholars" (Hayhoe's email to Seeberg in March 1994), Qiang at SU and J. Huang at NU. They had been successful in promoting at their institutions an orientation toward research that was open to multiple analytical approaches, and they welcomed international collaboration; hence, their institutions were added as sites to Seeberg's investigation into enrollment patterns in higher education (Seeberg 1998, 1999).

In 2000, Qiang invited Seeberg to deliver a keynote address (Seeberg 2000) for her conference on *University Curriculum Development for Gender Equity Education* at SU where Qiang, Seeberg, and Xue met up again. The *Gender Equity Education* conference was a second-generation project organized by Qiang and sponsored by the United Board for Christian Higher Education in Asia to produce a textbook series on gender in education for normal universities in China. Qiang had previously invited Hayhoe, Seeberg, and Xue to serve on the advisory editorial board for the textbook series (Qiang et al. 1999–2002). The three circles of relationships had been carefully seeded in the original government development aid project by Hayhoe, and conscientiously nurtured and cultivated over the years by the three scholars at the core of each circle to touch many scholars and students in both continents.

As on previous occasions, this intersection too grew new offshoots, new circles. L. Zhang, Qiang's colleague who had comanaged Hayhoe's library and scholarship project, over an informal lunch with Seeberg mentioned some of its unexpected effects. The scholarship girls who had been able to go back to school had become known in the village as "little intellectuals," and enjoyed newfound respect. The girls had risen in value in the villagers' eyes portending better lives and futures for them and other village girls.

As a feminist, Seeberg saw in this story an opportunity to pay back for years of scholarship in China and for being able to adopt a daughter there. She and her family immediately established a new scholarship fund in the name of their daughter, Guanlan. Zhang of SU made it happen through a former schoolmate who headed the Women's Association of a remote mountainous county in Shaanxi Province. By 2011, more than 86 daughters of a cluster of villages had returned and continued in school on the scholarship; a few have even made it into tertiary institutions as the first-ever girls from those villages. Research on the progress and lives of the Guanlan Sisters has resulted in several publications (Seeberg et al. 2007; Seeberg 2011), and television documentaries (Jacobs and Seeberg 2011). In 2007, Seeberg established a "China girls' education" research team to track and explore the meaning of girls' schooling for social change. From a serendipitous intersection of two circles of scholars grew this enduring project enhancing the lives of families and enabling young women in one part of China to experience a degree of social justice. This offshoot of a second-generation collaboration has taken on a life of its own and made Chinese village girls part of the worldwide *girl effect* movement.

Reflecting on the fruitful and successfully bidirectional, cross-cultural collaborations recounted above, Seeberg pointed out that a shared interest in social justice research and activism ran through the collaborations. Mutual respect was based on professional knowledge and cultural awareness, which were two fundamental elements that originally enabled collaboration. Another important aspect, according to Seeberg, was a shared personal feminism and interest in gender issues. Seeberg reiterated that it was this disposition of the activist scholar that led the participants to work creatively and effectively together over time.

Analysis

Each circle of scholars intersected with another at what were seemingly serendipitous points, which, upon closer inspection, showed that they were the necessary outcomes of each individual scholar's genuine and enduring interest in furthering scholarship and activism in her field. It is the sharing of the interest that revealed itself in continually sharper relief as the intersections of the scholars' circles of colleagues multiplied. The network of scholars strengthened itself in that fashion. With added persons and resources, it became increasingly sustainable.

The shared interest among the scholars in this case existed at the level of a presumptive, obvious, yet unspoken assumption rather than the careful hammering out of different stakes common to institutional collaborations. It was not until the present investigation that the key participants expressed their post hoc perceptions on how they had originally framed their initiatives or intentions in becoming involved in collaborations. A strong sense of commitment to a common goal and a willingness to cooperate were almost tangible qualities present from the beginning of each circle of relationships. Solomon, Boud, Leontios, Staron (2001, 143) suggest that "collaboration works best when everyone has a stake in it and this stake has both personal and organizational dimensions." That feeling was shared by the main participants.

Though Stead and Harrington (2000) recommend that objectives be specified before starting, only the governmental aid projects can be said to have followed this advice. However, as Stead and Harrington also advise, commitment to goals and willingness to cooperate are absolutely necessary and were present on the part of the main participants in all second-generation projects.

Culling the major themes in the stories told above, we suggest that the nature of the shared interest, multiculturalism in education, and a sense of enhancing social justice formed the essential foundation of the second-generation cross-cultural collaborations. Evidence from international collaborations in the natural sciences shows that the nature of the shared research is not necessarily crucial (Johnson 2001). However, in the collaborations discussed here, the nature of the shared interest is of primary importance, because it defines both content and process. Attempting to create a democratic, bidirectional, cross-cultural collaboration is by its very nature defined by process. The interests the collaborators shared were based on a presumption of commitment to mutuality, balanced power relations, and cross-cultural knowledge, which are foundations of multiculturalism. The key participants held an a priori multicultural awareness, and this was a known, though undeclared, characteristic in the formation of the circles of relationships and the collaborations that sprang from them. This assumption provided safety and trust in the networking process that reinforced itself over time. Furthermore, multicultural awareness includes acceptance of cultural differences and adjusting one's behavior, which, as Stead and Harrington (2000) suggest, is essential for facilitating international collaborative relationships. The skills they mention as being indispensable in maintaining collaborative relationships, social skills, and intercultural sensitivity, such as understanding partners' perspectives, as well as knowledge of participants' cultural mores, are cornerstones of multiculturalism and cross-cultural theory.

Through past and consistent cross-cultural contacts, work, and study, the key participants had practiced the skills of intercultural communication. One of the foremost elements of such skills is the formation of a strong personal–social identity. Relevant here are both cultural and gender social identities. In terms of social identity formation theory (Helms 1997; Cross 1999), not only was her own cultural identity salient to each of the scholars involved, but it was expected to be salient for the collaborating partner of the other culture as well. As is often the case, an awareness of one's own social identity allows an individual to understand other dimensions of personal identity, for example, gender, and an understanding of social hierarchies and power distribution. The key participants were aware of the sociohistoric positions of their respective countries in the global research community and global economy in general, and worked to redress the imbalances of social and economic hierarchies. Stead and Harrington (2000) warn researchers to be vigilant against coworkers dominating; multicultural theory suggests that social power, such as being from a globally dominant nation, also must be confronted and negotiated. In the present case, solidarity as opposed to hierarchy was an expected feature of the collaborations due to the commitment to multiculturalism, rather than something to be carefully built as is suggested in international collaboration literature.

The theoretical foundation of *social identity formation* or *development* referred to above is found in social psychology (see, for example, Carter 2005 and multicultural counseling literature; e.g., Helms 1997; Cross 1999; Hollins 1999).

The key participants in this international collaboration had taken advantage of many opportunities to examine their individual and social identity and had developed a commitment to acting on social justice prior to embarking on the creation of the circles of relationships into a network of collaboration on multiple projects. As Ruth Hayhoe (Hayhoe's email to Seeberg in March 2003) summarized so well, these stories do "show the fact that we were not in continual contact at all—it was just that we embraced the same values and these drew us together!"

Conclusion

Our study describes a case of multiple international collaborations that do not fall within the borrower–lender model. The case study illustrates relating cross-culturally to mutual benefit and ever-expanding impact that brain drain is not a necessary outcome of international collaborations in higher education.

The projects under study here were vital educational programs originating and operating in civil society in and beyond academia. The collaborations were knit together by the actions of individuals in the pursuit of scholarship—rather than grants. This case shows that collaborative, private efforts associated with public, nongovernmental organizations can create locally controlled, appropriate projects that have far-reaching and beneficial effects both locally and internationally.

We propose that scholarly exchanges, when they are approached from a shared stance of genuine scholarly commitment and democratic relations, have the potential to establish a pattern of mutually beneficial, sustainable international collaborations. To sustain over time, the participants need to hold shared values, to understand and respect each other's personal–social identity, and to act equitably. Cultural and political dynamics are a constant in international collaborations, and the study suggests particularly that cross-cultural and bidirectional models need to be based in a practice of social justice in order to be sustainable, long term, and to cast ever-wider ripple effects.

Ruth Hayhoe's (1986) ruminations on China's prior educational cooperation presaged the findings of this study and show that her understanding of mutuality of social justice values laid the foundation of these projects:

> Equity suggests aims and forms of organization that are reached through full mutual agreement; autonomy suggests a respect for the theoretical perspective rooted in peripheral culture that would require center participants to gain a thorough knowledge of this culture; solidarity suggests forms of organization that encourage maximum interaction among peripheral participants and growing links between them and their fellow researchers; participation intimates an approach to knowledge that does not stratify in a hierarchical way but assumes the possibility of a creative peripheral contribution from the very beginning.

On a practical level, the commitment to sustainable collaboration has to be accompanied by communication and nurturing of relationships. The relationships as shown in this study are by nature multilayered and are strengthened by the interaction of the layers. By that we mean personal relationships are primary but are strengthened by institutional ties and professional networks.

Robert Arnove (2003) explains "the workings of a global economy and the increasing interconnectedness of societies pose common problems for educational systems around the world . . . A dialectic is at work between the global and the local" (1). Our work provides one model defining an egalitarian dialectic, giving evidence that democratic and cross-cultural projects can be constructed and maintained—despite a global context of growing structural hierarchies.

The intersections of the three circles continue to yield additional undertakings, which generate more circles, wider ripples across generations. On a personal note, we and all key participants have remarked on how personally rewarding the collaborations have been and remain.

NOTES

1. The names of the institutions and participating scholars other than the authors, Haiyan Qiang and Vilma Seeberg, and Ruth Hayhoe, the originator and creator of the three circles, have been changed to respect confidentiality as their permission was not sought.

2. *Reverse flow* is a term used in the study of international flows of scholars in the natural sciences conducted by such offices as the National Science Foundation in the United States (Johnson and Regets 1998). It is based on a center"periphery model of international relations and recognizes the fact of the *brain drain* from the developing world to the postindustrial, technologically advanced countries of the *North*.

3. Johnson and Regets hasten to add in their 1998 study of international mobility that "more recently, however, the mobility of highly talented workers is referred to as 'brain circulation,' since a cycle of study and work abroad may be followed by a return to the home country to take advantage of high-level opportunities" (p. 1), "yet 47.9% of Chinese origin S&E doctoral recipients had firm plans to stay in the U.S. in 1988–96" (p. 2).

4. Key educational institutions receive special funding and attention from the educational department of the respective administrative level, in this case, the Ministry of Education of China.

5. Xue had previously completed a Master's degree at Seeberg's university in North America.

REFERENCES

Arnove, Robert F. 1980."Comparative Education and World Systems Analysis."*Comparative Education Review* 24 (1): 48–62.

Arnove, Robert F. 2003. "Reframing Comparative Education: The Dialectic of the Global and the Local." In *Comparative Education: The Dialectic of the Global and the Local*, ed. Robert F. Arnove and Carlos Alberto Torres (pp. 1–23). Lanham, MD: Roman and Littlefield Publishers.

Boli, John, and Francisco O. Ramirez. 1992. "Compulsory Schooling in the Western Cultural Context." In *Emergent Issues in Education: Comparative Perspectives*, ed. Philip Altbach, Robert F. Arnove, and Gail P. Kelly (pp. 25–38). Albany, NY: State University of New York Press.

Boyd, Dwight, and Julia Pan. 2001. *Women and Minorities as Educational Change Agents: Final Report, Canada-China Special University Linkage Consolidation Program*. Toronto: Ontario Institute for Studies in Education of the University of Toronto.

Cao, Xiaonan. 1996. "Debating 'Brain Drain' in the Context of Globalization." *Compare* 26 (3): 269–284.

Carter, Robert T, ed. 2005. *Handbook of Racial-Cultural Psychology and Counseling: Theory and Research (vols. 1 and 2)*. Hoboken, NJ: Wiley.

Cross, William E., Linda Strauss, and Peony Fhagen-Smith. 1999. "African American Identity Development across the Life Span: Educational Implications." In *Racial and Ethnic Identity in School Practices: Aspects of Human Development*, ed. Rita H. Sheets and E. R. Hollins (pp. 29–48). Mahwah, NJ: Lawrence Erlbaum.

Hayhoe Ruth. E-mails to Seeberg Vilma, 1994; March 13, 2001; May 23, 2001; March, 2003.

Hayhoe, Ruth. 1986. "Penetration or Mutuality? China's Educational Cooperation with Europe, Japan, and North America." *Comparative Education Review* 30 (4): 532–559.

Hayhoe, Ruth. 1989. *China's Universities and the Open Door.* Armonk: M.E. Sharpe.

Hayhoe, Ruth. 1996. *China's Universities 1895–1995: A Century of Cultural Conflict.* New York: Garland Press.

Hayhoe, Ruth, and Julia Pan, eds. 1996. *East-West Dialogue in Knowledge and Higher Education.* Armonk: M.E. Sharpe.

Hayhoe, Ruth, with Hilda Briks, Andrew Gordon, Ray Kybartas, Jane Moes de Munich, Frank Moody, Julia Pan, Edward Synowski, Lorraine Wilson, Ian Winchester, eds. 1993. *Knowledge across Cultures: Universities East and West.* Toronto: OISE Press, and Wuhan, PRC: Hubei Education Press. [Published in English and Chinese.]

Hayhoe, Ruth, and Julia Pan, eds. 2001. *Knowledge across Cultures: A Contribution to Dialogue among Civilizations.* Hong Kong: The University of Hong Kong.

Helms, Janet E. 1997. "Toward a Model of White Racial Identity Development." In *College Student Development and Academic Life: Psychological, Intellectual, Social and Moral Issues*, ed. Karen Arnold and Ilda Carreiro King. New York: Garland Publishing.

Hollins, Etta R. 1999. "Relating Ethnic and Racial Identity Development to Teaching." In *Racial and Ethnic Identity in School Practices: Aspects of Human Development,* ed. Rosa H. Sheets and Etta. R. Hollins. Mahwah, NJ: Lawrence Erlbaum Associates.

Jacobs, Tom A., and Seeberg, Vilma. 2011. "Guanlan's Sisters: A Family Journal." PBS stations. Cleveland, OH: WVIZ.

Johnson, Jean M. 2001. "Human Resource Contributions to U.S. Science and Engineering from China." Arlington: National Science Foundation. Available online at: www.nsf.gov.

Johnson, Jean. M., and Mark C. Regets. 1998. "International Mobility of Scientists and Engineers to the United States: Brain Drain or Brain Circulation?" Arlington, VA: National Science Foundation. Available online at: www.nsf.gov.

Qiang, Haiyan, X. Deng, and L Shi, series eds. 1999–2002. *The Role of Gender and Women in Development, Vol. 1; Gender Equity in Psychology, Vol. 2; Gender Difference and Education, Vol. 3; The Development of Women's Education: International Perspectives. Vol. 4.* Shaanxi, PRC: Shaanxi Renmin Jiaoyu Chubanshe [Shaanxi Peoples Education Press].

Yang, Rui. 2011. "A Tribute to Dr. Ruth Hayhoe." Paper delivered at the Education and Global Cultural Dialogue Conference, Toronto, May 6, 2011.

Seeberg, Vilma. 1998. "Stratification Trends in Technical-Professional Higher Education." In *Higher Education in Post-Mao China*, ed. R. Adamson and M. Agelasto. Hong Kong: Hong Kong University Press.

Seeberg, Vilma. 1999. "Rampant Capitalism Meets Confucian Traditions: Resolution of Value Conflict among Chinese College Students: A Case Study." *Educational Practice and Theory* 21 (2): 51–67.

Seeberg, Vilma. 2000. "Equity for Girls in Education: What is Important for the Future." Keynote presented at the Conference on Gender Equity and Teacher Education Course Development, Sha'anxi Normal University, Xi'an, Sha'anxi, PR China.

Seeberg, Vilma. 2008. "Girls First! Promoting Early Education in Tibetan Areas of China, a Case Study." *Educational Review* 60 (1): 51–68.

Seeberg, Vilma. 2011. "Schooling, Jobbing, Marrying, What's a Girl to do to Make Life Better? Empowerment Capabilities of Girls at the Margins of Globalization." *Research in Comparative and International Education* 6 (1). Available online at: www.wwwords.co.uk/rcie.

Solomon, Nicky, David Boud, Maria Leontios, and Maret Staron. 2001. "Tale of Two Institutions: Exploring Collaboration in Research Partnerships." *Studies in the Education of Adults* 33 (2): 135–143.

Stead, Graham B., and Thomas F. Harrington. 2000. "A Process Perspective of International Research Collaboration." *The Career Development Quarterly* 48 (4): 323–331.

Chapter 13

Parallel and Diverging Paths: Hong Kong Higher Education and Ruth Hayhoe

David Post

Many universalists—humanists and monotheists alike—favor a common narrative template, one that Joseph Campell called the "mono-myth." Many of us are drawn, like moths drawn to light, by the clarity of a universal archetype: journey out, journey home. Ideal protagonists return enlightened, and eventually they also enlighten their brethren with the journey's song. At least, that is one ideal. In fact, however, many real lives look and are played only forward and not backward; despite the appeal of the return, there may be simply a journey out toward a new world. This template offers a less-reassuring myth. The worry over whether our path goes in any consistent direction, or toward what could be called individual "growth" or collective "progress" is, of course, a central dilemma both in world literature and psychosocial development.

Ruth Hayhoe is still reading—still living—the classics of her girlhood: of Moses and Odysseus, of the Buddha and the Journey to the West, and, of course, the Gospel. This chapter attempts the improbable, trying to unify into one account—in audacious parallel—the narratives of Hayhoe's intellectual and spiritual growth alongside the concomitant changes experienced by Hong Kong's education system and norms. I will assume that the readers of this collection are well acquainted with the *dramatis personæ*, Ruth Hayhoe and Hong Kong, how the two first met and how they have maintained a cordial, familiar, and mutually productive relation. I could refer novice readers to *Full Circle*, the first installment of Ruth's projected multivolume memoir. For an understanding of Hayhoean thought, you also should get hold of two important lectures she delivered to the Comparative and International Education Society ("A Chinese Puzzle" and "Redeeming Modernity"). For an introduction to Hong Kong education during the years of Ruth's relationship since the mid-1960s, I could refer readers to any of the scholarly studies of Hong Kong's schools and universities written by the authors of the other chapters in this book, or by such writers as Ng Lun Ngai-ha, Anthony Sweeting, Tsang Wing-Kwok, Wing Wah Law, and Mark Bray (and I myself have attempted modestly to add to this literature).[1]

From Hayhoe's first memoir, readers get some idea of the ultimately flexible guidance she received from two accepting and loving parents. We know about Hayhoe's early excellence in Greek and Latin, through the tutelage of a dedicated high-school teacher who led Hayhoe to an elite program at the University of Toronto. Outside the classroom, and beyond her biological family, she also tells readers that an exclusive Christian community rigidly structured most of her childhood and coming of age. We know that Ruth came close to moving to Rome to continue her study of Latin literature and history, but, fatefully, and with strong support from her Church, she opted to become a missionary educator in Asia.

One memory of Hayhoe's move to Hong Kong that she decided to share is meaningful both for what it says about choices she made in 1967 and what it tells us about the memories she retained and chose to record 35 years later. It was the selection of her Chinese name. Years after the decision, Ruth recalled how she had considered maintaining her biblical name. But she did not. She called herself *Mei Dak* (Beautiful Virtue) instead of *Louh Dak* (by convention, the Biblical "Ruth"). Let me offer an interpretation both of this decision and the significance of its recollection.

The archetypical Ruth—the protagonist of the eponymous book of the Jewish and Christian Bible—never looked back on her own nation or its gods when she left to follow Naomi and converted to the faith of the Hebrews. Ruth Hayhoe, by the time she arrived in Hong Kong, must have made her peace with verses 16–17:

> And Ruth said [to Naomi]: "Entreat me not to leave thee, and to return from following after thee; for whither thou goest, I will go; and where thou lodgest, I will lodge; thy people shall be my people, and thy God my God; where thou diest, will I die, and there will I be buried; HaShem do so to me, and more also, if aught but death part thee and me."[2]

Peace, yes, but unquestioned acceptance? The Biblical Ruth never returned. How could Ruth Hayhoe, a devout single woman for the first time far from family, not have questioned whether her own odyssey would ever permit clear passage home or whether, lacking familiar signposts, she had begun a journey without end? Perhaps, to a committed, faithful, and very young person 6,000 miles from Toronto, "Ruth" would have been less reassuring in Chinese than in English. Questions of constancy, departures, and growth trouble every healthy adult, and the trajectory of Ruth Hayhoe could be the model for these questions and their resolution.

In 1967, Hong Kong was also wrestling with its identity as Ruth Hayhoe arrived and began volunteer teaching at the Exclusive Brethren Christian School *Yan Kwong* (Grace and Light). Hong Kong, as a colonial entrepôt and then as a refugee magnet, had never used schools for the purposes of national development or national identity (some critics would say it still does not). Lacking a strong rationale for public support, in 1967, basic schooling was largely the province of political parties, patriotic associations, profit-making businesses, and religious organizations such as those operating the Exclusive Brethren *Yan Kwong* mission and the Anglican school (*Heep Yunn*) where Hayhoe was more formally employed as a staff. Even primary schooling was far from universal, and relatively few of those who did attend went to government schools.

Historically, at the time of Hayhoe's arrival, the government's approach had been more reactive than proactive. The 1913 Education Ordinance, for example, was prompted by the creation of democratic movement schools opposed to the Qing Dynasty. Only in that year and through the first Ordinance did the colonial government—anxious not to create conflict with China—require that all schools at least register with the HK Education Department. Subsidies grew slowly and gradually as the price the government had to pay for maintaining very tentative control over independent schools before very gradually expanding control over education.

Although Hong Kong's world had, in some ways, been turned upside down by 1967, the basic charter for state–society relations had been retained and the government still interfered little in the provision of education. Just four years prior to Ruth Hayhoe's 1967 arrival, the Chinese University of Hong Kong had been recognized and funded, thanks to the efforts by Hong Kong refugee intellectuals from the mainland and with political support from the Anglican Bishop as well as the Kuomintang of China (Nationalist Party of China) (KMT) in Taiwan, US missionaries, and the Yale-in-China Association. The British administration, rather than pushing either "manpower planning" or nation building, acceded only reluctantly to pressures from Chinese intellectuals.

"Wrestling with its identity" perhaps overstates the self-consciousness and purposeful introspection within Hong Kong society in the mid-1960s. Hong Kong, heir to multiple spiritual and intellectual traditions, responded through its basic education system to demands from industrialists for workers and from parents for greater opportunities. Hong Kongers seemed to be at various crossroads in terms of their identity in education just as in their spirituality and their political allegiance. Although the history curriculum prescribed by the Education Department said little about China post-1949, everyone understood that, just across the border, the Cultural Revolution was in full swing. Ruth's first-hand experiences with the generational conflict manifest in Hong Kong by this social movement—including the previously unheard-of disrespect to educators—left a lasting mark on Hayhoe's view of China. The conflict was not only cultural: Many died in riots instigated by anticolonial and pro–Communist Party organizations.

The reticence of the colonial government to prioritize a purposeful public education is clear in comparative perspective. Taiwan, for example, had made nine years of schooling free and compulsory about the same time that Hayhoe arrived in Hong Kong. By contrast with Taiwan, ten more years were to pass before Murray MacLehose, a progressive governor with a Labour Party background, would make the same level of schooling free and compulsory in Hong Kong. At the time that Hayhoe arrived in 1967, responsibilities for Hong Kong's (noncompulsory) primary schooling had devolved to a multitude of organizations, some more serious than others about the quality of the schools they sponsored. Because access to university and the upper forms of secondary education was economically out of reach for most families, there was in practice no unified course of study preparing students to sit for a single examination. From the historical perspective, and probably from Ruth's standpoint of an outsider, Hong Kong seemed to offer a diverse array of educational experiences. For parents in the mid-sixties, most of these options were confusing, not to mention quite expensive. This is because Hong Kong's government, instead of creating a unified curriculum, controlling the examination regime, or employing directly Hong Kong's teachers, had allowed hundreds of providers to establish primary schools and then secondary schools. Rather than building, owning, and operating schools, a capitation system of finance had evolved, reimbursing private schools for a determined number of non-fee-paying students. As we will see, the numbers of government-paid slots were limited, far lower than the actual demand for schooling.

In 1967, apart from the few government-owned and government-operated schools, many primary and most secondary students attended private schools. These were organized similar to the Exclusive Brethren Christian *Yan Kwong* School (belonging to Hayhoe's cousin) where Hayhoe volunteered. Some schools actually functioned on the rooftops of public housing estates. In addition to a great deal else that Hayhoe learned (language, history of China, and making a traumatic break with a key figure in her religious community), Hayhoe also began to contextualize the role of schools such as *Yan Kwong* and the rooftop schools run by the other missionary in this close-knit community. Her awareness of the social context grew such that she began to place her individual experiences within the evolution of Hong Kong education, noting that such "rooftop" schools began to disappear as the government finally made primary education more available in schools willing to meet certain curricular requirements.[3] In my own research on Hong Kong, I have tried to show the chronology of government expansion into the chaotic and unsystematic provision of secondary schooling, in order to gauge its consequences for particular birth cohorts (Post 1993, 2010).

There are several possible measures of the increasing state role in the formerly devolved school systems of Hong Kong. Government subsidization offers a convenient indicator. The annual statistical digests of the years when Hayhoe taught in Hong Kong can be used to illustrate the emergence of "free" opportunities for families. Conversely, the government's increased funding shows the growing challenge for non-government-supported religious schools such as *Yan Kwong*. Hong Kong has long recorded the numbers of all students attending all types of schools and levels, even when the students did not attend a government-owned or government-subsidized school. By the time Ruth Hayhoe arrived in Hong Kong in 1967, most children were finishing primary school either at government or family expense. However, not all children who finished six years of education could afford to continue to the lower secondary level. From government records, it is possible to know precisely the numbers of children finishing primary schooling in a particular year who then continued their secondary schooling during the subsequent year. It is also possible to ascertain whether these children continued in a government-supported slot or in a school, such as *Yan Kwong*, which received no such funding.

At the time Ruth Hayhoe arrived in Hong Kong, fewer than 20 percent of primary-school graduates who continued on found secondary-school slots that were either government subsidized or provided directly in government-run schools. The vast majority of families who wished their children to go on to secondary school had to pay private fees unless they received scholarship support from the church or sponsoring organization. By the time Ruth Hayhoe left Hong Kong in 1978, the situation was changing rapidly. Half of those seeking secondary-school admissions were being financed through government support. The numbers of participating children and the participation rates increased apace. It is almost certain that a rapid growth in number of the absolute secondary school students was prompted by the fact that free and compulsory education was adopted in 1978 (the same year that Hayhoe extended her own education at the

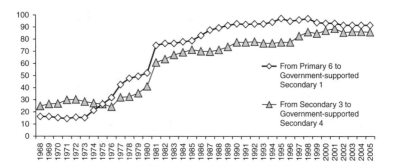

Figure 13.1 Hong Kong government support of education. Percentages of students who completed primary school and lower-secondary school and who in subsequent years continued their educations in a government-funded school space.

University of London's Institute of Education). The same pattern can be found in the history of the continuation of students from the first three years ("lower") to the last years ("upper") of secondary school. Figure 13.1 shows the consequences of the government's sudden expansion into the education sector.

Figure 13.1 could be interpreted as showing that—at least in the area of education—the state "woke up" during the years Ruth Hayhoe taught in Hong Kong from 1967 to 1978. However, this picture and this interpretation are too simplistic. A deeper question would ask about the reasons why this change occurred and about the rationales behind it. Did Hong Kong's government or its churches, trade unions, and civil organizations indeed develop a common rationale for the expansion of education? Were there stakeholders? Who was committed to increasing the governmental role? And what exactly were the "stakes?" On these questions, although the record is complex, the evidence seems clear enough even for foreigners like myself who cannot read Chinese. The debates in Hong Kong's legislative council are preserved in the archives of the Hansard, and fortunately they are available today online and in English. These debates reveal no general agreement about the reasons why the government first began to expand its support for education. However, when the rationales finally did begin to be offered by government, they tended to use the language of manpower planning.

The decision by Governor Murray MacLehose to extend free and compulsory education for nine years, and, a dozen years later, Governor David Wilson's decision to expand university construction and openings, were both implemented as top-down directives that did not reflect mass mobilization or even elite mobilization (as had been the case during the earlier mobilization leading to Chinese University's creation in 1963). To the extent that public rationales for expansion were debated at all in these two key moves, manpower planning and economic concerns for Hong Kong's growth were loudest, drowning out any possible expression of the concerns over the political integration of a diverse immigrant and refugee population, nor was there any vocalization of demands for social mobility, the other concern leading to mass mobilization that characterized the educational histories of most democracies. What, then, happened to the dynamism and fervor for education that Hayhoe witnessed—and aided— as a young Hong Kong educator? Did the energy disappear after the late 1970s, after her departure? Where did the energy go that, in days gone-by, had created hundreds of private schools from dozens of churches and interest groups?

I cannot answer these questions. However, it seems that, while many community-based schools in 1967 had embraced spiritual, political, scholarly, or humanistic objectives in their curriculum, these passionate commitments were wholly absent when the government began its expansion of funding. A more neutral and politically liberal orientation (i.e., neutral about the plural visions of a good life) emphasized human capital accumulation as the underlying rationale for public support of education. The net result of this shift in discourse was that, by the time Ruth Hayhoe returned to Hong Kong as the first president of the newly build campus of the Hong Kong Institute of Education (HKIEd), the basis for HK's lavish subsidies of schools and universities was neither well understood nor widely accepted.

As already mentioned, the intentions of Hong Kong's British governors in supporting education were, at least during two critical junctures, buried beneath the language of manpower planning and bureaucratese. Thus, the accelerated provision of free and compulsory lower secondary schooling in 1978 was justified as a human capital investment (even if the ultimate causes were political). Later, following the Tiananmen Massacre in 1989, Hong Kong accelerated the construction of universities so as to offer places to up to 18 percent of the population of that age. Eighteen years later, former governor David Wilson recalled in an interview that he was quite conscious about demands for upward mobility among working-class parents and also that the political aspirations of a university-educated public were taken into account, albeit very implicitly.[4]

Before Hong Kong's 1997 Handover to the People's Republic of China, this implicit, barely articulated rationale for government support by the government was echoed by the silence of civil society. The Professional Teachers Union, the Federation of Hong Kong Students, the staff associations of the polytechnics, and the nascent political parties were not outspoken about their reasons for supporting education, nor were Hong Kong's religious leaders active in the way that Bishop Hall had been in the late 1950s in mobilizing support for creation of the Chinese University. Such quiescence was understandable because the colonial government, until the early 1980s, had no formal institutional accountability to the public over educational decision making. Only after the Llewellyn Committee report in 1982 did Hong Kong create the Education Commission in an attempt to offer a means for channeling input to the decision-making process. It is possible that the most important policy decisions about education in the late seventies and the late eighties were undertaken less in response to Hong Kong's own civil society demands and more in response to events occurring outside of Hong Kong. In the first case, in the 1970s, Governor MacLehose was sensitive to the demands by European trade unionists who opposed competition from underaged textile workers in Hong Kong at a time when the International Labour Organization had adopted restrictions on work by persons younger than 15 years. The solution was to accelerate the pending plan to universalize the first three years of secondary school, at government expense. In the second place, after the repression of university students at Tiananmen Square in Beijing, Governor Wilson accelerated the expansion of postsecondary participation, also entirely at government expense. In the contemporary political context, this expansion and the funding of autonomous Hong Kong universities through unrestricted block grants could be seen as a vote of confidence in Hong Kong youth.

It is worth noting that these two policy decisions in Hong Kong, while undertaken with little direct input from civil society, ultimately produced profound, long-lasting consequences for civil society. I have written previously about two such consequences, concerning gender and social-class educational inequality. In my own investigations, I have accessed Hong Kong's individual household census records since 1971 (the earliest year when census records were preserved electronically). I looked at the relative likelihood that girls and boys had obtained particular levels of education across each census year. If we define "parity" as the relation when equal numbers of girls and boys obtain a particular level, it seems that there were obstacles for girls in 1971, the earliest available year. As evident from subsequent census years, these obstacles were removed.

First, a note on the methods for studying educational opportunity. Most Hong Kong residents aged 19 and 20 years live in a household headed by a parent. More men than women live longer with a parent, since women tend to marry younger. Using census data, it is possible to attach information from parents to their children in households where they live together. Using this method over the multiple census years is admittedly a second-best solution to the study of educational access and differentiation. If Hong Kong had a large-scale social survey, especially if there were accessible multiple waves of longitudinal surveys, then these sources would eventually generate more reliable information about the family origins of students attending various types of secondary and postsecondary education. A random sample of individuals who were asked retrospectively about their family situations in their primary and secondary school years could give relevant information about the causes of the respondent's current school status (e.g., whether studying at all, and whether studying a two-year degree or a four-year degree in Hong Kong or overseas). However, even if this type of information becomes available, it will remain cost-effective to take full advantage of census record data. While these data can never compete with a purpose-built survey, there are some advantages for researchers concerned to disentangle the details of study fields and modalities. No random sample of Hong Kong's population can ever match the coverage of the census in terms of the sheer number of cases available for such an investigation.

Census data allow us to understand the tendencies of immigrant groups, women, and poorer families. My investigations, and those of Suet-ling Pong, showed the time period during which girls overtook boys in terms of access to all levels of education. We also showed the effects of sibling constellation and sibship size on attainment, and confirmed the diminution of these effects as the government took on a more active responsibility for sponsoring education. Prior to 1978, elder sisters tended to forego schooling when they had younger siblings. After this time, sisters were at no such disadvantage. We also confirmed the challenges facing new arrivals from the mainland and showed, too, how recent immigrants compensated for their disadvantages by deliberately holding back or "red-shirting" their children.

Figure 13.2 illustrates that girls overtook boys as the government stepped in and began to subsidize education. The figure shows that, in 1971, there were fewer girls attaining lower-secondary and upper-secondary education than boys. However, in subsequent census data, the ratio of girls to boys was either reversed (with more girls than boys attaining secondary education) or was equal (with the ratio close to parity). In terms of postsecondary education, there are two ways to define attainment: the broad category of postsecondary (including short course, technical degree, and vocational programs) or the narrower and more elite category of "university" leading to a Bachelor's degree in Hong Kong.[5] By both the broader and the more elite definition, girls' higher education attainment overtook that of boys in a single generation. In other words, girls have been the main beneficiaries of government support for secondary and postsecondary education.

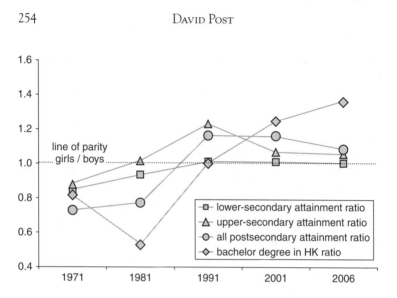

Figure 13.2 Educational attainment by girls, relative to boys, in lower-secondary, upper-secondary, postsecondary (includes university), and Bachelor's degree programs.

What about the dimension of social class background? A similar analysis can be made showing the likely impact of government policy on educational opportunities for children who had fathers with working-class jobs, as opposed to clerical and professional occupations. In each of the census years, the occupational categories were defined slightly differently, but it is still possible to group occupations broadly as involving office and professional work (what US sociologists term "white collar") and other manual jobs. In terms of social-class inequality, Figure 13.3 presents a similar account of the impact of government support for secondary schooling to the tendency seen in Figure 13.2 for gender inequality. Just as girls made gains since 1971 in terms of lower- and upper-secondary educational attainment, as compared with boys, so did children of working-class origins gain relative to children whose fathers were in "white-collar" employment. The gap between these two groups virtually disappeared over the past generation, a remarkable accomplishment that is not seen everywhere in the world (certainly not in the United States or Canada).

It is noteworthy that the social-class gap narrowed in terms of differences in the attainment of university education leading to the Bachelor's degree between 1981 and 1991. However, it is equally noteworthy that, in recent years, this social-class gap has slightly widened. Why Hong

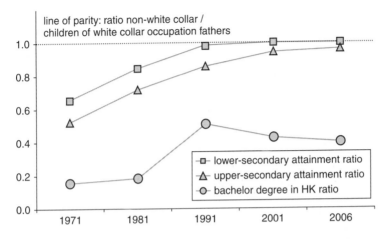

Figure 13.3 Educational attainment by working-class children, relative to children with white-collar-occupation fathers, in lower-secondary, upper-secondary, and Bachelor's degree programs.

Kong experienced this reversal is uncertain. Perhaps, the initial push to expand participation rates up to 18 percent, coinciding with Governor David Wilson's initiative following Tiananmen Massacre, created opportunities for the working class, at the same time that secondary education was becoming universal. In recent years, the 18 percent ceiling remained in place for the publicly owned and operated universities. However, the choices outside of these Bachelor degree-granting institutions changed. With a global recession and higher costs for universities in Europe, the Americas, and Australia, it is possible that families whose children might have pursued their studies outside of Hong Kong (and left spaces for working-class children) elected instead to take advantage of the high-quality and less-expensive local institutions. This would have reduced the opportunities for the working class in Hong Kong if working-class children were displaced by children from affluent families who might, in previous years, have sent their children overseas to study.

Another major change in Hong Kong's education system came following the 1997 Handover, and a major financial crisis. Hong Kong's first local leader of the new Special Administrative Region (SAR), Tung Che Wah, invoked a language of human capital and international competition in a call for greater postsecondary opportunities. "In developed countries and some major cities in Asia," noted Tung in his 2001 policy address, "up to 60% of senior secondary school graduates pursue tertiary education. For Hong Kong, however, the rate is just about half that. Not only are we lagging far behind, but failing to meet the needs of a knowledge-based economy. It is imperative we catch up. Our objective is that within 10 years, 60% of senior secondary school leavers will receive tertiary education."

The new postsecondary education policy, which began during Ruth Hayhoe's leadership of the HKIEd, was an acknowledgment that further expansion was not possible without cost-sharing from the students. Accordingly, new programs leading to "Associate degrees," and administered separately from the main faculties of the public universities, have accommodated about 40 percent of the age cohorts over the past ten years. The most recent year for which census data are available is 2006. Using these data, I have been studying the allocation of higher-educational opportunities to families who are wealthier and poorer. The goal is to uncover the story of who benefited most from the government's decisions to diversify the postsecondary finance system in Hong Kong.

Figure 13.3 illustrates that the gap in secondary-school completion, between the working-class and white-collar Hong Kongers, has narrowed substantially. This gap has not narrowed in terms of access to the Bachelor's degree programs funded by the University Grants Committee (UGC), however. Part of the reason for the failure to achieve greater equality of higher-education opportunity is from the mere fact that Bachelor's degree financing remains very expensive for the government and so has not expanded as much as secondary education. It is also possible that some of the demand for Bachelor access was redirected to the Associate degree programs, which began to proliferate ten years ago. From analysis of the 1996, 2001, and 2006 census (see Figure 13.4), it does not seem that these associate degree programs had become a diversion for poorer families in particular. Given that all those paying for studies to the associate degree level would have preferred to enter a Bachelor's degree program, there seems to be no great stratification between degree programs. That is, those who enroll in the Community College programs are not predominantly from the lower class, nor are those who are in publicly funded Bachelor's programs predominantly from the wealthiest sectors of Hong Kong. However, among the children who pursued higher education outside of Hong Kong, wealthier families predominated. Only time will tell whether continued expansion eventually does result in increasing concentration of social origin by institutional type and increasing inequality between institutions within Hong Kong.

How can we relate the development of Hong Kong higher education with Ruth Hayhoe's contribution? Most obviously, it was her leadership of the HKIEd that institutionalized the teaching profession as part of Hong Kong's higher education system. Beyond her administration, there are her contributions to educational thought. Most of her contributions have been

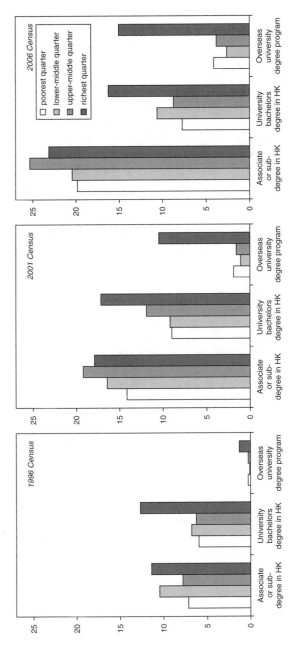

Figure 13.4: Postsecondary educational attainment rates for usual Hong Kong resident children aged 19–20 years, by parental income quartile in 1996, 2001, and 2006 census.

in the history of Chinese educators, the focus of a different section of this book. However, Ruth has also contributed her own ideas about education, and some of these are now percolating into the discussions about the purpose of higher education as Hong Kong extends its Bachelor's degree from three to four years.

In a prescient article that was ultimately published only one month before Tiananmen Massacre, Hayhoe wrote that China's dilemma was to reconcile its aspirations for economic modernity, on the one hand, with "notions of political order that were conceived entirely in terms of the regulation and control of knowledge, on the other. The anarchy that historically accompanied attempts to deregulate knowledge, most dramatically evident in the Cultural Revolution period, has only served to reinforce adherence to the opposite pole. This is the problem of a dialectic without synthesis."

What would be a synthesis in the field of education? For Hayhoe, one suspects that it would be a humanistic and pluralistic valuation of many educational traditions and histories. How are these values to be inculcated? Here is where Hayhoe the educational leader finds her mission. As she explained in her presidential lecture to the Comparative and International Education Society, while she led the HKIEd: "I have read the story of comparative education as a kind of search for ways of dealing with values and ethical decisions within the patterns provided by a reflexive modernity. The concept of redeeming modernity, rooted in a Judeo-Christian value framework, has provided an overarching metanarrative for that search. It has also opened up space for listening to metanarratives coming from other spiritual traditions" (2000, 439).

Ruth's vision of education as part of a search for value and ethical decisions is at odds with the Hong Kong government's motives for supporting higher education in recent years. Rather than searching for "values," it often seems that the only rationale for higher education has been to increase the value of the Hong Kong workforce in competition with other cities of Asia. Listening seriously to Hayhoe, one can hear options for constructing a modern educational architecture that retain (or "redeem") an ethical vision of educational purpose, a purpose predating the current expansion.

Architecture is not merely a metaphor for the planning options before Hong Kong, but is also the literal embodiment of the choices. I will illustrate this point with a digression to Rome and Washington before returning to Hong Kong. Ruth Hayhoe's original passion was for Latin literature and, as previously mentioned, she nearly traveled to Rome rather than Hong Kong upon graduation from the University of Toronto. Had she made a home for herself in Rome, she would have often contemplated the Arch of Constantine (fine images of this monument could be found on the

Internet). The architecture of this monument was later appropriated by the world's first superpower as a monument to its own preeminent position in technology and industry. A hundred years ago, many in the United States saw their country as in same position relative to the rest of the world as they imagined was the relation of the Roman Empire. This is one reason that visitors to Washington, DC, can appreciate its twentieth-century architecture more if they have first studied the classics.

One of the grandest modern buildings of Washington, DC, is the 1907 Union Train Station, designed by Chicago architect Daniel Burnham. Burnham copied the Arch of Constantine for his façade (also evident in any search on the Internet). However, what is of most curiosity is the inscription he fixed above the portal of this busy thoroughfare, above, that is, the arch of the new empire. For over 100 years, all who entered this magnificent structure have hurried beneath its epigram: "The truth shall make you free." Abstracted from the original context, from John 8:31–32, this striking legend becomes the hallmark of modernity itself. Whereas Jesus stated that "ye shall know the truth, and the truth shall make you free" from sin, the modernistic vision of secular progress that is captured by Union Station, and by many contemporary design elements, equates spiritual progress with economic growth, commerce, and the mobility represented by the equivalent of the Internet in 1907 (i.e., the modern railway).

By contrast with the expansive historical and spiritual ambitions of Union Station, the utilitarian and functionalist architecture of Hong Kong's universities reflect a superabundance of concrete and engineering know-how. But a corresponding richness of vision and historical imagination? This seems doubtful. Yet, the ethical and humanistic vision of Hayhoe may still be emergent. Consider the architectural example of the next-door neighbor of Hayhoe's old *Yan Kwong* School at Diamond Hill. In her 1967 encounter, Hayhoe experienced the sights and sounds of a different spiritual tradition, the *Chin Ling* (Chi Lin) Buddhist Nunnery. Today, although the *Yan Kwong* School has been pulled down, its property has been incorporated into the grounds of the nunnery. And the nunnery's original structures have themselves been replaced with a spectacular replica of a Tang Dynasty monument, the likes of which never existed in Hong Kong in the historical past (any more than did the Arch of Constantine exist in the early United States). The attempt by a key Hong Kong spiritual institution to connect with China's past indicates the unease with the ends-directed rationality of the modern, market-driven, competitive relationships that are being cultivated by most Hong Kong schools, with their obsessive drive for quantifiable and certifiable success.

There are other signs of Hayhoe's relevance to Hong Kong education in recent years. One is the affinity with her ideas of the medical doctor who now heads the Chinese University of Hong Kong, Joseph Jao-yiu Sung. It will be a happy encounter when he and Ruth Hayhoe finally meet in person, because Dr Sung has written eloquently about the need for a new vision of higher education. "I believe that a university should, while creating knowledge and nurturing talent with professional expertise, preserve and promulgate its culture and core values. Without culture and ideals, a university has lost its soul."[6] Another sign of movement away from the overly utilitarian view of education could be found in quite a different public intellectual, the barrister and progressive political leader Margaret Ng Ngoi Yee. When asked why Hong Kong invested money in higher education, she replied: "When we look at government rhetoric and setting the agenda for the public discussion, basically they're about the economy, about getting the jobs—and about less getting the jobs as pushing Hong Kong's economy. I see a minority view—but a very, very minority view—which doesn't actually get heard, which is that education is not about the economy. Education is about bringing up people who will be the future leaders."[7]

The sentiments of Joseph Sung and Margaret Ng may appear anachronistic in the immediate present, but their ideas are deeply rooted in the Chinese educational traditions documented by Hayhoe. In the larger history of China, arguments based on manpower planning, instrumentalism, and materialism are actually more anachronistic than are the arguments by Sung and Ng. To appreciate the Hong Kong traditions that support both the physical architecture of the *Chin Ling* Buddhist Nunnery at Diamond Hill and the rhetorical architecture used by Sung and Ng, consider first the arguments invoked by the Englishman who held Hong Kong University's professorship of education, K. E. Priestly. Writing in the *South China Morning Post* in November 1957 in opposition to the creation of a second university for the Chinese population, Priestly employed the language of manpower planning:

> In days past when higher education was the privilege of a small exalted class of gentlemen in England or would-be mandarins in China, it was no doubt a proper and sufficient justification to say that higher education cultivated knowledge for its own sake. Indeed, in those days reference to its uses was felt to be undignified. Today, so far as individuals or benefactors are concerned, higher education need seek no new justification; but insofar as it demands that the taxpayer should pay, it must embrace courses which meet community needs; and the less sectarian or racial or political it is, the more easily will it attract unanimous support. Hongkong government might fairly and squarely be asked to pay for higher education which keeps Hongkong in the main stream of the development of modern science,

technology, commercial, social, and pedagogical techniques; or which is calculated to reduce our dependence upon the expatriate officer in all these spheres; or which contributes to the process of cultural fusion of two great civilizations, the process by which Hongkong lives and breathes.

Second, consider the response to Priestly by three prominent intellectuals and educators, who drafted a rejoinder in English and published their arguments in the *South China Morning Post* in December 1957. The three heads of the Chinese Colleges Joint Council, D. Y. Lin (*Chung Chi* College), Chien Mu (New Asia College), and F. I. Tseung (United College) offered a compelling (and ultimately successful) reframing of Priestly's architectural elements:

> China has its own educational ideals and traditions, fully as ancient and as well tried as those of the west....There is....an important connection between language and leadership. Very few students can ever be expected to become completely bilingual in the sense that they would be entirely at home in the classical literature of both England and China. If the function of a university is to train leaders for a given society, it is very important to decide in what language these leaders shall be trained to think. The graduates of a Chinese university may not be able to read Chaucer, but they will be able to read the great classical writers of their own civilization....The debate between advocates of "early specialization" and those who would continue to emphasise "general education" in the university is by no means a closed issue even in England itself. In Hongkong, it may be argued that there is a still greater need for general cultural education beyond middle school for Chinese young people who live in a rootless and over-commercialised environment. The development in them of a sense of social responsibility alone requires it. Furthermore, this is consistent with China's own tradition of higher education.

Today, the spiritual and humanistic argument for education is being combined with a new concern for civic (or, sometimes, patriotic) curricula in Hong Kong. Liberal Studies is a new element in the secondary-school curriculum, and the three-year course of studies at Hong Kong's universities has just been extended to four years so that general studies and humanistic nonprofessional classes can be offered to all students. Were Ruth Hayhoe to return to participate in Hong Kong's higher education system, she might feel at home.

I wish to conclude this chapter conventionally by recapitulating and then ending at the beginning, for the question reposes itself insistently: Journey out or journey home? Will Hong Kong's higher-education system grow to offer not merely opportunities for access to all, but real opportunities for intellectual and moral development? I believe it will. Hong Kongers are no longer satisfied with the 1957 rationales used by Professor Priestly to justify public support of universities. Hong Kong higher education is no longer exclusive, and the numbers of students as well as their social origins have expanded massively. Until now, mass higher education has been justified mainly though arguments based on technological production and human capital formation. However, these arguments are being contested as never before, so that now there is wide acknowledgment that universities have a broader role, making responsible, caring citizens while preserving a space for debate. In this sense, Hong Kong higher education "returns" to the architecture of ideas cherished in classical Chinese civilization, even while departing from utilitarian rhetoric sharpened in the late colonial period.

The journey of Ruth is equally clear. The Biblical Ruth did not return to her roots or come "full circle." She left behind her original exclusive society and joined a different community.[8] Hence, the real, nonmetaphorical and non-archetypical Ruth Hayhoe. She has contested her own assumptions and moved to an inclusive, humanistic view of beauty and virtue. The legacy of Hayhoe's educational thought for Hong Kong is part of a broad-based turn both forward and toward ideals of Chinese education and even spirituality. Not only as an administrator but also as a creative thinker, Hayhoe will be remembered in Hong Kong higher education.

NOTES

1. For further exploration on the history and politics of Hong Kong education, please consult the references to these scholars in the bibliography to this chapter.
2. "Hashem" was and is a common Hebrew reference for God, meaning "the name," spoken to avoid mentioning God directly. The Biblical Ruth here is being specific in referencing the God of the Hebrews in particular, as opposed to one of the gods of her original native community.
3. *Full Circle*, p. 53. Hayhoe does not tell readers whether she thinks that *Yan Kwong* could have adapted to the new requirements in order to accept Education Department subsidies.
4. "We looked at [educational expansion] in terms of what it was desirable to do, and if further down the road there were consequences for the type of political organizations that society would want for change, then that's fine. We were certainly not going to do something simply because there might be that sort of issue down the road. We were entirely in the business of an evolving society, an upwardly mobile society." Interview with Lord Wilson at Peterhouse, Cambridge University, June 2007.

5. In census surveys since 1996, parents have been asked about the educational activities and attainment for all children, even for children who resided temporarily outside Hong Kong in pursuit of higher education or for temporary employment. However, to make the analyses depicted in Figures 13.2 and 13.3 comparable across all census years, I have restricted the definition of postsecondary and university attainment to mean attainment in a Hong Kong institution. This restriction also focuses the analysis on the consequences of Hong Kong government support of its own education system.
6. Online Chinese University blog space of Vice-Chancellor Sung.
7. Interview, David Post with Margaret Ng Ngoi Yee, May 2007.
8. A community in which she became a great-great-grandmother to the Biblical "David!"

REFERENCES

Campbell, Joseph. 1972. *The Hero with a Thousand Faces*. Princeton, NJ: Princeton University Press.

Chan, Joseph, and Elaine Chan. 2006. "Charting the State of Social Cohesion in Hong Kong." *The China Quarterly* 187: 635–658.

Cheng, Kai Ming. 1987. *The Concept of Legitimacy in Educational Policy-Making: Alternative Explanations of Two Policy Episodes in Hong Kong*. Unpublished Ph.D. Thesis, University of London.

Choi, Po-King. 1990. "A Search for Cultural Identity: The Students' Movement of the Early Seventies." In *Differences and Identities: Educational Argument in Late Twentieth Century Hong Kong*, ed. Anthony Sweeting (pp. 81–108). Faculty of Education Papers No. 9. Hong Kong: University of Hong Kong.

Hale, Sir Edward. 1965. *The Financing of Universities in Hong Kong*. Hong Kong: Government Press.

Hayhoe, Ruth. 1989. "A Chinese Puzzle." *Comparative Education Review* 33 (2): 155–175.

Hayhoe, Ruth. 2000. "Redeeming Modernity." *Comparative Education Review* 44 (4): 423–439

Hayhoe, Ruth. 2004. *Full Circle: A Life with Hong Kong and China*. Hong Kong: Comparative Education Research Centre, The University of Hong Kong.

Keswick, John. 1952. *Report of the Committee on Higher Education in Hong Kong*. Hong Kong: The Government Printer.

Leung, Benjamin K. P. 2000. "The Student Movement in Hong Kong: Transition to a Democratizing Society." In *The Dynamics of Social Movement in Hong Kong*, ed. Stephen Wing Kai Chiu and Tai Lok Lui (pp. 209–226). Hong Kong: Hong Kong University Press.

Ng, Lun Ngai-ha. 1984. *Interactions of East and West: Development of Public Education in Early Hong Kong*. Hong Kong: Chinese University Press.

Post, David. 1993. "Educational Opportunity and the Role of the State in Hong Kong." *Comparative Education Review* 37 (3): 240–262.

Post, David. 2010. "Postsecondary Educational Expansion and Social Integration In Hong Kong." *Research in Sociology and Socialization* 17: 231–270.

Post, David, and Suet-ling Pong. 1998. "The Waning Effect of Sibship Structure on School Attainment in Hong Kong." *Comparative Education Review* 42 (2): 99–117.

Sweeting, Anthony. 1993. *A Phoenix Transformed: The Reconstruction of Education in Post-war Hong Kong.* Hong Kong: Oxford University Press.

Sze, W. T. (Anthony Sweeting). 1990. "The Cat and the Pigeons: Relationships between the Government and the Universities in Hong Kong." In *Differences and Identities: Educational Argument in Late Twentieth Century Hong Kong,* ed. Anthony Sweeting (pp. 127–159). Faculty of Education Papers No. 9. Hong Kong: University of Hong Kong.

Chapter 14

Hong Kong's Potential for Global Educational Dialogue: Retrospective and Vision

Ruth Hayhoe

This chapter is based on a keynote address given for a historic ministerial round-table conference held in Hong Kong on July 14, 2011, to celebrate the completion of an educational reform process begun in 1997, the year Hong Kong was reunited with mainland China after 155 years as a colony of Britain.[1] Invited to comment on the educational reform process and its importance for human resource development, I began by noting that the concept of human resources has broader connotations than human capital, the concept often used by economists concerned with competition in the global knowledge society. It includes moral, aesthetic, emotional, and social dimensions, alongside the cognitive. In reviewing many of the reform documents, I discovered a recurring concern with the moral aspects of education and the need to strengthen connection with China's classical heritage, while learning lessons from all that is most advanced in global educational and scientific developments: "It is the society's expectation that education should enrich our moral, emotional, spiritual and cultural life so that we can rise above the material world" (Education Commission 2000, 38). This mention of the spiritual dimension intrigued me, and I have taken it up in the concluding section of the chapter.

I had the privilege of studying under Professor Brian Holmes at the University of London Institute of Education in the early 1980s, and one of his deep insights as a comparative education scholar related to the fact that education reforms are often carefully formulated and adopted at the policy level, yet fail to be fully or effectively implemented, since teachers and parents do not connect at a deep level to the values expressed in the reforms. The Hong Kong government certainly undertook extensive consultation at every stage of the reform process, with substantive input from teachers, parents, and community groups, as well as local and international experts. Nevertheless, I felt it might be helpful to reflect on the resources of educational thought and culture that Hong Kong has to call upon, as it moves forward to implement and build upon the reforms that have been put in place.

In the first decade of the twenty-first century, China's rise has become increasingly clear, and also the recognition that its achievement is not merely a result of the strategic policies and decisions of its leaders. Rather, it reflects the richness of its educational resources, rooted in a Confucian civilizational heritage that goes back 2,500 years. Over its 155 years as a British colony, Hong Kong had access to educational values that undergirded Britain's remarkable rise and extensive empire, from the seventeenth century to the mid-twentieth century. Much has been written about the parallels between the Chinese commitment to nurturing scholar officials and the British concept of the scholar gentleman, but only Hong Kong has had such a lengthy experience of the blending of these two traditions. The recent reform has brought about a fundamental change in the structures left by British colonialism, yet positive elements in the values that have made Hong Kong such a dynamic city remain a significant resource for the future.

The second half of the twentieth century has been dominated by American educational ideas and values, which have an ongoing global influence. The structural reform of Hong Kong's educational system has resulted in a move from a 6-5-2-3 pattern to the widely influential American pattern of 6-3-3-4. Efforts to foster student-centered learning, to integrate different parts of the curriculum and encourage creative thinking, also resonate with Deweyian educational values. Interestingly, this structural change also makes the Hong Kong education system fully compatible with that of China. The reason for this goes back to the early twentieth century, when John Dewey's visit to China influenced China's educational reform legislation of 1922. The 6-3-3-4 structure put in place at that time has persisted in mainland China until now (Hayhoe 1984, 37–40). Of even greater significance was Dewey's influence on Tao Xingzhi, one of modern China's most influential educators, as well as the resonances between Dewey's educational ideas and the educational thought of such progressive Confucians as Wang Yangming in the sixteenth century and Liang Shuming and James Yen Yangchu in the twentieth century (Keenan 1977).

As Hong Kong goes forward in implementing the courageous and visionary reforms undertaken since its return to China in 1997, it thus has the possibility of drawing upon values and ideas from classical China, Britain, and the United States. These have already demonstrated their capacity for the enrichment and enlargement of human potential in a range of historical settings, both singly and in various combinations. Hong Kong is in the unique position of being able to build upon these three influential traditions at a deep level and create an approach to education that integrates best practices from China, Europe, and North America. This should make it possible to optimize the potential of each and every child, enabling Hong Kong's people to live fulfilled lives and contribute to their community, the Chinese nation, and the world.

In this chapter, I begin by sketching out my personal experience of Hong Kong's educational development, from the perspective of a Canadian whose education was also profoundly influenced by the British tradition. Then I look at some of the expressed goals of the reform in terms of the full development of each individual in a student-centered learning environment; effective communication in Cantonese, Putonghua (Mandarin), and English; responsible citizenship at the local, national, and global levels; and creative contributions to fundamental knowledge that will enable Hong Kong to remain competitive in the global knowledge economy.

From there, I turn to potential areas of synergy among Chinese, British, and American educational values and ideas. First, the dynamic educational reforms under Song Neo-Confucian ideas of moral transformation are compared with Renaissance English ideas of civility to develop the concept of humane talent. Then a parallel is drawn between the educational thought of John Dewey and the progressive ideas of the twentieth-century Confucian Liang Shuming, to introduce the idea of an inclusive individuality. Finally, a new way of thinking about childhood in a Chinese context, based on Daoist thought, draws attention to Chinese roots for a radical creativity in education. My conclusion demonstrates how these deep-rooted values, which are all a part of Hong Kong's rich heritage, could be drawn upon in implementing an approach to education that integrates Chinese and Western educational ideas and has the potential to enrich global educational discourse.

Personal Reflections, from 1967 to the Present

My personal perspective on Hong Kong education reform goes back to June 30, 1967, when I got off an airplane at Kaitak Airport and began to look for my first job as a novice teacher in a Hong Kong secondary school. I had just completed an honors degree in Classics at the University of Toronto, which my professors boasted was identical in curricular content to Greats at Oxford. My secondary school had been similar to a British grammar school. Much more attention was given to English literature and history than that of Canada, let alone the nearby United States. And I had written Grade Thirteen examinations similar to British A-Levels, a structure that only disappeared in Ontario in the 1990s. Efforts at building Canadian identity through education and influences from American progressive education came along with the student radicalism that unfolded in the late 1960s, shortly after my departure for Hong Kong. I thus felt comfortable with the ethos and curricular patterns of a fairly traditional Anglican girls school, Heep Yunn, where I taught from 1967 to 1978, while setting myself to master both Cantonese and Mandarin.

With the Cultural Revolution raging in China in 1967, a third wave of refugees was finding its way to Hong Kong, following the influx after the revolution of 1949, and the flow escaping from the Great Famine of 1959–1961. I was impressed at the efficiency of the colonial government in building six-story resettlement estates to provide basic housing as quickly as possible, with rooftops that served as schools for the children. Since I had family connections with two elderly Christian missionaries, one of whom ran a rooftop school in Wong Tai Sin and the other a mission school in Diamond Hill, I had the opportunity to get to know some of the families and children. A patchwork of such schools filled in the gaps left by the government system, and made it possible for most children to have access to primary education. Secondary schooling was a different matter, however, and the majority of the children from the refugee areas and resettlement estates were working in factories for plastics, toys, and electronics by the time they reached their teens. In 1978, the year that I left Hong Kong to pursue graduate education in London and university teaching work in Shanghai, the colonial government initiated a reform that ensured nine years of compulsory education for all children, six years of primary and three years of lower secondary.

The story of one refugee family whose children attended my cousin's school gave me some insight into the human resources that could not be developed in those years. This family had five young children, all of whom attended Yan Kwong or Grace and Light, my cousin's school in Diamond

Hill. The father worked as an orderly in a local hospital, and through a church connection, he got the opportunity to immigrate to Canada and work as a personal assistant to an elderly man with Alzheimer's. Within a year, his family followed him and settled in Toronto. His oldest daughter found a job as a bank teller, but the other four children completed secondary education and subsequently studied at the University of Toronto. All of them had successful professional careers. This would have been impossible had they remained in Hong Kong of the 1970s.

The introduction of compulsory nine-year education for all children in Hong Kong coincided with the dramatic reform and opening up of China under Deng Xiaoping in 1978. As China's economy began its rapid revitalization, many Hong Kong factories moved inland and Hong Kong's landscape changed noticeably. The expansion of a diverse yet largely public higher-education system that thrived under the British-modeled University Grants Committee (UGC) has been one of the important stories of reform. As I pursued an academic career that involved periods of teaching, diplomatic work, and higher-education development in China, it was always a pleasure to pass through Hong Kong and see how it was transforming itself. I followed the negotiations for Hong Kong's historic return to China with interest, and reflected on the consequences for education, but never expected to be personally involved.

It was a surprising turn of events that brought me back to Hong Kong in September 1997, 19 years after I had left in 1978 and at the historic juncture of Hong Kong's return to China on the first of July of that year. As the newly appointed director of the Hong Kong Institute of Education (HKIEd), I had to think through the consequences of Hong Kong's new identity for teachers at all levels. I also served as a member of the Education Commission that drafted the first major reform document, *Learning for Life Learning through Life* (Education Commission 2000) and chaired the subcommittee for early childhood education. While higher education had blossomed, with 18 percent of the age cohort entering universities, teacher education had lagged behind and the majority of teachers for basic education were still being trained in two-year certificate programs. What kind of content should our new Bachelor of Education courses have in order to ensure teachers who could be well prepared to carry out the reforms that were being planned?

Our first task at HKIEd was to develop a vision that went to the heart of the reform's purpose. It took immense focus and intellectual effort to formulate this in a concise and clear way, using 12 words in English and 12 Chinese characters: "Optimizing each child's potential through the shared joy of learning and teaching" 共享學教喜悅盡展赤子潛能 (Hayhoe 2001, 337). This was the vision we hammered out over a year of deliberation, with a committee consisting of colleagues, students, and community representatives. It goes to the heart of educational reform and human resource development. We also developed guiding values that touched upon core areas addressed in the reforms, including civic and moral education, language policy, and effective communication, an approach to educational quality that called for the integration of academic excellence with social and professional practice, as well as the importance of a strong foundation in early childhood education.

Major Achievements of the Reform

Since I left Hong Kong in the spring of 2002, I did not have the opportunity to observe, at close hand, the unfolding of the various stages of the reform movement, culminating in the implementation of four-year undergraduate programs in Hong Kong's public universities in 2012. It was thus a moving experience to read or reread the major reform documents as I prepared to write this chapter. I was struck by the determination to effect major reforms that will open up opportunities for all of Hong Kong's people to fully develop their potential and talent, while at the same time preserving and building upon the heritage of the past: "Our education system is infused with the essence of eastern and western cultures, preserving the basic elements of traditional Chinese education while absorbing the most advanced concepts, theories and experiences from modern western education" (Education Commission 2000, 3–4).

The reason I emphasize this point is that I believe it provides conditions for Hong Kong's reformed education system to contribute to the global community in unique ways. There is an increasing awareness globally that China's rise owes a great deal to its educational values and patterns, and that these have much to offer to the world. Yet, in spite of China's newly developing cultural diplomacy and the proliferation of Confucius Institutes around the world, there are few educators who can articulate the relevance of these values clearly. Fewer still can demonstrate the ways in which they can effectively integrate the dominant streams of educational influence in the Western world within a Chinese framework. That is precisely where the success of Hong Kong's reform could be important not only locally but also in a wider global context.

Let me begin with a consideration of the structural reforms that have been put in place. I remember vividly the sense we had in our early deliberations that there was a need for space to be created, in which children could stretch their minds, open their hearts, and learn freely and with joy.

There was a need to lift the high-stakes examination barriers, which had led to a culture of constant testing and teaching to the test.

This has now been done at two crucial junctures in the structure. At the interface between six years of primary education and the beginning of secondary education, schools have been encouraged to create a "through train" (Education Commission 2000, 18) in order that the majority of children would move smoothly through their nine years of compulsory education, before entering a three-year senior secondary program. The purpose of testing was changed from a mechanism for allocating life chances to a tool for analyzing learning difficulties and facilitating effective diagnosis and assistance. It is difficult to judge how far this has been successfully implemented in the complexity of the Hong Kong school environment but the vision is a compelling one and a model for progressive education everywhere.

The second change, which has been even larger and more consequential, was the decision to develop a single Hong Kong Diploma of Secondary Education and benchmark it to parallel university entrance examinations in other jurisdictions. Hong Kong students no longer face two sets of high-stakes examinations in their upper-secondary years at Form 5 and Form 7, similar to British O and A Levels, but one common examination for all school leavers (Education and Manpower Bureau 2005). Given the fact that only about 35 percent of Form 5 graduates had had the opportunity to study in Forms 6 and 7 and compete for university entrance in the past, this has been a dramatic opening up of space and opportunity for all young people on an even playing ground. It is also a step that has brought the Hong Kong system in line with that of mainland China and most jurisdictions in North America.

This has in turn created the need for a four-year university system in which students have greater latitude in their first two years for general studies and a range of electives while still being able to focus on an academic or professional major. In addition, a large number of new programs at diploma and associate degree level have opened up, with an opportunity for articulation to the public university system for high-achieving students. Every effort has been made to ensure a "no-loser" principle with opportunities for early and late bloomers and for students from disadvantaged backgrounds alongside those from more privileged families (University Grants Committee 2010, 46).

The new structure has in turn opened up space for a wholly different approach to curriculum, as learning experiences rather than fixed bodies of knowledge to be transmitted. The reform documents are replete with phrases such as "life-wide learning" and "student focused learning." A curriculum framework has been put in place for the nine years of compulsory education that sets forth eight key learning areas, generic skills to be mastered, and values and attitudes to be nurtured. Of particular significance is the place of Chinese history and culture within this new curriculum. The first of six strands within general studies in the primary curriculum, history is an independent subject in junior and senior secondary education. A crucial decision was made to teach history as one subject, with Chinese history providing the frame from which world history is to be examined (Curriculum Development Council 2001, 23). This may prove difficult to implement, but it expresses a new and more integrated way of looking at the world from Asia.

The new curricula for senior secondary education focus on the three core areas of Mathematics, Chinese, and English, with the addition of a fourth core area called Liberal Studies. All students are required to take two or three elective subjects to fill out their program, either from such traditional disciplines as physics, chemistry, biology, and geography, or from more applied and career-oriented areas. There have been many debates over the development of liberal studies, with its three broad areas relating to the human condition and the contemporary world: Self and Personal Development; Society and Culture; Science, Technology, and the Environment. Clearly, Liberal Studies aim to give students a sound foundation in basic knowledge that will enable them to be responsible citizens at the local, national, and global levels.

The intention of these curricular documents is to provide a common core of education for all of Hong Kong's children and young people. It will give them a strong foundation in Mathematics, Chinese, and English, an opportunity to build their own well-founded understanding of current personal, social, and environmental issues, to master several other basic or applied subject areas and gain an examination qualification that is recognized in Hong Kong and abroad. All will be given the opportunity for some form of further or higher education that will enable them to find employment and contribute to their community. Making all of this happen constitutes a huge ongoing task, but one can see an educational structure and curricular philosophy that should make it possible for children's potential to be developed and for learning to be so enjoyable that it becomes a lifelong habit.

A third part of the picture in Hong Kong's educational reform is that of language and the issue of medium of instruction. While Putonghua is mandated as the medium of instruction in all of China, Hong Kong made the firm determination at the time of reunification to maintain and strengthen the role of Cantonese, a local dialect of Chinese, as the main medium of instruction for most primary and secondary schools. Research showed that Hong Kong young people learned subjects such as chemistry and geography more effectively when teaching was done in their mother tongue, and many secondary schools were required to change from English to Cantonese medium, with exceptions for those that could demonstrate high standards in English.

While I understand well the parental opposition to this policy, often based on their sense of the higher status of English-medium schools, it seemed absolutely clear to me, as a scholar of education, that this was a wise decision. In fact, I believe Hong Kong's language policy is one of the great strengths of the educational reforms. English remains an important language, indeed the language of global engagement, yet the role of Cantonese, the mother tongue, has been maintained and enhanced, while measures have also been put in place for all children to become fluent in Putonghua, the language in common use throughout mainland China. A further intriguing angle to this trilingualism is the notion of bi-literacy in English and Chinese. Given a history of the use of traditional Chinese characters in Hong Kong, contrasting with the simplified characters used throughout mainland China, this has its own complications.

The curricular goal is for Hong Kong students to be able to "engage in discussion actively and competently in English and Chinese (including Putonghua)" (Curriculum Development Council 2001, 6). My personal observation while at the HKIEd was that Hong Kong students were enthusiastic about gaining proficiency in Putonghua and excited by the new frontiers it opened in their lives. One of my proudest moments was when HKIEd students came second in a national university debating competition in Shanghai, using fluent Putonghua to argue some complex and controversial propositions. On the other hand, there has been some concern as to whether the added emphasis on mastery of Putonghua would influence levels of English-language competency. Trilingualism and bi-literacy in two very different kinds of written language sets a high bar for Hong Kong young people.

The preservation of local and national languages in the face of globalization has become a major concern for many educational jurisdictions around the world. Long ago, Ali Mazrui wrote eloquently about his native Kenya, and the need for education reforms that embraced local tribal languages, the East African regional language of Swahili and the colonial language of English (Mazrui 1975). With the sweep of globalization, English is becoming more and more dominant, giving Hong Kong an advantage with the strengths of English in its educational history, and also an opportunity to model a balanced approach to language policy in education. Local culture is preserved and enhanced by the use of Cantonese as the main medium of instruction in the early years and fluency in Putonghua is promoted, alongside English.

When we were putting together the guiding values for HKIEd's vision in 1998, we decided on a somewhat broader language vision, and expressed it as follows: "We support multilingualism to encourage flexibility of mind and access to the wisdom of the world's diverse cultures" (Hayhoe 2001, 340–341). There are many statements in Hong Kong's curricular reform documents that endorse this value and indicate that the learning of other languages, beyond Chinese and English, will also be encouraged.

Before concluding this section on the major achievements of the reform, something should be said about the areas of early childhood education and higher education, which might be seen as bookends of the reform. Although my expertise lies in the area of comparative higher education, I found myself passionate about the importance of reforms in early childhood education during my Hong Kong years and was pleased to be entrusted with chairing a subcommittee in this area. One of the constantly recurring themes of the reform documents is the importance of lifelong learning, and this was endorsed in one of HKIEd's guiding values: "We affirm early childhood education as the foundation of lifelong learning" (Hayhoe 2001, 339). While most early childhood educational provision is in the private sector, a crucial aspect of the reforms has been the provision of much more substantive and academically demanding teacher formation for the early childhood sector. This indicates a recognition of how important are a child's earliest years, when the patterns that take shape in the brain set the parameters for a lifelong capacity to learn.

At the other end of the spectrum of reform, it is not surprising that the rethinking of higher education has taken some time. The recently published report of the UGC (2010) lays out the contours of a higher-education system that seeks to maintain a considerable degree of diversity while promoting the highest possible standards of excellence in teaching and scholarship. Plans for a fully integrated framework of qualifications and a unified approach to quality assurance are notable. Also of note is the high priority given to internationalization, an internationalization rooted in the "deeply embedded character" of Hong Kong's history as "a point of encounter between different cultures and influences and ways of thought" (University Grants Committee 2010, 68). To be brief, this document lays out the promise that 65% of Hong Kong's young people will be able to benefit from some form of higher education in future. This diverse higher-education system is also to embrace an increasing number of students from mainland China and from the international community, and emphasis will be given to developing "curricula that combine Western and Asian problems and responses, experiences, sources and cultural roots" (University Grants Committee 2010, 60).

"'Teaching without any discrimination' has been a cherished concept since ancient times. We should not give up on any single student but rather let all students have the chance to develop their potentials," stated the first of the reform documents (Education Commission 2000, 36). "The concept that everyone is educable, everyone can become a sage, and everyone is perfectible forms the basic optimism and dynamism towards education in the Confucian tradition," commented Lee Wing On (Lee 1996, 38). By contrast, Brian Holmes has noted how the Platonic view of human beings as having innate intelligence passed on by heredity resulted in long-persisting structures and patterns of education in Europe that nurtured a limited elite to a high level, while creating barriers impassable for the majority (Holmes 1981, 135–141). I mentioned earlier the four children from a refugee family who had no chance for secondary education in colonial Hong Kong of the 1970s, but managed to graduate from the University of Toronto after immigrating to Canada in those same 1970s. Hong Kong's return to a foundational Chinese belief in the potential of each and every child and the creation of a system with no losers is thus something worth celebrating!

At the same time, there is a realization that the full implementation of the reforms will be a challenging process. We live in an era of globalization that emphasizes intense competition on the part of individuals and nations for a fuller share in the global knowledge economy. There is a concomitant tendency to see human resources in a one-dimensional way as human capital—highly skilled individuals who are able to obtain a personal return on their investment in education through high-paying jobs and good social status. Furthermore, some of the progressive ideas of inquiry and project-based learning in the curricular reform documents are premised on a Western assumption of the autonomous rights–bearing individual that does not fit comfortably with the Chinese idea of the person as a social being, deeply connected to family and community. In addition, the task of nurturing global citizens who have a balanced and critical understanding of national identity and a commitment to social justice remains elusive. The definition of the nation state that arose in nineteenth-century Europe still tends to dominate global discourse, and realist conceptions of national interest often take precedence over genuine commitment to a peaceful and sustainable global community.

Hong Kong's educational reforms have taken on a courageous commitment to the blending of the essence of East and West. The determination to teach one history, rather than Chinese history and world history as separate subjects, is both significant and difficult. It means integrating Western values and achievements into a Chinese frame and searching for a deep level of connection between the two sides. It might be seen as a reversal of the longstanding practice of interpreting China's historical development through a Western lens. Ironically, because of its lengthy experience of a British colonial regime, Hong Kong may be somewhat better situated to undertake this task than China, given the speed and scale of change that is unfolding there.

Let me return to the triangle of influences in global education—British, American, and Chinese—that were mentioned earlier in this chapter. Hong Kong's reform documents have asserted over and again the determination to build upon core Chinese values and equip her young people to be able to articulate these effectively in Cantonese, Putonghua, and English. At the level of higher education, there is an explicit commitment to a "fusion" between Chinese and Western approaches to knowledge. The structural aspects of the reform give evidence of a determination to move away from the British legacy, yet reforms in curriculum and pedagogy reflect awareness of significant innovations in both Britain and America for the improvement of teaching and learning. The most demanding task, in my view, is finding a deep foundation for connecting Chinese and British values, on the one hand, and Chinese and American values on the other. The end goal is to build a Chinese educational approach that absorbs the best values from these Western systems while carrying the global education discourse forward, and enabling it to move "beyond the Enlightenment," to use a phrase from Harvard Confucian scholar Tu Weiming (Tu 1998, 13–14).

In the next part of this chapter, I will take you on a journey with three young women scholars. Each of them felt compelled to dig into comparative history and philosophy in order to explore the ways in which China's educational heritage might contribute to the global educational community and enable humanity to move beyond the Enlightenment heritage, while absorbing and building upon its crucial contributions to human history. The first deals with issues of higher education and economic development, proposing an ideal of nurturing "humane talent" in place of the notions of human capital or human resources (Bai 2010). The second takes up the notion of quality at the level of basic education, one of the oft-repeated words in Hong Kong's reform discourse. She suggests the possibility of education fostering an "inclusive individuality" rooted in progressive Confucian thought (Zhang 2010). The third explores the Chinese world of childhood in order to uncover a radical source of freedom for human creativity in Daoist ways of thinking about human nature (Zhao 2010). All three scholars had the problems of China's educational reform in mind, when writing their essays; yet, they are equally relevant to Hong Kong. In fact, I am suggesting that Hong Kong's remarkable reform efforts have created conditions for a genuine synthesis between Chinese and Western educational values that has much to offer global educational circles.

Human Capital or Humane Talent? Synergies in Chinese-British Educational Thought

The move to mass higher education in Hong Kong took place over a longer period of time than in the mainland, with less-serious consequences for graduate unemployment. Nevertheless, Hong Kong education is subject to pressures of globalization and intense competition for recognition in global ranking systems that tend to turn education into a competitive exercise in the production of human capital. The strongly instrumentalist ethos that easily results can lead to neglect of the moral, spiritual, and aesthetic dimensions of education in favor of drilling for examination success. While Hong Kong has eliminated the two sets of high-stake examinations equivalent to British A and O Levels in favor of a single set of examinations for secondary-school completion and university entry, there is still intense competition for entry into tertiary programs most likely to yield status and attractive employment opportunities. Many of those who do not make the grade for university entrance and turn to associate degree programs find it hard to gain employment. They thus eagerly seek opportunities to gain a university-level qualification (University Grants Committee 2010, 40).

In both Hong Kong and the mainland, the global atmosphere of neoliberalism, with its focus on human capital, has combined with the firmly engrained belief in meritocracy through written examinations that is part of the Chinese tradition. In her research on higher-education massification in the mainland, Bai Limin has been deeply concerned about the dilemma of an increasing number of university graduates viewing higher education as an investment for personal advancement, an experience that has left them facing a similar disappointment to that of Hong Kong youth in associate degree programs.

Bai uses the ideas of British Asianist Ronald Dore (1976) to analyze the difference between education as a process of learning for pleasure and schooling as a process of certification with career advancement as a primary goal. She goes on to question the basic assumption of human capital and neoliberal ideology that the primary purpose of education is an investment promising high economic returns. Through an insightful comparative analysis of the educational ideas of Song Dynasty Neo-Confucianism and English Renaissance thought, she uncovers a historical synergy between a much broader set of British and Chinese educational values. She notes the expansion of the examination system in twelfth-century China to include many who were not from aristocratic families, yet who were enabled to join a ruling class in which "moral and intellectual qualities were more important than good birth." In the same era, she comments, "newly risen social groups in Renaissance England led to a redefinition of nobility and gentility on the basis of people's own virtue and wisdom, not of hierarchy." Neo-Confucian scholars emphasized "learning for the sake of the self….and self-cultivation became the basis of a good government and a harmonious society" (Bai 2010, 112). English scholars emphasized civility in place of nobility. There are striking parallels between civility as a model of behavior and the Chinese notion of *li* or rites of conduct.

The aim of humanist teachers in the subsequent centuries was to mould the complete citizen, with a liberal education that included the study of morals, history, law, ancient and modern languages, mathematics, and astronomy. That of neo-Confucian teachers, as expressed in *The Great Learning*, one of the famous *Four Books*, was to combine self-cultivation with keeping good order at home and dealing with the affairs of state as a whole principle. The notion of talent was thus much broader than the narrowly economistic concept of human capital or even the somewhat wider term human resources. It embodied all of the five core concepts that undergird curriculum in the Chinese context: the moral, cognitive, physical, social, and aesthetic (德智體群美 *de zhi ti qun mei*). It could be summed up in the term "humane talent." Bai noted how the core Confucian term "*ren*" (仁) or "benevolent" is very close to the English word "humane." Etymologically, both terms arise from the word human (人 *ren*) with the addition of an "e" in English and the character for two added to the human person in Chinese!

What we see here is a deep concurrence between English and Chinese views of the purposes of education in historical periods of significant transition—leading to the industrial revolution and the building of empire in Britain, to a period of flourishing in the Ming and early Qing dynasties that was subsequently followed by decline in China. Ronald Dore sums these up in his concept of "productive self-fulfillment" and his distinction between two different sets of intelligence-linked qualities: "qualities expressed in self-fulfilling activities that include curiosity, creativeness, productiveness and craftsmanship" and "acquisitive achievement," which he associated with "cunning and the ability to manipulate things and other people in order to acquire for oneself wealth or power or prestige" (Dore 1976, 177–178).

Mainland Chinese educators are struggling to counter tendencies toward a highly competitive examination-oriented culture that provides significant material and social rewards to the few who make it into elite institutions and leaves the rest demoralized. They are using the term quality education in this effort. Hong Kong's education reforms have put in place a structure and set of curricular patterns that have also been inspired by the idea of quality as one of the five major underlying principles (Education Commission 2000, 6) and a commitment to learning that encompasses moral, aesthetic, physical, and social elements alongside the cognitive tasks that are measured by examinations. At the higher-education level, the recent UGC report deals with this in a balanced and sensitive way: "It would be a mistake to regard universities exclusively in terms of a direct utility to the Hong Kong economy....Students should acquire a greater sense of the wider world and the moral or ethical tools with which they can contribute to that world" (University Grants Committee 2010, 15–16).

These thoughts on comparative history suggest that Hong Kong has a set of educational resources arising from the British heritage and its synergies with neo-Confucian values that could be extremely valuable in the implementation of the reforms. These resources are not just words found in public documents but deeply held beliefs passed down through the family and community. Hong Kong has the heritage of Christian churches, both Catholic and Protestant, which continue to provide education for many, and that exemplify the British notion of civility in their ethos. In reading the early history of education in nineteenth-century Hong Kong, for example, I was touched by the leadership of James Legge, the great missionary, professor and translator of the Confucian classics into English, who labored long ago to lay a foundation in which all students would learn Chinese and English, so that they could benefit from the richness of both of these heritages (Bickley 2001, 60–64, 91–92).

If Hong Kong is serious about a genuine integration of the essence of East and West, as expressed numerous times in the reform documents, reflection on the British educational heritage and its synergies with Song neo-Confucian educational values may be of particular importance. In short, can Hong Kong's educational reforms enable all of its people, its human resources, to become humane talent? Can Hong Kong nurture the kind of Confucian or Christian humanity that includes a high level of moral and spiritual capacity, alongside the scientific and social knowledge necessary to contribute effectively to all around development in an increasingly globalized world?

Inclusive Individuality-Synergies in Chinese-American Educational Thought

Probably the most fundamental curricular change in Hong Kong's educational reforms is the view of curriculum as experience, something that changes and evolves, rather than fixed documents outlining the knowledge that is to be mastered. This notion of curriculum as experience goes back to the celebrated American educator, John Dewey (1938). It has been noted earlier that Dewey spent two years in China around the time of the May Fourth Movement (Keenan 1977). Before going to China in 1919, Dewey had supervised a number of influential Chinese students, including philosopher Hu Shi and educator Tao Xingzhi. Through these and others, his educational ideas had a considerable impact on China's emerging modern educational structure, as well as experimental efforts with progressive school curricula in some urban settings.

Dewey's writings were translated into Chinese by a number of enthusiastic followers, including Tao Xingzhi. Deeply influenced by Dewey's view that knowledge arose from problem solving in the process of life experience, and in turn should be tested in action, Tao adopted a name that means "knowing through action." After returning to China, he came to believe that an even more radical version of this progressive epistemology could be found in Ming neo-Confucianism, particularly the writing of the sixteenth-century scholar, Wang Yangming. Wang had turned his back on book learning in favor of a "learning of the mind and heart" (心學 xinxue), to be achieved through a four-step process of reflection on experience (Hayhoe 2006, 33–34). This progressive thread in Ming Neo-Confucian philosophy might be seen as an indigenous foundation for a student-centered pedagogy.

While Hong Kong has not had the historical connections with Dewey's ideas that can be seen in mainland China, efforts to reform the curriculum toward progressive child-centered practices go back several decades, and can be seen in projects such as the "target-oriented curriculum." Further remarkable resources have been available through the support of the Curriculum Development Council to support the implementation of pedagogical reforms toward experiential learning. Now that a much larger space has been created, through the changes in structure and the reduction in the number and character of the examinations, we may hope for a genuine unfolding of curriculum as a progressive series of learning experiences that expand the child's knowledge and understanding of the self, the community, the nation, and the natural world.

However, fundamental differences between Chinese and Western views of the human person persist. While the West tends to think in terms of the autonomous rights–bearing individual, Chinese philosophy tends more toward social being, the person defined by family and community as having both obligations and rights. If the curricular reforms are to take deep root in the Hong Kong context, where the majority of children and families are fundamentally Chinese in mindset and heritage, there needs to be a way of conceiving individuality that fits this context.

Here the concept of inclusive individuality, developed by Zhang Huajun, may be helpful. Zhang has found inspiration in the resonance between the ideas of John Dewey and Liang Shuming, a twentieth-century Confucian whose signature work was titled *Eastern and Western Cultures and Their Philosophies* (Alitto 1979). Dewey's view of education might be summarized as the pursuit of genuine interest in ways that develop a sense of the self, suggests Zhang. Dewey saw interest as developed through activities in which the individual is engaged and education as a change process that continues to open up new possibilities for young people to gain broader perspectives and create connections between the past and ongoing experience. This process demands that the learner be willing to face uncertainties and unexpected challenges, which require a strong self-identity. Individuality is developed when genuine interests are identified and unknown or unfamiliar others are drawn into the inclusive self.

Resonating with this idea of Dewey's, Liang Shuming identified an inner self, which is not autonomous or essentialist, yet provides continuity as the child learns through interactive experience with the world. It is described as the "deep self" (深心 *shen xin*) and might be compared with the deep water at the bottom of a river. Liang's conception of the inner self is seen as developing through social interaction and the integration of others into the self. The individual reaches an independent capacity for self-reflection wherein the inner self is built up and a consistent self can be maintained, even in conditions of radical social change. Liang Shuming's notion of inclusive individuality may thus provide a strong foundation on which parents, teachers, and students can build, as they embrace the new curricular practices promoting learning through experience in the classroom, the home, and the community.

"The conception of inclusive individuality....responds to the call of the quality education reform movement for the development of the individual's full potential. By understanding their own mission in life, individuals gain their own vision of learning and are motivated to try their best to expand the boundary of the existent self and reach toward a more enriched self." For the teachers, who are to implement the curricular reforms, "to discover the richness of students' individuality, teachers first need to discover the richness of their own lives" (Zhang 2010, 232). Teacher education is thus crucial to the full implementation of the reforms, and Hong Kong is to be congratulated for its foresight in this regard. The vision of creating a purpose-built campus for teachers in a beautiful part of the New Territories under the hills of the eight immortals indicates a realization that teachers need the fullest possible experience of a liberal and progressive education themselves, if they are to be capable of optimizing the potential of each child in their class and creating conditions for "the shared joy of learning and teaching" (Hayhoe 2001, 237).

If Song neo-Confucian ideas have significant synergy with the values of Christian humanism that blossomed in the centuries before Britain's industrial revolution, Ming Neo-Confucian values connect well with progressive ideas of the American educational tradition, and indeed have been seen by Chinese educators as pre-dating them. Thus, there are real possibilities of an authentic indigenous notion of educational quality emerging in the Hong Kong context, and absorbing into itself these two streams of Western educational thought, while carrying them forward in ways that could revitalize global educational thought.

Recent years and the repeated results of the Programme for International Student Assessment (PISA) testing have shown children in Confucian heritage societies as being in advance of many other parts of the world. Shanghai's stunning debut as Number One in the world has reinforced this sense, and it is noteworthy that Hong Kong has maintained the fourth position, behind Korea and just ahead of Singapore (Hargreaves 2011, 21). Given that PISA tests give attention to problem-solving skills and social, emotional, and intellectual capacity, these results are interesting (Mundy and Farrell 2008, 202). Hong Kong's wonderful series about "The Chinese Learner" sheds considerable light on the reasons for this success (Chan and Rao 2009). The full implementation of Hong Kong's recent reforms could constitute a vivid demonstration of them in action! Here I am trying to suggest that Hong Kong has a unique capacity to integrate the strong threads of educational progressivism from Britain and America into a new vision for global education that is rooted in China's rich educational heritage.

One more piece to this puzzle may illuminate a part of the philosophical heritage that has challenged while also strengthening the unfolding Confucian tradition. That is Daoism and most particularly the radical educational ideas of the philosopher Zhuang Zi. To reflect on this possibility, I turn to a third scholar, who has recently written on Chinese childhood in a way that belies the common stereotypes about conformity and filial piety and gives insight into a significant source of energy for the implementation of educational reform from this part of China's rich heritage.

Chinese Childhood and the Roots of a Radical Creativity

If Confucianism has provided a remarkable continuity in China's educational culture, this has been largely due to its openness and ability to absorb impulses and ideas coming from the opposite values of the Daoist tradition. Historically, these provided a context that enabled Buddhism to make the transition from a foreign to an indigenous religion in China. Thus, Wang Yangming developed his "philosophy of the heart," Ming neo-Confucianism, after a period of experimentation with both Daoist and Buddhist philosophies. Similarly, Liang Shuming was deeply influenced by Buddhist ideas in developing his twentieth-century version of Confucian educational thought.

In a recent article on Chinese Cultural Dynamics and Childhood, Zhao Guoping has suggested the possibilities of this alternative tradition for the development of a truly radical creativity in education. She notes that there is "a hidden side that contradicts and undermines the dominant cultural project (of Confucianism) and because of it, the precious root for the development of individuality is preserved" (Zhao 2010, 583). Highlighting the "unity of heaven and humanity" (天人合一 *tianren heyi*), she identifies a Chinese notion of transcendence that does not seek to confront or overcome the world but rather connects the divine to humanity. From this comes the principle that it is possible to embrace all experiences unconditionally and positively, and to preserve and accommodate individual needs and interests, no matter whether or not they fall within the range of the cultural project. The philosopher Zhuang Zi was the ultimate defender of individual freedom and creativity in Chinese culture. His lively poetic approach to depicting the integration of the person with the larger whole opens up a radical freedom from all social and political constraints.

Zhao notes a fascination with the revival of subjectivity (主體性 *zhutixing*) in recent Chinese educational scholarship. While some have interpreted this as reflecting the influence of Western ideas of individualism, she counters this by saying "the remarkable Chinese dynamic that rejects and yet embraces individual needs and experiences has helped preserve and nourish individualistic sentiments and thus makes individual flourishing possible." She sees this as quite distinct from the search to emulate the kinds of individualism that have emerged in Western capitalist culture, which "has mostly resulted in a shallow market-oriented and one-dimensional individual self, that is only marked by the person's monetary success or failure" (Zhao 2010, 584).

Zhao introduces some interesting literature from the writing of poets, which gives insights into the lives of children in Chinese society that are quite different from the official literature. Since this genre was not intended for moral or historical purposes, it provides vivid affectionate descriptions of young children and their relationships with their parents that indicate how far children's individuality and creativity were nurtured. Zhao ends her article with a challenge to persist in the search "for a new concept of human beings and a new individuality." She suggests that "an understanding of the potential as well as the problems of the Chinese understanding of men and women may contribute to the emergence of a new concept of humanity that not only centers on social harmony, but also nurtures individual flourishing and self-realization" (Zhao 2010, 593).

Conclusion: Cultural and Spiritual Resources for the Implementation of a Courageous Reform

I come to the end of this chapter with a strong sense of my own limitations. I stand in awe at all that has been achieved in the educational reforms unfolding in Hong Kong, and have little to offer in the way of new pedagogical or curricular patterns or ideas, more effective approaches to testing or more exciting ways of using educational technology in the classroom. Hong Kong educators are already so remarkably good in all of these areas! All that I can bring is a deep sense of the significance of the new structures and patterns that have been created and a kind of anticipation of the immense possibility of an educational approach emerging that may carry us "beyond the Enlightenment." What I love about Tu Weiming's emphasis in this expression is the affirmation of the many positive contributions of Enlightenment science and individualism, combined with a recognition of certain limitations, and a conviction that humanity cannot stop here.

I have tried to identify synergies between various strands in Confucian and Daoist thoughts and the British and American educational values that have been part of Hong Kong's historical experience. It is my conviction that a deep understanding of these values, as they exist in the hearts and minds of Hong Kong people and as they inform the work of teachers, the learning patterns of children and the attitudes of parents, is the key to an effective implementation of the reform.

I am heartened by the suggestion in the UGC report on the future of higher education that a small number of centers should be given public support to "develop research and graduate programmes that bring together Western and Asian perspectives" (University Grants Committee 2010, 66). Let me take this opportunity to propose that one of these centers should focus on the development of an educational approach that is consciously rooted in values from Song and Ming neo-Confucianism as well as Daoism, and that identifies synergies with various Western values and patterns that may serve to enlarge or enhance this Chinese frame. This new approach could offer the fullest possible support for optimizing the potential of children and young people in a balanced way across five major human dimensions: the moral, cognitive, aesthetic, social, and physical, while also recognizing the importance of the spiritual dimension.

Thinking about this in terms of a deep level of bridging between East and West, I felt I could not bring this chapter to a conclusion on my own. So I went back to the three young scholars whose work I have used and asked for their thoughts. I also turned to an older colleague and mentor who has built his rich contributions to education in North America on the work of John Dewey, among others. Respected as the father of narrative inquiry in education and an inspired academic leader in the areas of teacher development and curriculum theory, Michael Connelly surprised me with a quotation from the final paragraph of John Dewey's educational credo, first published in January 1897: "I believe that every teacher should realize the dignity of his calling; that he is a social servant set apart for the maintenance of proper social order and the securing of the right social growth. I believe that in this way the teacher always is the prophet of the true God and the usherer in of the true Kingdom of God" (Dewey 1897, 80).

This brought me face to face with the reality that we cannot ignore the connection between humanity and the divine, in reflecting on how educational reforms are to be implemented—the kinds of moral responsibility, cognitive brilliance, aesthetic beauty, social capacity, and physical ability we hope to optimize through education may all be understood as a gift of grace. We could begin with the Confucian relationship between Heaven and Humanity, and reflect on how the Chinese word for Heaven (天 tian) was used by Jesuit missionaries to convey the Christian message in a way that could be understood in China. The fact that Tian "expresses an order that is both divine and natural, both social and cosmic" (Gernet 1985, 194) made it possible to accommodate Christianity into Confucianism, and Western learning into the Chinese system. There is also a resonance between the egalitarian spirit of Renaissance Christianity, the notion of all being equal before God, and the Confucian idea that in education there should be no distinction by class. There is a further connection between physics and metaphysics in the Confucian concept of "extending knowledge through the investigation of things." One's mind and the world meet in self-cultivation, learning for the sake of the self, whether it be the mastery of physics or the development of morality (Bai 2011). Next, there is the fundamentally different nature of the individual-society relationship in Chinese and Western cultures. Hong Kong reforms could be viewed as an embodied experiment of the "unification of knowing and action," the motto shared by Dewey, Tao Xingzhi, and Wang Yangming (Zhang 2011). Dewey saw the self as being made through education; his focus was on the democratic social order and interaction with the changing environment.

Liang's focus was more on the importance of the inner self. The great contribution that the Chinese concept of the inclusive individual might bring to global society is the capacity to develop an individuality that warmly embraces the other while still maintaining strong individualism. It stands in contrast to the Western notion of the individual, which divides the self from the other and objectifies the other, making encountering the other peacefully a great challenge. This may be at the heart of the realist concept of international order, with each nation primarily concerned with defending its interests against external encroachment. There is a need, somehow, to integrate Chinese and Western views in the acknowledgment of a self that is both related and separate, and moving from there to nurture the kinds of international and global relations envisioned in China's ancient ideal of the Great Harmony (大同 *datong*) (Zhao 2011).

In this chapter, I have shared some of my personal experience of Hong Kong's educational development over a 44-year period and commented on the major reforms carried out since Hong Kong's return to China in 1997. Three core concepts have been articulated which I believe could be developed into a unique educational approach rooted in Chinese civilization, open to the world and capable of moving us beyond the Enlightenment: humane talent, inclusive individuality, and a radical creativity rooted in Daoist naturalism. I view Hong Kong educators as uniquely capable of developing these concepts in the spacious environment that has been provided through the reform process. They could therefore contribute in a significant way to mutually enriching global educational dialogue between the Chinese and the Anglo-American worlds.

NOTE

1. I am grateful to Dr Catharine K. K. Chan, deputy secretary (Curriculum and Quality Assurance), Education Bureau, Hong Kong Special Administration Region, China, for giving permission for this keynote address to be adapted for publication as a book chapter.

REFERENCES

Alitto, Guy. 1979. *Liang Shuming and the Chinese Dilemma of Modernity*. Berkeley: University of California Press.

Bai, Limin. 2010. "Human Capital or Humane Talent? Rethinking the Nature of Education in China from a Comparative Historical Perspective." *Frontiers of Education in China* 5 (1): 104–129.

Bai, Limin. 2011. Personal Communication via e-mail, February 15.

Bickley, Gillian. 2001. *The Development of Education in Hong Kong 1848–1896, as Revealed by the Early Education Reports of the Hong Kong Government 1841–1896*. Hong Kong: Council of the Lord Wilson Heritage Trust.

Chan, Carol, and Nirmala Rao, eds. 2009. *Revisiting the Chinese Learner: Changing Contexts, Changing Education*. Hong Kong and Dordrecht, The Netherlands: Comparative Education Research Centre, University of Hong Kong and Springer.

Curriculum Development Council. 2001. *Learning to Learn: Lifelong Learning and Whole-person Development*. Hong Kong: Government of the Hong Kong SAR.

Dewey, John. 1897. "My Pedagogic Creed," *School Journal* 54: 77–80.

Dewey, John. 1938. *Experience and Education*. New York: Collier Books.

Dore, Ronald. 1976. *The Diploma Disease, Education, Qualification and Development*. Berkeley, CA: University of California Press.

Education and Manpower Bureau. 2005. *The New Academic Structure for Senior Secondary Education and Higher Education—Action Plan for Investing in the Future of Hong Kong*. Hong Kong: Government of the Hong Kong SAR.

Education Commission. 2000. *Learning for Life Learning through Life: Reform Proposals for the Education System in Hong Kong*. Hong Kong: Government of the Hong Kong SAR.

Gernet, Jacques. 1985. *China and the Christian Impact*. Trans. by Janet Lloyd. Cambridge, UK: Cambridge University Press.

Hargreaves, Andy. 2011. "Content to be Canadian," *Toronto Star*, January 26, A21.

Hayhoe, Ruth. 1984. "The Evolution of Modern Educational Institutions," In *Contemporary Chinese Education*, ed. Ruth Hayhoe (pp. 26–46). London: Croom Helm.

Hayhoe, Ruth. 2001. "Creating a Vision for Teacher Education between East and West: The Case of the Hong Kong Institute of Education." *Compare* 31 (3): 329–345.

Hayhoe, Ruth. 2006. *Portraits of Influential Chinese Educators*. Hong Kong and Dordrecht, The Netherlands: Comparative Education Research Centre, University of Hong Kong and Springer.

Holmes, Brian. 1981. *Comparative Education: Some Considerations of Method*. London: George Allen and Unwin.

Keenan, Barry. 1977. *The Dewey Experiment in China*. Cambridge, MA: Harvard University Press.

Lee, Wing On. 1996. "The Cultural Context for Chinese Learners: Conceptions of Learning in the Confucian Tradition." In *The Chinese Learner: Cultural, Psychological and Contextual Influences*, ed. David A. Watkins and John B. Biggs. Hong Kong: Comparative Education Research Centre, University of Hong Kong.

Mazrui, Ali. 1975. "World Culture and the Search for Human Consensus." In *On the Creation of a Just World Order: Preferred Worlds for the 1980s*, ed. Saul Mendlovitz (pp. 1–37). New York: Free Press.

Mundy, Karen, and Joseph P. Farrell. 2008. "International Education Indicators and Assessment." In *Comparative and International Education: Issues for Teachers*, ed. Karen Mundy, KathyBickmore, Ruth Hayhoe, Meggan Madden, and Katia Madjidi. Toronto: Canadian Scholars Press.

Tu, Wei-ming. 1998. "Beyond the Enlightenment Mentality." In *Confucianism and Ecology: The Interrelation of Heaven, Earth and Humans*, ed. Mary Evelyn Tucker and John Berthrong. Cambridge, MA: Harvard University Center for the Study of World Religions, distributed by Harvard University Press.

University Grants Committee. 2010. *Aspirations for the Higher Education System in Hong Kong.* Hong Kong: Government of the Hong Kong SAR.

Zhang, Huajun. 2010. "Cultivating an Inclusive Individuality: Critical Reflections on the Idea of Quality Education in Contemporary China." *Frontiers of Education in China* 5 (2): 222–237.

Zhang, Huajun. 2011. Personal communication by e-mail, February 11.

Zhao, Guoping. 2010. "Chinese Cultural Dynamics and Childhood: Towards a New Individuality for Education." *Frontiers of Education in China* 5 (4): 579–595.

Zhao, Guoping. 2011 Personal communication by e-mail, February 1.

Index